USING THE
MASS MEDIA
COMMUNICATION
PROBLEMS IN
AMERICAN
SOCIETY

USING THE MASS MEDIA
COMMUNICATION PROBLEMS IN AMERICAN SOCIETY

STEVEN H. CHAFFEE
University of Wisconsin

MICHAEL J. PETRICK
University of Maryland

McGRAW-HILL BOOK COMPANY

New York · St. Louis · San Francisco · Auckland
Düsseldorf · Johannesburg · Kuala Lumpur · London
Mexico · Montreal · New Delhi · Panama · Paris
São Paulo · Singapore · Sydney · Tokyo · Toronto

**USING THE
MASS MEDIA**
COMMUNICATION
PROBLEMS IN
AMERICAN
SOCIETY

1 2 3 4 5 6 7 8 9 0 KPKP 7 9 8 7 6 5

This book was set in Times Roman by National ShareGraphics, Inc. The editors
were Lyle Linder and Susan Gamer; the cover was designed by Joseph Gillians;
the production supervisor was Judi Frey.
Kingsport Press, Inc., was printer and binder.

Library of Congress Cataloging in Publication Data

Chaffee, Steven H
  Using the mass media.

  1. Mass media—Social aspects—United States. 2. Mass
media—Psychological aspects. 3. Communication—United States. I. Petrick,
Michael J., joint author. II. Title.
HN90.M3C5   301.16'1'0973   74-26944
ISBN 0-07-010375-5

To the
memory of
Ralph O. Nafziger

Contents

Acknowledgments

We wish to thank the following persons, whose assistance and patience helped us plan and complete this book: Professors Scott M. Cutlip of the University of Wisconsin and James E. Grunig of the University of Maryland; Stephen Dragin, Dave Edwards, Susan Gamer, Orville Haberman, and Lyle Linder of McGraw-Hill; Mary Ann Coffman, Bob Givarz, Arlene Goldberg, Dennis Hogan, and Irene Kolb for manuscript assistance and typing; and for special help and encouragement, Sheila Chaffee and Mathline and Tony Petrick.

Steven H. Chaffee
Michael J. Petrick

USING THE MASS MEDIA
COMMUNICATION PROBLEMS IN AMERICAN SOCIETY

me-di-um, *n. (pl.* **me-di-ums** *or* **me-dia**) *[L.] 1. Something that is intermediate or in a middle position. 2. A means through which a force acts or something functions. 3. A material or method for artistic expression. 4. A surrounding substance. 5. A person through whom messages are thought to be sent from the dead. 6. A channel of communication . . .*

Part One

Mass Communication

Introduction

"Mass media" is a term that most of us do not hear until long after we have come to look on television, radio, newspapers, magazines, and films as commonplace elements of our everyday lives. Because we have learned to take them for granted, it is hard for us to imagine what life might be like without them.

As individuals in a world without mass media, we might picture ourselves as having a great deal of leisure time to spend—time that we now devote to viewing, listening, and reading. Our imaginations have to stretch a bit to realize what the absence of the media would mean to us as individuals in a larger society. We would be without so many sources of information and entertainment that none of us would be the same person; in many ways, we would be lesser persons, and so would those around us. Finally, it is most difficult to comprehend what radical changes there would have to be in the organization and operation of American society at large without the mass media.

But, of course, the media have not always been with us, and there are many countries in the world today where the development of media is minimal. Where few citizens are literate, for instance, there are correspondingly few newspapers and magazines. Where electrical energy is in short supply and electronic technologies are underdeveloped, television is unknown and radio is a carefully husbanded national resource. So we can, by comparison with earlier times and other places, get some idea of the ways in which our society would have to operate if we had a less plentiful supply of mass media. It is still not easy, though, for us to look at our own lives and our own society and comprehend the many ways in which we do use the media we have. This book is dedicated mainly to introducing the reader to that kind of self-awareness of the ways in which we use our mass media in dealing with the problems of our diverse society.

This is not a textbook in the details of operation of the mass media, nor an outline of abstract theories of mass communication. Many books deal extensively with those topics, and we will provide in the first few chapters here a bare-bones introduction to concepts that we feel are essential for readers to grasp in order that they may understand the communication industry. We will review very briefly the historical development of mass communication, in the context of more fundamental considerations based on interpersonal communication. We will also sketch an outline of the factors that enter into the decisions that are made within the media about what material will—and what will not—reach us as members of the vast media audience.

Beyond that we see only limited value in analyzing the communication industry as a whole. The media provide society with tools, but it is the problems of society that present the material on which those tools might be used. For the remainder of the book, then, we will consider, one by one, a series of major problems that have been closely intertwined with mass communication in American society.

It is a characteristic trait of American public discourse to talk in terms of "solutions" to problems. But in other societies it has usually seemed sufficient to attempt to work on a problem, without necessarily promising to solve it. We will take that more modest approach here. The issues raised in these chapters have been selected partly because they have proved very difficult to solve. They have been with us for some time, and we expect them to endure as societal problems.

To offer to solve them would, then, be reckless and highly presumptuous. We will, where we can, suggest new approaches that we think might alleviate a few of the problems to some extent. But the solutions, if any, will have to come from many elements of our society, working through mass communication. Our prime hope is to provide a guide for such media-centered action programs.

Part One of this book is introductory. In Parts Two through Five, we will discuss four major problem areas, which represent four distinct types of social goals that people try to achieve by means of the mass media.

In Part Two we consider problems having to do with *public information*. There are a number of institutions in our society which find that they suffer from widespread ignorance of their activities and purposes. At the same time, consumers are often called on to make judgments and decisions for which they are ill-informed. Mass media channels are the logical mechanism for disseminating information to a broad range of people. No other channels reach as diverse and extensive an audience. We have selected for analysis four institutions that represent a range from those with purely informational and educational functions, to those for whom public information is of decidedly secondary importance.

Part Three deals with *influencing behavior*. We have avoided here the pop psychology notion of "attitude" management. Instead we want to focus directly on what people *do*—in terms of spending their money and casting their votes. These two concrete behaviors constitute the principal mechanisms by which American society regulates itself. The mass media are widely seen as a primary source of influence over these acts, although of course there are other "more real" influences on voting and personal spending as well.

Part Four examines the role of the media as agencies of *social control* over several kinds of behavior that are deemed undesirable by one or more major sectors of American society. Of the topics we will consider—violence, environmental pollution, sexual excesses, and political radicalism—none is noncontroversial. That is, all have some base of popular support as well, if only from those many persons who contribute to the controversy by persisting in the behavior at question. Without taking sides for or against any of these kinds of activity, and without denying that there may be more severe societal problems in need of control, we will examine these as representatives of a large variety of human behaviors that many people have attempted to eliminate through mass communication controls.

Finally, in Part Five we take up the role of the media in *social change*. Here our approach shifts from that of existing problems to certain kinds of changes in society—and in the media—that might arise in the future. We first deal with technological innovations that are being introduced in the communication field and consider some dimensions of change in people's social relationships and functioning that these changes in media might bring about. Then we turn the question around and consider some shifts in the demographic structure of society that might create needs for change in mass media organization and performance.

In the last two chapters we must necessarily be speculative. We limit our discussion mainly to changes that are already under way, or to elements of the media and social systems that have undergone major changes in the past. The topics that are taken up are illustrative, and certainly not intended to be an exhaustive listing of the potential relationships between mass communication and social change. Our hope is to stimulate people's thinking and study of this very broad and vague sort of social problem. To do that, we have had to make assumptions and statements that will sound much more conclusive than we intend them to be. We would ask that the reader approach this book as a collection of hypotheses, subject to testing against evidence. We believe the statements we make here to be true, and we have evidence to back up most of them. But it is not the conclusions that are important in a developing field of knowledge; it is the questions that are asked and the larger conceptual structure in which they are related to one another. If the things we have written stir students of communication to undertake research that will prove us wrong, we will be as satisfied as if the result were the opposite and our statements were borne out. On the other hand, we will have failed if the book is simply read and either believed or disbelieved—and if readers do not follow up with their own inquiry into the social role of mass communication, within or beyond the topics dealt with in this book.

A book devoted to goals of this kind cannot hope to be complete and comprehensive. Chapters 2, 3, and 4 are not in themselves adequate for the type of understanding we would wish our readers to have of mass media institutions and processes. The problem-centered sections that follow represent topics that we consider important, to be sure; but there are many other important problem topics that do not appear in this book. Still, we hope our readers will study the book with some care. We have designed it, to an extent, in the form of a textbook, with the idea that students who seek an introduction to the role of mass media in their own lives will find some of these topics relevant and involving. We are fairly certain that no one person will find all of these problem areas to be of interest to him or her as an individual; our hope is that our analysis of such matters will nevertheless provide insights into the role of the media in complex modern society as it impinges on the reader's own life.

We have a larger hope, too. As the following pages will make clear, we are not blind supporters or apologists for the media. We are critics to some extent, and we will spend many pages discussing ways in which the media could serve society better. But we do work from a basic belief that our mass media can operate most effectively under basic conditions of freedom. We assume in our analysis that they are free institutions, working in the marketplaces of both commerce and ideas. President Richard Nixon, in discussing his Watergate problems with an aide, commented: "Well, one hell of a lot of people don't give one damn about this issue of the suppression of the press, etc." Even as we want this assessment to be wrong, we know that to some extent it is correct. Our larger hope, then, is that this book might help to reduce the number of people who "don't give one damn" about the role of mass communication in American society.

REFERENCES

The Presidential Transcripts (New York: Dell Publishing Co., 1974), p. 48. (Meeting between the President and John Dean, Oval Office, Feb. 28, 1973.)

SUGGESTED STUDY PROJECT

As an experiment in "abstinence," try to avoid all contact with the mass media for one twenty-four-hour period. Keep notes on those media contacts that you couldn't avoid; those that you missed but needed; and the other things you did instead of spending time with the media. From this experience, what can you conclude about the role of mass media in your daily life?

Chapter 2

The American Mass Media System

The mass media are important to our society because we use them so much. When the media are a controversial aspect of American life, it is largely because of who uses them and why.

As this country developed, more people found more ways and more reasons to use more new forms of mass communication. Practically every generation in the last 200 years embarked on its own new "age of mass communication." We now have more mass media than ever before—both in quantity and form—available for our use. And most of us have more time and more reasons for using them. So the interest and concern about the people, machines, and procedures which make up American mass communication is legitimate and likely to grow stronger.

Today, many citizens use the mass media as aids for coping with an increasingly complicated and often frustrating society. Entrenched interest groups, both public and private, continue to use the media to solicit support for the status quo. Proponents of new ideas continue their efforts to use the media as a vehicle for social change. Professional media communicators—

persons who have careers in mass communication—will use the organizations and machines of the media to construct and deliver information, education, persuasion, and entertainment to millions. And all the while, the owners of the mass media will be using their personnel and machines to make money and stay in business.

If we are to put the media to effective and responsible use—as citizens, professional communicators, or whatever—we first need to understand how the media are structured, how they operate, and how they came to be that way.

The American mass media system is an exceedingly complicated combination of individuals, organizations, circumstances, and technology. To refer to the media as "society's suggestion box" (whereby citizens provide input to decision makers) or as "the concentration of more and more power over public opinion in fewer and fewer hands" (as Vice President Spiro Agnew said in 1970) does little to enhance understanding of our media system. Simplistic slogans can only detract from an obvious and genuine need for insight into the workings of mass communication.

We need to know about the major parts of the American mass media system and how these parts fit together to make mass communication work.

A "MASS MEDIA SYSTEM"

We use the term "system" deliberately, to convey three important characteristics of the American mass media:

1   Many individuals and groups (or organizations) of individuals use the machines of mass communication in various ways and for various purposes. In so doing, they *interact* with one another and influence the total performance of mass communication.

2   Over time, these interactions have had certain common, recurring patterns which have become the major uses, or *functions*, of mass communication.

3   Major social forces—such as changing life-styles, government policy, technology, and economics—have been *outside influences* on the strength and the uses of the mass media.

We will examine each of these qualities in turn.

Interaction in the Mass Media System

It is fairly common, but not terribly realistic, to view mass communication as a process in which professional communicators (such as reporters, editors, advertising copy writers, and television newscasters) produce material which is injected by a one-way, single-step flow into the bloodstream of the masses. The American mass media system is more ingenious, if less romantic, than that.

We can categorize the persons involved in a mass media system. As we spell out six major categories below, we remind the reader that these groupings are oversimplified, that each has further subcategories, and that in the end the individual member of the group is importantly unique in many ways.

One grouping consists of the *owners or managers* of the mass media. They own or control the machines which make mass communication possible, and they employ persons to construct and transmit messages over media machinery. In general, they use both the employees and machines to make money.

Professional communicators make up a second category. These are individuals (a reporter, for instance) working as part of an organization (such as the newsroom staff of a newspaper). They use the mass media to make a living by constructing messages appropriate to the task of the organization.

Audiences constitute a third category. These are large groups of persons who use the media to get such things as entertainment, information, education, and advice.

Then there are *economic supporters* of the mass media: persons, such as advertisers, who buy audiences from the media, and who use the media to communicate with the audiences they have purchased.

A fifth category consists of *professional utilizers* of the media. Although not actual employees of the media, they actively and deliberately use mass media as vehicles to deliver their personal messages to audiences. (And the professional communicators working for the media often use these *utilizers* as sources for material.) Persons in this category include public relations personnel and anonymous but "informed" news sources.

Finally, *servicers* of the mass media perform auxiliary but vital services which keep the media operating. Proofreaders, newsprint suppliers, and radio station engineers are examples.

All the kinds of people listed above, interacting with one another and with the broader social environment, make up the complex *institutions* of the American mass media system.

In a literal sense, "the mass media" are inert objects: lifeless combinations of paper and ink, of electronic signals and cathode-ray tubes. It is the people, using such channels of mass communication, who give life to mass communication—with all that life implies.

One implication is growth. As society developed, new forms of media technology became available. More and more people entered mass communication as a business or career. More audiences became available, so there were more audiences to be sold or bought. The media grew into specialized

Aggregate financial data can be used by a media industry to stress that industry's stability and growth. The data for the television industry shown below give total revenues, expenses, and income for all American television stations and networks. The original data came from official Federal Communications Commission reports and were republished by Broadcasting Yearbook, a sort of annual report of the broadcast industry.

Television

(In millions of dollars)			
Year	Revenues	Expenses	Income
1952	324.2	268.7	55.5
1960	1268.6	1024.5	244.1
1969	2796.2	2242.6	553.6

Source: Adapted from 1972 Broadcasting Yearbook.

structures built around particular traditions, technologies, and social goals; mass communication, in short, became institutionalized.

At one level, institutionalization has meant separation and competition between the two super-giant mass media institutions—the print media and the electronic broadcast media. Each is dramatically and inherently different from the other in basic technology and, of course, historical origin. Consequently, each has unique advantages and disadvantages which have affected its status. The American print media, spawned from a heritage of resisting suppressive English licensing and other censoring mechanisms, attained virtual freedom from prepublication censorship. But American broadcasting, born as a product of American industrialization and urbanization, has been subjected to government licensing because its technology required use of "public property," that is, the airwaves; yet broadcasting has prospered because even the most modern printing technology is no match for instantaneous coast-to-coast electronic delivery.

We have already introduced the major dividing line of American mass communication: the technological differences between print media and broadcast media. Each of these media forms, in turn, consists of what we will call media industries. These industries differ from one another primarily in terms of the mass communication product they provide. The newspaper, magazine, and book industries are the principal examples in the print media. Radio, over-the-air television, and cablecasting are the main broadcast industries.

The concept of *media industry* is worth considering here because it often is used as an economic barometer, a rallying point, and an inlet for innovation. Accumulations of industrywide statistics on audience size and advertising revenues, for example, give an indication of past, current, and

American Mass Media Units in 1971

Industry	Number of units
Newspaper	
Daily	1,749
Weekly	8,800 (approx.)
Magazine	
Public magazines	10,000 (approx.)
Company "house organs"	10,000 (approx.)
Radio	
AM stations	4,327
FM stations	2,649
Television	
VHF stations	596
UHF stations	296

Source: Compiled from Editor & Publisher Year Book, Ayers Newspaper Directory, Broadcasting Yearbook.

future economic health. Moreover, representatives of an industry can, and often do, band together to promote a common cause (such as admitting television cameras to courtrooms) or fight a common foe (such as anti-trust actions against newspapers). And industrywide publications and convocations provide a focal point at which marketers and proponents of new technology and practices can aim their efforts. But mass media industries, by and large, are loose, ad hoc organizations.

Most of the day-to-day work—the actual decision making in mass communication—takes place in the individual *units* of the media industries. Most editing of news, selling of audiences, and allocation of resources occurs in the office of the weekly magazine, the local radio and television station, the community newspaper.

In order to carry out those tasks with efficiency, many individual media units have become divided into specialized organizations; this is particularly true in larger units, where expertise and division of labor are considered necessary to enhance the effectiveness and integrity of the tasks performed. A typical daily newspaper, for example, has separate departments to handle news, advertising, circulation, and printing. Often these specialized departments are physically separated from one another; advertising, after all, shouldn't interfere with news.

In general, the larger the media unit, the more specialized departments it will have. The news department of a large daily newspaper (often called the "editorial department") might well be broken down into several smaller divisions—one for national and foreign news, one for sports, one for city news, and so forth. Each of those subdepartments might become an entity unto itself, occupying a distinct space and headed by a separate editor. And within such departments, individuals often have distinct specialized tasks. A newspaper journalist working for a city editor might be one of several reporters assigned to the "city government beat" or to the "rewrite desk" or to the "general assignment."

Obviously, coordination mechanisms have to be established in order that the total media unit can put out its product. And someone has to arbitrate disputes between competing departments. Media units usually have managers, editors, and boards to do those things.

Media units are serviced by a number of special organizations. Some are adjuncts which supply a unit with part of its product. Wire services such as the Associated Press and United Press International feed large amounts of foreign, national, and state news to television and radio stations, magazines, and newspapers. Syndicates make entertainment, educational, and advertising materials available to all media units. Radio and television networks provide the great bulk of programing for many stations.

Other special organizations act on behalf of persons working in the mass media. There are national and regional associations of television station managers, newspaper publishers, and magazine publishers. There are professional societies for photojournalists, editorial writers, broadcast news directors, etc. And there are labor-oriented groups such as the American Newspaper Guild and the American Federation of Television and Radio Artists. Each in its own way impacts on the structure and operation of the media industries and the individual media units. In general, these groups help set media standards, try to promote favorable government policies toward the media, enhance professionalism, and define employer-employee relationships.

The American mass media system is not structured according to a particular task or function; there is no structured "news industry" or "advertising industry" in this country. Instead, each media industry, and each unit within each industry, is organized to carry out those tasks most appropriate to its traditions and technology. We turn now to the common tasks which, over time, people involved in mass communication have considered appropriate.

Functions of Mass Communication

Homo sapiens has always used communication to share information and ideas. The dawning of *mass* communication—which usually is traced back to the mid-thirteenth century when the Chinese and later Johann Gutenberg invented movable type—made it possible and profitable to spread knowledge and opinions more widely and more quickly. The benefits of newly discovered printing technology were not universally acclaimed in those early years, however.

European government and church leaders, whose wealth and position had given them exclusive possession of expensive hand-lettered writings of previous ages, were apprehensive and hostile. But the printers were persistent, and people were eager for more knowledge and information than that provided by messengers, minstrels, or storytellers. And so, despite some successful attempts by the authorities to control printing, an increasing number of writers committed their thoughts and observations to print.

Large numbers of people took an interest in those early products of mass communication. By the last quarter of the fifteenth century, thousands of books had been printed and circulated among millions of persons on the European continent. Many of them, such as the works of Jean Jacques Rousseau, challenged established political doctrine. Others were classical works such as the Bible; but no longer did ecclesiastical leaders have an exclusive prerogative to tell people what the Bible said.

During the first quarter of the seventeenth century, writers and printers began to introduce the first "news-papers." They were books and pamphlets containing information about commerce, wars, and politics, printed at frequent intervals. The news-papers were popular, and their number increased throughout England and the European continent.

As printed media spread throughout Europe in the sixteenth and seventeenth centuries, they took on three basic tasks: spreading new information, teaching established views, and persuading people to support causes. That tradition carried over to the American colonies. The first colonial printers produced textbooks at Harvard in the 1630s. Colonial newspapers, though impeded by a strict licensing and censorship system, eventually started appearing regularly in the 1720s. They contained mostly information and gossip about European affairs, as well as efforts at persuasion in the form of "letters" from anonymous or pseudonymous writers who criticized and ridiculed colonial authorities.

As discontent with English rule grew in the colonies, printers and writers became bolder. Propagandistic pamphlets and newspaper items, urging colonists to take a particular side in the conflict, became common.

From its earliest stages, then, mass communication succeeded because some persons found it rewarding to inform, teach, and persuade, and because others were willing to be informed, taught, or persuaded. In the eighteenth and nineteenth centuries industrialization, literacy, and urbanization brought about new techniques and formats in American mass communication. But our mass media developed largely as profitable menus of news, education, and influence. They remain so today.

The functions of mass communication, then, are those tasks which the media traditionally and routinely perform. In that respect, American mass media have three major social functions:

1   To share information with the public about important and relevant events and problems

2   To teach people about matters considered necessary or useful

3   To build support for ideas and activities

Professor Wilbur Schramm, a leading researcher and scholar of mass communication, has called these the *watcher, teacher,* and *forum* functions of mass communication. In the first function, media personnel seek out, observe, and report situations which are considered important enough to share. This public information function most commonly takes the form of news reports and is carried out primarily by journalists.

In their education function, the media provide people with material about society's traditions, norms, and prevailing attitudes. In teaching these things, the media help keep stability in a society—acting, in effect, as an agent of social control.

The media also provide messages of persuasion—that is, content designed to bolster current values (the status quo) or to transform new ideas into social change.

Some scholars of mass communication have added entertainment as a fourth major function of the American mass media. With new technology, mass communication became more readily available; and with changing life-styles, more Americans had more leisure time for mass communication. Some mass media entrepreneurs found that providing enjoyment to people can be very profitable indeed.

Making money is sometimes listed as a separate function of the mass media. We do not consider it separate at all. The media have been used for information, persuasion, education, and entertainment because each of those functions has been profitable under certain conditions. The major functions of the media have persisted largely because media owners can make money by using the media for those purposes. That, we feel, will continue to be the case so long as people want to be informed, advised, and taught.

Since the media are social institutions, we may object to instances where, for the sake of sheer profit, they give up—or bastardize—their important functions of informing, teaching, and persuading. Media institutions demand a great many indulgences from American society. So it is entirely proper that they be called to account when they fail to deliver in return.

OUTSIDE FORCES: MASS MEDIA AND SOCIETY

The people and organizations involved in mass communication have always responded to the technological, economic, and political-legal forces of American society. They have taken advantage of new developments in order to survive, to operate more profitably, and to serve more efficiently. The mass media have consequently become a pervasive part of American life. They have fed upon the diverse tastes and life-styles of a pluralistic society. They have become huge business enterprises because they could attract, then sell, audiences on a grandiose scale. And yet they have managed to perform their social tasks under constitutional guarantees of freedom of expression.

The American mass media have become so pervasive, so widespread, that it is impossible for most of us to avoid routine contact with them—unless we really work at it.

Media Technology

The thrust of mass communication into nearly every section and segment of American life depended partly on technological developments which allowed the media to use techniques of mass production and led audiences toward mass consumption. High-speed printing presses and more efficient typesetting mechanisms made production of the urban daily newspaper feasible in the 1830s; and such mass production techniques helped make it economically feasible to distribute the "penny papers" of that era for a single cent per copy. Progress in electronic technology transformed the sending and receiving of radio signals into a practicable commercial venture in the 1920s. Development of the cathode-ray tube made television a technological possibility as early as the 1930s (although economics and World War II delayed the "age of television" for nearly twenty more years).

Increased incomes and more leisure time for Americans spurred mass consumption of media products. And increased use of advertising as the major subsidizer of media operating expenses helped keep subscription prices at bargain levels.

As America entered the 1970s, the pervasiveness of mass media had reached these spectacular heights:

One copy of a daily newspaper was sold for every three persons in the country.

Some 62 million American homes (98.6 percent of them) had at least one radio set.

Americans in 96 percent of the country's homes had television sets (nearly half of them color), which were viewed an average of six hours and eighteen minutes per day per home.

Readers could select from about 10,000 paid-circulation magazines, most of them devoted to specialized leisure and occupational interests.

Pervasiveness need not mean sameness. American mass media have not spread evenly throughout society; they have, in fact, developed with considerable diversity.

Technology played a role in the diversity of the media. Consider the media which attempt to cover and distribute news on a daily basis. Print technology has never allowed large-scale nationwide production and distribution of a daily newspaper; the country is too large and the printing process too slow. Consequently, daily newspapers have sprung from the country's many urban areas (primarily to serve local and regional audiences), and most continue to place a heavy emphasis on local and regional news. Broadcasting, on the other hand, allows for instantaneous nationwide presentation over the airwaves. Radio and television network news programs are therefore geared to national and international news. But since television technology permitted audiences to see as well as hear, the popularity of video soon helped displace radio as the most used nationwide medium for daily news.

Media Economics

In order to survive, each media industry has had to attract and hold a particular audience which it could then sell to advertisers. As new forms of media develop, they inevitably cut into the established audiences of the older media. In some cases, the cut has been so serious that the older media have had to look for a different type of audience.

The impact of television on magazines, radio, and (to some extent) newspapers graphically illustrates the relationship between the economics of the media and their diversity. Before broadcasting, magazines had been the major nationwide medium for information, opinion, and entertainment. Because they did not compete with newspapers for "hot news," magazines could be distributed nationwide by mail and by magazine-stand sales. Then broadcasting—especially television—began attracting huge nationwide audiences, and national advertisers started buying them, inevitably at the expense of national magazine audiences. Venerable mass-circulation general magazines such as *Collier's, Look,* and *Life* ceased publication. The magazine industry, however, did not succumb; it became apparent that people would support magazines aimed at special interests—at hobbies, occupations, income levels, sex, and so forth. It also became clear that advertisers of specialty products would advertise in the specialized magazines. Because advertising rates are usually determined by the size of the audience, it is more economical for a manufacturer of sporting equipment to buy the smaller yet more interested audience of *Sports Illustrated* than the larger but generalized audience of *Reader's Digest*. Likewise, the radio industry found it could attract a local audience by offering a diet of background entertainment (chiefly music on most stations).

By and large, radio has ceased to be a national entertainment medium, with the radio networks acting as supplier of hourly newscasts to their affiliate stations. In recent years, radio has followed the magazine industry toward specialization; "all news" stations, "hard rock" stations, classical music stations have found and sold sufficient audiences to make a profit. Newspapers, too, have adopted some aspects of specialization which proved successful for magazines and radio. Some dailies, for example, publish separate editions for various parts of their circulation area. And the number of special newspaper sections—devoted to travel, food, the arts, recreation, and the like—is generally increasing.

Specialization of media audiences and content in many ways reflects overall changes in American life-styles. As people had more leisure time, they developed and pursued more special interests—directly through personal participation and indirectly through mass media. As society itself became more specialized industrially, politically, and economically, a need developed to keep abreast of specialized fields. And as income levels rose, people had more money with which to purchase messages that could help them deal with both the pleasures and pains of specialization.

A country as large as America needs a pervasive mass media system to reach all its citizens. It also needs a media system which can serve the diverse needs of individuals and groups for information, education, advice, and entertainment. Can the American mass media reconcile those social tasks with the economic task of selling its audiences to advertisers? The seeming disparity between social and economic tasks of the media has disturbed many observers. When a medium sells its audience, must it also sell its soul? Does the fierce competition for audiences result in monopolistic (rather than pluralistic) control over the content of mass communication? Answers to such questions are neither as easy nor as bleak as they may seem.

The mass media do not necessarily have to sell audiences. We could, for example, have a system of government subsidy in which the media would be supported by tax dollars. That suggestion raises the bogey-man of government control, of turning the media into an official propaganda arm of the government; for "he who pays the piper calls the tune." The media could also be supported entirely by subscription, thereby doubling or even tripling subscription costs. A few magazines are able to operate that way because fiercely loyal subscribers are willing to pay. Experiments in coin-operated television ("pay as you watch") have not been very successful; but

Ownership Concentration in American Mass Media

—Out of 1,511 cities with daily newspapers in 1971, only 37 (or 2.5 percent) were served by papers with competing owners. In 1930, 20.6 percent of the cities had competing newpaper owners. In 1880, the figure was 61.4 percent.

—Of 4,327 AM radio stations licensed in 1971, magazines or newspapers owned 402 (or 9.3 percent). Of the 2,203 commercial FM stations in the country, 248 (or 11.3 percent) were so owned.

—Newspapers and/or magazines owned 191 (or 28.9 percent) of the country's 696 commercial television stations in 1971.

—In 1968, newspaper "chains" owned 828 (or 47.1 percent) of the country's 1,749 dailies.

many subscribers to cable television systems pay a fee for getting some channels without advertising plus some with regular commercials. Overall, privately owned media supported at least in part by advertising are likely to continue.

The media have generally recognized the internal conflict between their status as profit-making corporations and their service roles as social institutions. They have had to live with, and try to deal with, what media critic Ben Bagdikian has called a "built-in schizophrenia." Today, advertising pays for the biggest share of operating costs of most magazines, broadcast stations, and newspapers.

There is ample evidence of control by advertisers over the entertainment content in the broadcast media, to be sure; entertainment programs live or die by commercial sponsorship. In the news media, direct advertiser control over information and opinion content has fortunately been a rare phenomenon. A fairly strong sense of professional journalistic ethics and integrity has managed to enforce a tradition of independence of news content from advertising. When this wall of separation occasionally breaks down, public outcry is as justified as it is vociferous.

An economically strong, healthy medium is usually the most resistant to pressures from advertisers; it can afford to be. But to stay independently healthy in an atmosphere of rising costs, many media operations have bought out competitors and increased their media holdings, making ownership of mass communication concentrated in the hands of fewer and fewer firms. The Federal Communications Commission prohibits one firm from owning more than one television station in a single city, but in many large cities one company will control a newspaper, a television station, and a radio station. And it is not too uncommon for one firm to own two newspapers, an AM and an FM radio station, and a television station in a single city. Newspaper chains (companies which own newspapers in several scattered markets) have spread.

Conditions like that naturally cause concern about the effect of concentrated ownership on the content of the media: Does concentrated media ownership eliminate diversity and competition in news and opinion? Some critics argue that it inevitably does. There have been some documented instances of one media unit withholding news that may be harmful to a sister unit. Some studies show that ownership concentration often results in higher advertising rates and higher subscription rates. Media which operate under monopolistic conditions usually do compete with one another, but in a peculiar way: they make their separate products appear to be different. Such "monopolistic competition" accounts for the differences in news content, editorial policy, and design frequently found between two newspapers serving the same city but owned by the same company. The situation is analogous to the one where a firm makes and sells two different brands of fluoride toothpaste—one with red stripes and one with mint flavoring.

Government policy in recent years has favored diversification of mass media ownership. FCC rules and anti-trust actions by the U.S. Department of Justice have tried to break up concentrations of media ownership. The success of such moves has been lukewarm at best, counterproductive at worst. The trend toward monopoly and conglomerate ownership does not appear to have been blunted. And in some cases, the government has forced a company to get rid of one of its units—only to have that unit go out of business for lack of a new buyer.

Freedom of the Media

If the American media are not free from the tyrannies of economic pressures, they at least are granted some protection to keep government from interfering with their products of information, education, and opinion. The First Amendment to the Constitution says that "Congress shall make no law abridging . . . freedom of speech or of the press." That guarantee—unique in that it is the only freedom specifically granted in the Constitution to a private enterprise—culminated a long and bitter struggle by early American mass communicators against censorship and harassment by the English colonial governments. But freedom of the press is not an absolute immunity from regulation; American society has yet to confer any absolute freedoms. What does the First Amendment mean, then? In order to answer that question, we must deal with several others which have posed perplexing and recurrent problems throughout the last 180 years.

Who decides what freedom of the press means? All public policy-making agencies do to some degree. Mostly, though, the judicial system, headed by the U.S. Supreme Court, has enunciated the great principles of constitutional law which define the parameters of the First Amendment. In so doing, the courts act as arbiters between communicators and those who would regulate or suppress communications.

Boundaries of Freedom of the Press as Described by the U.S. Supreme Court

The question in every case is whether the words used are in such circumstances and are of such a nature as to create a clear and present danger that they will bring about the substantive evils that Congress has a right to prevent. It is a question of proximity and degree.

Justice Oliver Wendell Holmes, in *Schenk v United States,* 1919

. . . (D)ebate on public issues should be uninhibited, robust, and wide-open, and . . . may well include vehement, caustic, and sometimes unpleasantly sharp attacks on government and public officials.

Justice William Brennan, in *New York Times v Sullivan,* 1964

Liberty of circulating is as essential to that freedom (of the press) as liberty of publishing; indeed, without the circulation, the publication would be of little value.

Justice Stephen Field, in *Ex Parte Jackson,* 1877

"Any system of prior restraints of expression comes to this court bearing a heavy presumption against its constitutional validity." . . . The Government "thus carries a heavy burden of showing justification for the enforcement of such a restraint."

Statement "by the court," in the "Pentagon Papers case," 1971

Who is protected by freedom of the press? Everyone, in a broad sense. The guarantee belongs to the ordinary citizen who produces a mimeographed statement of his political views as well as to the industries and units of mass communication.

What kinds of communication does freedom of the press protect? Courts have struggled with this question on an issue-by-issue basis. In general, the First Amendment protects all expressions (as opposed to overt actions) of information and opinion which do not clearly and directly jeopardize some other basic right or value. In some situations (such as statements advocating violent overthrow of the government or posing a threat to the integrity of a court), expression which poses a "clear and present danger" to evoke a great evil can be suppressed or punished. Censorship prior to dissemination usually requires that the would-be censor meet a heavy burden of proving such a danger, thus giving press freedom a "preferred position."

To whom is the First Amendment addressed? In the words of the Amendment itself, to Congress. But subsequent Supreme Court decisions, relying chiefly on the Fourteenth Amendment, have extended the prohibition to include all branches and levels of government. In effect, the First Amendment now means that "government shall not abridge freedom of the press."

What does the First Amendment seek to do? In the view of Supreme Court justices, freedom of the press exists to promote vigorous debate on matters of public importance. To promote that end, the First Amendment prohibits censorship of information and opinion prior to its dissemination (except for communications found immediately and clearly threatening to the national security or patently pornographic). It also protects communicators against unreasonable prosecutions and lawsuits which might result from disseminating certain types of statements.

What kinds of prosecutions and lawsuits against the media are permitted by the First Amendment? Prosecutions are possible for criminal contempt (interfering with a court, grand jury, or legislator), obscenity (which the courts have never really been able to define), blasphemy, and some other offenses against the public order. Private lawsuits are permitted for such offenses as civil libel (damaging the reputation of a private citizen by a false, injurious statement), invasion of privacy (intruding upon the solitude or mental well-being of a non-public personage), and copyright infringement (theft of another person's style of expression without consent).

Does freedom of the press apply uniformly to all mass media? No. Because broadcast stations are licensed, the FCC can establish, and has established, criteria by which broadcasters are to operate in "the public interest." The "fairness doctrine," for example, requires balanced treatment of controversial subjects on station editorials and public affairs programs. In addition, Congress has decreed that broadcasters provide "equal time" to all bona fide candidates for public office. Regular newscasts generally are exempt from both requirements, but broadcast journalists claim that the rules still discourage bold and controversial news programing. The Supreme Court held in 1969 that under the First Amendment the right of the audience to fairness, rather than the right of the broadcasters to do what they want, is paramount.

Does the First Amendment cover all aspects of mass communication? Advertising of commercial products is not protected by the First Amendment's guarantees. Material judged obscene is not protected by freedom of the press. Freedom of the press does not grant the mass media immunity from anti-trust laws. And "freedom of information," the right of journalists and others to attend public meetings and inspect public documents, is a statutory or common law right in most states, but oddly enough has not been held to be part of the First Amendment.

Freedom of the press, then, is a complex, evolving liberty. Over the years it has been stretched by courts to protect more and more forms of expression. But the expansion has been slow—often painfully so. The First Amendment, like other areas of American law, has been victimized by a legal lag which keeps social norms several decades ahead of legal doctrines. It must be remembered, though, that courts do not go around seeking business—from the mass media or anyone else. If freedom of the press is to continue to expand, the media and other communicators will have to keep challenging government restrictions through the courts.

Effectiveness and Responsibility

The historical, institutional, economic, and legal underpinnings of American mass communication all affect and reflect the workings of our mass media. The nagging but crucial questions of responsibility and effectiveness remain. Are the media being used effectively? Can they be used more responsibly? Later chapters of the book consider those questions in several contexts.

REFERENCES

Ben H. Bagdikian, *The Information Machines* (New York: Harper & Row, 1971).
Wilbur Schramm, *Mass Media and National Development* (Stanford, Calif.: Stanford University Press, 1964).

SUGGESTED STUDY PROJECT

Keep a good record of this evening's news program on one of your local television channels. Then compare it with today's issue of your local newspaper. What are the main differences, in terms of the amount and kinds of news covered in each medium? To what extent do you think these differences are due to the different communication technologies of the two media? In what ways do you think the news you get from each channel is limited by advertisers and other commercial factors? In what ways do you think the different audiences of the two media influence the kinds of news you get from each?

Chapter 3

Decision Making in Mass Communication

In his book *The Brass Check* (1936), the muckraker Upton Sinclair compared profits made by the media with the token used as barter in houses of prostitution. He addressed this cryptic statement to his journalistic contemporaries:

> The Brass Check is found in your pay-envelope every week—you who write and print and distribute our newspapers and magazines. The Brass Check is the price of your shame—you who take the fair body of truth and sell it in the market-place, who betray the virgin hopes of mankind into the loathsome brothel of Big Business.

With that graphic analogy, Sinclair leveled a charge that journalists prostitute themselves to the baseness of profit making. His assessment was almost as unrealistic as it was bitter. Yet similar assessments of the news media's decision makers are still echoed today by persons—some of them well-meaning—who ought to know better.

Statements such as the following are not too uncommon:

"*The New York Times* and the *Washington Post* printed the Pentagon papers in order to sell more newspapers."

"Jack Anderson broadcast a false report about Senator Thomas Eagleton's driving habits to gain attention for himself and make more money from his column."

"Editors suppress stories unfavorable to their advertisers because they want to get more advertising revenue."

Assessments like that, more often than not, are ill-informed. They also are too simplistic, given the complicated decision-making mechanisms operating in contemporary mass communication. The overwhelming bulk of newspaper sales today, for one thing, are based on subscription home deliveries, not on newsstand or street sales. While the *Times* and the *Post* may have sold additional copies of those issues containing the Pentagon papers, the economic benefit was insignificant in terms of the newspapers' overall revenues; and any extra money from street sales was likely wiped out by the legal costs of defending their constitutional right to publish the documents.

American media, of course, have to make money to stay in business. As we pointed out in Chapter 2, they do this chiefly by gaining and holding an audience which they can, in turn, sell to advertisers. So major *business* decisions made by media executives commonly are influenced by profit-making considerations. But day-to-day decisions about much media *content* typically are made by persons other than business executives, and they are based on criteria other than profit making. This is particularly the case in the news media—and appropriately so. Citizens have a stake in the end results of all media decision making; but with information and opinion, that stake is particularly high. If news decisions—such as whether to use a particular story and how much to emphasize it—were based directly on profit motives of media executives, Sinclair's description of journalism would be apt and his outrage justified.

In this chapter, we outline the common kinds of decision making in mass communication—particularly those in the news media—and describe the criteria usually employed in making those decisions. Citizens have a right and an obligation to be aware of the techniques which determine the media products they receive. Only then can evaluation of the mass media's performance be well-informed. On the other hand, simplistic, misinformed evaluation, we feel, deserves the same contempt as irresponsible decision-making practices.

Decision-making practices are important, since they determine the final products (or "outputs") of mass communication. What will appear on page one of today's evening newspaper? Will the network newscast include a dramatic film, in living color, of a bloody massacre? Which phonograph records will the radio station disc jockey choose to play and promote? How will the staff of a news magazine organize its coverage of a presidential election? Such questions suggest only a few examples of the host of decisions made every day by media personnel.

INFLUENCES ON DECISION MAKING

Regardless of the particular media industry (radio, magazine, television, newspaper) and regardless of the particular way the medium is being used (for information, entertainment, opinion, or instruction), four aspects of mass media institutions typically influence decision making: the need to filter, specialization, humanness, and traditions of "worthiness."

The Need to Filter

Most media operations face a situation of having more material available to them than they have time or space to use. A large daily newspaper, for example, might be able to use only one-tenth of all the materials which flow into the newsroom on any given day. In radio and television newscasts, the fraction is quite likely even smaller than that.

The problem is likely to intensify in the future as the amounts of available information increase. New knowledge will continue to "explode" at an ever-growing pace, technological advances will make it possible to transmit and store more information more quickly, and activities of professional utilizers of the media (particularly public relations people) will probably intensify as more private groups attempt to get their messages into the media.

So the simple but crucial need to filter will probably have an ever-growing impact on the content of the mass media. The procedures of filtering, however, are not simple. Media institutions and media units have developed traditional mechanisms and norms for making such decisions. The mechanisms are supposed to allow for efficient filtering; the norms try to ensure responsible filtering.

Media personnel who filter material are sometimes called "gatekeepers." That's an apt description in the sense that they man strategic points along the way in the process of producing and packaging media content. The gatekeepers accept or reject material; and often, material they accept will go to another gatekeeper, who may also accept it, or modify it, or reject it. Gradually, enough material gets filtered out to reduce the amount to manageable proportions. The chart on the next page illustrates one example of such filtering. It shows how an original possible 125,000 words of news copy available to the Associated Press during a four-month period in 1952

Filtering of News

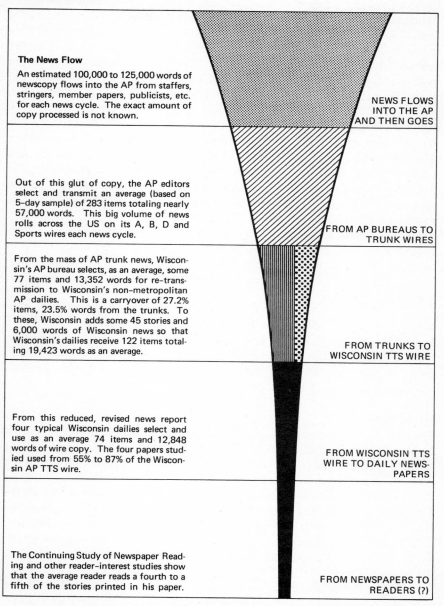

The News Flow

An estimated 100,000 to 125,000 words of newscopy flows into the AP from staffers, stringers, member papers, publicists, etc. for each news cycle. The exact amount of copy processed is not known.

NEWS FLOWS
INTO THE AP
AND THEN GOES

Out of this glut of copy, the AP editors select and transmit an average (based on 5-day sample) of 283 items totaling nearly 57,000 words. This big volume of news rolls across the US on its A, B, D and Sports wires each news cycle.

FROM AP BUREAUS TO
TRUNK WIRES

From the mass of AP trunk news, Wisconsin's AP bureau selects, as an average, some 77 items and 13,352 words for re-transmission to Wisconsin's non-metropolitan AP dailies. This is a carryover of 27.2% items, 23.5% words from the trunks. To these, Wisconsin adds some 45 stories and 6,000 words of Wisconsin news so that Wisconsin's dailies receive 122 items totaling 19,423 words as an average.

FROM TRUNKS TO
WISCONSIN TTS WIRE

From this reduced, revised news report four typical Wisconsin dailies select and use as an average 74 items and 12,848 words of wire copy. The four papers studied used from 55% to 87% of the Wisconsin AP TTS wire.

FROM WISCONSIN TTS
WIRE TO DAILY NEWS-
PAPERS

The Continuing Study of Newspaper Reading and other reader-interest studies show that the average reader reads a fourth to a fifth of the stories printed in his paper.

FROM NEWSPAPERS TO
READERS (?)

Source: Scott M. Cutlip, "Content and Flow of AP News—From Trunk to TTS to Reader," *Journalism Quarterly,* Fall 1960, p. 386.

and 1953 was reduced. First, AP gatekeepers at the New York central head-quarters cut the amount of material almost in half, and sent it over the national news wire. Gatekeepers at the state AP bureau then rejected about three-fourths of the material sent from New York, and added some new material of their own. After that, gatekeepers working at the newspapers rejected about two-fifths of the material. The points demonstrated by the twenty-year-old AP filtering study still hold. If the study were repeated today, the proportion of material weeded out might be even more dramatic.

Specialization

As the study of filtering by the Associated Press implies, decisions about what to use and what to reject are not made only at a single point by one person, but at several places throughout the process. Most gatekeepers working at those points are specialists, and they use special tools to perform specialized tasks. In addition to filtering, they decide how to organize and emphasize those materials which they accept.

Gatekeepers in a newsroom—whether of a television network, news magazine or daily newspaper—include personnel who make assignments to reporters, the reporters themselves, editors who evaluate and perhaps modi-fy the stories done by reporters, and editors who plan and package all or part of the final product.

Frequently, a gatekeeper does his work independently, without con-sulting the other gatekeepers. In some ways, media gatekeepers are like inspectors scattered along a production line. Each has his own particular part of the product to evaluate. If that part passes inspection, it gets rou-tinely passed along to other inspectors, and, hopefully, a quality product emerges at the end of the process.

Humanness

Because media gatekeepers are human beings, their decisions are colored by very human conditions. Whims, habits, preferences, and personal ethics all play a part in the decisions they make. Researchers have found some common human forces which seem to be particularly influential on their decision-making practices. An often-cited study by David Manning White, for example, concluded that a newspaper telegraph editor (the gatekeeper who decides which wire service stories to place in the newspapers each day) based many of his choices on his own highly subjective value judgments; he frequently rejected stories because he considered them "trivial" or "slop" or "propaganda."

"What the boss expects" and a reporter's sympathy for news sources can also play a key role. A study of television news reporters by Dan G. Drew showed that their "role expectations" (whether the reporter viewed his function as being a "watchdog over government" or a "promoter for the community" or an "entertainer") influenced the decisions they made in covering and writing the news. George Bailey and Lawrence Lichty have documented how an NBC news broadcast showing a color film of an execution in Vietnam was influenced by a producer's opinion that a close-up of a corpse's bloody head might be in poor taste.

Another example of how personal viewpoints influence decisions is shown in the following statement by A. M. Rosenthal, managing editor of *The New York Times*, explaining why that newspaper decided to publish the Pentagon papers in 1971:

> . . . Not to print the documentation when it was available would have been a great disservice to American society. All kinds of rumors and speculation would have built up: What is in these documents? About the atom bomb? China? What great secrets? I think it would have been very divisive. People would have been debating this forever. What is in the documents? What are they afraid to reveal? It would have created ghosts in people's minds where none really need exist.[1]

Traditions of "Worthiness"

There are also institutionalized guidelines for helping decide whether something is worthy of being included in a media product, and, if so, how to present it. History, technology, inter-media competition "codes of ethics," and the law have all influenced the development of these standards.

One controversial American journalistic tradition—that events involving conflict are usually "newsworthy"—goes back to the penchant of the first colonial editors to dwell on conflicts between the mother country and other European powers. Various kinds of conflict, from politics to wars to natural disasters, have been a major staple of worldwide news ever since.

The role of technology in helping to shape traditions of "worthiness" is well illustrated by the impact of television on other media. As Paul Hirsch, a sociologist, has noted, television

> . . . threatened radio's existence to such an extent that it had to seek new and different markets which could complement those of television. The movie industry was affected similarly. . . . Rock-and-roll emerged in the fifties as part of the radio industry's confused responses to the onslaught of television.[2]

Thus, Hirsch maintains, radio programers came to consider rock music

[1]A. M. Rosenthal, "Why We Published," reprinted from *Columbia Journalism Review*, September–October 1971, pp. 16–17. By permission of the author and publisher.
[2]Paul M. Hirsch, "Sociological Approaches to the Pop Music Phenomenon," *American Behavioral Scientist*, January 1971, pp. 380–381.

(and later the "top forty" format, "progressive rock," and even "underground music") worthy only after the new technology of television had jolted them out of their old programing habits. Decision makers in the movie industry started accepting new, more liberalized standards after television became the number one video entertainer of the American family. Likewise, newspaper and magazine editors began to engage in more interpretative and in-depth treatment of information—a function which television has not yet attempted to any great degree, although it is capable of doing so.

As new forms of media develop, then, older media are forced to redefine their standards of decision making in order to compete with the new media. Cable television, and the cassette media, will surely have an impact on the traditions of other media. That is why competition helps set standards of "media-worthiness." The reporter's almost innate drive to "get a scoop"—and the editor's likely inclination to play up whatever "scoops" his reporters get—comes from the satisfaction of outperforming the competitor.

Ethical codes established by media institutions may also influence the behavior of media decision makers, and in many cases these "codes of ethics" lay down fairly specific guidelines.

Consider the Code of Broadcast News Ethics of the Radio Television News Directors Association as one example. It admonishes broadcast journalists that

> . . . factors such as race, creed, nationality or prior status will be reported only when they are relevant; that comment or subjective content will be properly identified; and that errors in fact will promptly be acknowledged and corrected.

Most journalists do try to abide by the ideals set forth in such codes. That is about all citizens can ask for, since in most cases compliance is voluntary, and concepts in the codes are subject to personal interpretation. One reporter's "decency," after all, might be another one's "obscenity."

Legal restraints constitute yet another force determining standards of media-worthiness. Many potential items never appear in the media because gatekeepers fear they might evoke a lawsuit for such things as libel, invasion of privacy, or infringement of copyright. Still other materials may be judged "unworthy" because the law defines them as being illegal; obscenity, sedition, and false advertising are examples of that.

MAKING NEWS DECISIONS

We turn now to a more detailed examination of decision making *in the news media.* Since public affairs information is assigned a high value in the work-

News is an intellectual artifact fashioned under a code of professional ethics and received as a cultural experience.

But it is also the product of a bureaucracy with employees, unions, and stockholders, processed in a manufacturing plant that has some of the same characteristics as its sister factories that produce hubcaps and monkey wrenches.

—Ben H. Bagdikian, in *The Information Machines*
(New York: Harper & Row, 1971), p. 115

ings of a democracy, the news media have a special obligation to exercise responsibility in their decision-making techniques, and those techniques deserve scrutiny.

Units of the news media—the individual newspapers, television news departments, etc.—generally organize themselves to process and package material efficiently and effectively. In that respect, they are no different from other media. But the types of decisions that are made, and the standards on which those decisions are based, make journalistic decision-making techniques special. To analyze them, we will look at the news process—the major steps by which the content of a newspaper, newsmagazine, or newscast is determined. In doing so, we will examine decisions involving (1) assignments, (2) reporting, (3) editing or evaluating content, and (4) matters of news policy.

Assignments

In general, most journalists would agree, the more news covered by a media unit's own staff, the higher the quality of the news product. Those media which thrive merely on wire service news and public relations "news releases" are cheap imitations of journalism. Most news operations consequently have a staff of reporters, along with photographers or cameramen, to "cover" the news. But *what news*?

The possible number of events and problems worthy of reportage usually exceeds the staff capacity to adequately report all of them. So decisions are required. What proportion, if any, of staff resources will be devoted to a particular event? Will one reporter be assigned, or perhaps a team of reporters? Does the story warrant visual coverage as well? Decisions of how to allocate staff resources are of primary importance in an examination of news decision making; for if an event is judged unworthy of staff attention, it will not be transmitted to the citizenry, regardless of its significance.

Media personnel who give assignments, therefore, are crucial decision makers. Their titles vary according to the medium. Some larger operations have "assignment editors" whose sole job is to think up and give out assignments.

"News Value" Personal preferences and idiosyncracies undoubtedly affect the decisions made by these "assigners." But some criteria typically pervade assignment making regardless of the type of medium or the individual's own foibles. Perhaps the most important criteria are notions of "news value"—a set of journalistic traditions which may trigger an almost automatic response from news decision makers. The notion of news value is that certain attributes, when connected to an event, are prima facie evidence of "newsworthiness." The major attributes traditionally include the following:

Conflict An event which demonstrates antagonism, opposition, or disturbance of the status quo is likely to be judged newsworthy. Such events include conflict between individuals (e.g. crime), groups (e.g. riots and election campaigns), nations (e.g. wars), and between humans and the forces of nature (e.g. natural disasters).

Magnitude The larger the event, or the more people it affects, or the more money it involves, the more likely it will be judged newsworthy.

Oddity If something is unusual enough, it will be covered. An old saying puts the notion well: "If man bites dog, that's news."

Proximity The closer the occurrence, the more likely the news coverage. A Detroit radio station would likely cover a story about a $1,000 bank robbery in downtown Detroit, but it's doubtful that a Boston station—or even a Chicago one—would use the Detroit story.

Prominence Well-known persons tend to have their activities covered; persons of low social status are more likely to be ignored.

Timeliness Things that happen relatively close to "deadline" might get preference over earlier occurrences. Most journalistic decision makers prefer to deal with "the latest news."

Other Criteria These "news value" criteria have their detractors. Critics call them artificial and out of date. Such standards, they claim, encourage sensationalism but discourage coverage of long-range problems. And the critics have had an impact. While news value criteria such as those above continue to play some part in determining which stories the news media will cover, other standards have been added in recent years. The result has been to give audiences a larger menu of news items in place of a rigid diet of conflict, bigness, physical closeness, and "bulletins." Decision makers in many news organizations now use other standards, such as the following:

Significance An occurrence or a problem should be covered if it is likely to have an impact on people. Inadequate health care, for example, would be a newsworthy topic; and staff resources would be devoted to it before the problem developed into one of conflict (such as a political campaign issue) or magnitude (such as an epidemic).

Explanation and problem solving   Items which shed light on how some current problem developed, or which report on how others may have tried to solve the problem, are considered worth covering.

Empathy   A happening or a problem may be psychologically close to people even though far removed physically. Thus, features about common incidents in the lives of common people—such as the episodes in Charles Kuralt's "On the Road" series on CBS—can be considered newsworthy.

Decision makers who give out assignments do not deliberately and systematically compare each potential assignment against a listing of news value criteria. By and large, they act out of habit. But their habits are formed in part by those of the organization—including its traditions of newsworthiness.

Other factors also play a role. The organization may have a deliberate policy of playing up certain kinds of news, and it may have developed a reputation or "image" of specializing in certain types of stories. Convenience is often a consideration too; a considerable amount of news often can be generated easily just by permanently assigning a single "beat" reporter to a certain "news center" such as the courthouse or the police department. Regardless of the criteria used, giving assignments is only the first of a series of decision-making situations common to all news media.

Reporting

The reporter has two main roles. He or she is an observer (or news gatherer) and a describer (or news teller). Few reporters consistently operate like robots. In carrying out both roles, they make many decisions—some deliberately, others almost mechanically—which affect the finished news product.

The nearly mechanical decisions result largely from organizational constraints imposed upon the reporter. There is the "deadline," for example, which requires a routine of working rapidly (sometimes resulting in superficiality) on some items. If the reporter is assigned to a "beat," there are routine persons to talk to, documents to look at. Moreover, the reporter usually knows what the editor wants; and most reporters try to please their editors.

Influences on Reporters   But despite those constraints, reporters have a lot of leeway in helping prepare the day's menu of news. The choice of persons to be interviewed often may be the reporter's to make. The choice of questions the reporter will ask inevitably molds the nature of the news presentation. Such decisions by reporters are influenced by several factors. Among the common factors are these:

Role perception   Does the reporter view him- or herself as a "watchdog" whose duty it is to expose corruption and other evil? Or is the perceived role that of a neutral "transmission belt" which simply relays "facts"? Or that of a "promoter" whose main job is to make newsmakers look good? Or that of "representative" who seeks out information that "average citizens" supposedly want or need? Or of "activist," who creates news and then reports it?

"News values"   Like assignment editors, reporters are aware of journalistic traditions which so often place a premium on the antagonistic, the large, the unusual, the prominent, the recent. The news sources they seek out, and the questions they ask, often are influenced by those considerations.

View of source   Like all of us, reporters like and trust some persons more than others. Newsmakers favored by reporters come to be "reliable sources," and they are more frequently sought out.

View of topic   Reporters sometimes frame questions in a way to elicit answers which coincide with the reporter's personal assessment of the topic being reported. Leading questions (such as "But isn't it true that . . . ?") are often used as a tool in this type of reportorial decision making.

In most instances, reporters also write their own copy; they transcribe what they have observed or learned into a format suitable for presentation in the media. In this "describer" function, reporters also make decisions which affect the final news product. For example, they engage in "filtering" by deciding what to include in the stories they write. All aspects of an occurrence, or all statements made during an interview or news conference, usually cannot be included in the reporter's story; space and time regulations dictate that some things be left out.

Reporters also must decide how to structure or organize their stories— what to emphasize, what to play down. The conventional practice in most news media is to use the beginning of a report as a spot for emphasis. So, in most cases, reporters put what they consider to be the most important aspects of the story at the beginning and the least important at the end. This "inverted pyramid" practice has pragmatic value. For one thing, it allows editors to shorten the story, should they decide to do so, more quickly; they can routinely cut off the last sentences or paragraphs of the story and thereby eliminate the least important material without spending too much time or effort. For another, editors can judge the relative importance of one story, compared with other stories, on the basis of the first few sentences or lines. Editors generally will give the biggest headlines or most prominent display to stories they consider the most important. And since most reporters like to see their own stories displayed prominently, they may be tempted to structure their stories more for the attention of editors than for edification of citizens.

Reporters who engage in deliberate distortion, however, are likely to get wrathful attention rather than admiration. Standards of professionalism in reporting, including honesty and fairness, are assigned a heavy weight by most reporters and their editors. Consequently, the decisions that reporters make when they organize their stories tend to revolve around the more routine "news values" commonly followed in journalistic decision making: emphasis on conflict, prominence, timeliness, and so forth. Reporters are aware that other decision makers are going to "inspect" their products, and that if a story is to pass through the newsroom filtering process, it will have to meet expected standards.

Editing

Sources of News Materials Editing basically involves evaluation of the materials that flow into the newsroom. It is no small task, and most news operations employ specialists to get it done. Consider the vast amount of different kinds of news materials which must be evaluated at the editing level in a typical news operation.

Staff-generated news These are stories covered and written by the organization's own staff or reporters.

News purchased from outside news agencies That includes news from the major wire services (the Associated Press and United Press International), specialized news services (such as *The New York Times* News Service), and syndicates (such as Newspaper Enterprise Association).

Material supplied by a parent or affiliated company Members of Scripps-Howard newspapers, for example, receive stories from Scripps-Howard News Service; network radio and affiliated stations can use portions of network news programing on the locally originated newscasts.

Items supplied by professional utilizers of the media (particularly public relations firms) A typical newsroom receives a great quantity of prepackaged "news releases," photographs, sound tapes, films, and videotapes. PR operations supply these materials free of charge to get free publicity for their company or client.

In evaluating all this material, editors face two kinds of decisions. They must "filter"—that is, decide which items will be used. And they must "package"—that is, decide how to organize and arrange the items they select for use.

Filtering   Earlier in this chapter, we took up the need for filtering. Now we will explain, in general terms, the *mechanisms* and *criteria* which editors typically employ in the filtering process.

Mechanisms   By *mechanisms,* we mean the established procedures or routines which are established to allow for quick, efficient filtering of mammoth amounts of materials. Specialization through division of labor is a common strategy. At an initial stage, a newspaper "city editor" might be responsible for filtering local-oriented items, the sports editor will take care of sports-oriented copy, and the "telegraph editor" will filter wire service news. (Wire service news, as we have seen, already has gone through a formidable filtering process before it ever reaches the individual newspaper or broadcast station.) At a newspaper, items that make it through the first checkpoints might then go on to the "copy desk," where copy editors check them for errors and style, and perhaps shorten the item. A third stage involves the actual placement of items on particular pages. This usually is a shared responsibility of various editors or other decision makers.

Similar filtering procedures take place in radio and television newsrooms for production of newscasts, with the elaborateness of the procedures depending on the size of the production staff. A small operation may rely on the news director, producer, and anchorman. Larger television operations also employ a news editor, copy editors, and several film editors.

Criteria   The *criteria* used to filter material will vary with the individual gatekeeper. Sometimes highly personal, subjective standards are used. More often, criteria related to "news values" are determinant. The chart on page 39 illustrates the broad spectrum of criteria employed by "Mr. Gates," the telegraph editor in White's study of gatekeeping. As implied in the chart, major criteria for filtering include the following:

How the gatekeeper personally feels about the story's topic. If the filterer "doesn't care for" certain kinds of stories, they're unlikely to pass through his inspection point.

Traditional "news values." Stories considered "too far away" (lack of proximity) or dealing with something that "goes on all the time" (lack of oddity) are prime targets for rejection.

Amount of available space. Some stories might be acceptable on other criteria, but are not used because there is "no space" (or time, in the case of broadcasting).

Quality of writing. Filterers are harried folk, and poorly written materials are readily dismissed as being "too vague" or "dull." Concise, interesting stories are generally preferred.

Competition. A story which is too old is likely to be rejected in favor of a version which gives "the latest" information and might be viewed as a scoop over competitors.

Ethical standards. Stories might be eliminated because they are considered below professional or community standards ("not in good taste").

Why a Gatekeeper Rejected News Items

Reasons for Rejection of Press Association News Given by a Newspaper Telegraph Editor During a Seven-Day Period

Reason	Number of times given
Rejecting incident as worthy of reporting	423
Not interesting (61); no interest here (43)	104
Dull writing (51); too vague (26); drags too much (3).............	80
No good (31); slop (18); B. S. (18)	67
Too much already on subject (54); used up (4); passed— dragging out*; too much of this; goes on all the time; dying out..	62
Trivial (29); would ignore (21); no need for this; wasted space; not too important; not too hot; not too worthy	55
Never use this (16); never use (7).......................................	23
Propaganda (16); he's too red; sour grapes	18
Wouldn't use (11); don't care for suicide stories; too suggestive; out of good taste	14
Selecting from reports of the same event....................................	910
Would use if space (221); no space (168); good—if space (154); late—used up (61); too late—no space (34); no space—used other press service; would use partially if space.	640
Passed for later story (61); waiting for later information (48); waiting on this (33); waiting for this to hatch (17); would let drop a day or two (11); outcome will be used—not this; waiting for later day progress	172
Too far away (24); out of area (16)	40
Too regional (36)...	36
Used another press service; better story (11); shorter (6); this is late; lead more interesting; meatier	20
Bannered yesterday...	1
I missed this one..	1

*In this and other cases where no number follows that reason was given only once.

Source: David Manning White, "The 'Gate Keeper': A Case Study in the Selection of News," *Journalism Quarterly,* Fall 1950, p. 386.

White's study is more than twenty years old, but his conclusions that gatekeepers rely on both personal and professional criteria are still valid. As journalist-scholar Ben Bagdikian concluded after a more recent study of gatekeeping practices, the gatekeeper of today is still influenced by a mixture of cultural, journalistic, and personal values.

Packaging   Those items that somehow make it through the filtering process need next to be packaged. In the print media, that usually means deciding about the size and style of type for the story and the headline;

deciding where to place the story; and laying out or designing the individual pages. In broadcasting, the typical packaging decisions concern arranging the stories (from opening to closing items of the newscast); adding transitions (called "coupling pins") between stories where appropriate; deciding whether and where to use "actualities" (filmed or taped on-the-scene reports) and other special effects (like background music or video slides); and editing the items to meet time requirements.

Criteria for packaging   These are similar to the criteria we discussed earlier. Indeed, some gatekeepers who filtered the items earlier might also become involved in packaging, so a brief outline of the common criteria will suffice.

Personal values. If an item simply strikes an editor's fancy for some subjective reason, it could get a large headline and placement on page one, or become the lead-off newscast item complemented with special effects. More often, though, criteria like the following three influence the packaging.

Traditional "news values." Stories, photos, or recordings dealing with prominent persons or involving conflict and similar standards are likely to get prominent display. In general, items containing a coalescence of several "news values" are given the most favorable packaging treatment.

Competition. News products are packaged to emphasize those items considered "exclusives" or "bulletins."

Departmentalization. A single news product is frequently divided into several smaller packages. Such treatment serves the special interests of audiences (for example, persons interested primarily in sports news can seize the sports section or tune in to the five-minute sports segment of a local newscast). Departmentalization also allows media to use division of labor to advantage in the packaging process. But, perhaps most important, it provides an added incentive for additional advertising. A weekly real estate section of a daily newspaper attracts real estate ads; and local newscast producers can squeeze in more commercials if they split up a half-hour program into separate segments dealing with news, weather, and sports.

Results   The *results* of the editing process are, of course, noticeable to media audiences. As readers, viewers, and listeners, we are aware only of the materials which *do* pass through the filtering process; and the way those materials are packaged ordinarily influences how we react to them. Editing procedures may vary somewhat from media unit to media unit, and inevitably involve complexities which we could not go into in one chapter. But the generalizations we have presented should provide a basic understanding of these important processes.

Policy Making

So far our discussion of news decision making has ignored media executives such as the publisher, editor-in-chief, station manager, or program director. That is because they usually do not play an active role in routine news decisions—except in small media units. But these executives do make decisions which influence the quantity and quality of news available in the media they oversee. They are instrumental, for example, in:

Determining the resources available for the news staff by setting employment standards, hiring key "gatekeepers," deciding how large the news staff will be, purchasing newsroom equipment, and setting salaries.

Formulating general policies, including codes of ethics, to guide the conduct of the news staff.

Setting editorial policy, by participating in the writing of editorials and occasionally by initiating and supervising various campaigns and crusades.

Making final decisions in major controversial matters, such as resolving disputes between staff members or determining whether particularly sensitive material (such as the Pentagon papers) should be used.

The history of journalism, both print and broadcast, is replete with biographies of media executives who have been tagged either heroes or villains. In years past, executives commonly used their media as personal mouthpieces; some of those have survived as stalwart and highly respected journalistic enterprises, while others have suffered scorn. Today, personal involvement by corporate executives in news decisions is quite rare. But in those instances where they do become actively involved in journalistic decision making, their employees and their audiences have every right to expect them to act as professional journalists rather than business managers.

REFERENCES

Ben H. Bagdikian, *The Information Machines* (New York: Harper & Row, 1971).
George A. Bailey and Lawrence W. Lichty, "Rough Justice on a Saigon Street: A Gatekeeper Study of NBC's Tet Execution Film," *Journalism Quarterly,* Summer 1972, pp. 221–229.
Scott M. Cutlip, "Content and Flow of AP News—From Trunk to TTS to Reader," *Journalism Quarterly,* Fall 1954, pp. 434–446.
Dan G. Drew, "Roles and Decision Making of Three Television Beat Reporters," *Journal of Broadcasting,* Spring 1972, pp. 165–173.
Paul M. Hirsch, "Sociological Approaches to the Pop Music Phenomenon," *American Behavioral Scientist,* January 1971, pp. 371–387.
A. M. Rosenthal, "Why We Published," *Columbia Journalism Review,* September/October 1971, pp. 16–18.

Upton Sinclair, *The Brass Check* (New York: Albert & Charles Boni, 1936).

David Manning White, "The Gate Keeper: A Case Study in the Selection of News," *Journalism Quarterly,* Fall 1950, pp. 383–390.

SUGGESTED STUDY PROJECTS

1 Take a current issue of a newspaper or newsmagazine and try to determine which criteria of "worthiness" are most frequently used by the editors. To what extent are traditional "news values" like conflict, magnitude, etc. reflected? What use is made of newer problem-oriented standards like significance, explanation, etc.?

2 Take detailed notes about packaging techniques employed by two competing radio or television stations in their news programs. By comparing the stations' newscasts for a single day, can you discern the criteria used by news packagers at the stations? What can you conclude from the differences, or lack thereof, in the packaging decisions of the two stations?

3 Ask an editor at a local newspaper, radio station, or television station to save all the wire service copy that gatekeepers have decided not to use during a given period, such as a single day. From studying the unused material, what do you conclude about the criteria used by those gatekeepers to filter the news?

Chapter 4

Mass Communication in Perspective

In the first few chapters we have discussed "communication" in terms of our modern mass media system, because that is the mechanism by which many concerted attacks on societal problems are undertaken. But "communication" should not be equated simply with the mass media. People were communicating long before methods of mechanical reproduction of messages had been invented. And even today, most of our communication takes place informally and without recourse to the media.

Still, in an age of widespread access to print, film, broadcast, and other forms of media, there are many qualitative differences in the way society functions—when modern life is compared to earlier times. In this chapter we attempt to relate mass communication to the more basic forms of interpersonal interaction, to provide a human perspective for our later discussions. This will also enable us to define some concepts that we will refer to throughout the remainder of the book.

COMMUNICATION FLOW AND STORAGE

The most basic concepts regarding communication technologies are those of message "flow" and "storage." Flow, or transmission, can be thought of simply as getting a message from one person to another. The main points of variation from one communication system to another are in terms of the speed of transmission and the number (and variety) of persons to whom the message can be transmitted. These factors are the ones most often used to distinguish mass communication from seemingly simpler interpersonal transmission. When a delivery system permits flow of messages to large and varied audiences, it is usually called a *mass* medium—reflecting the notion that the audience is a "mass" as well as the fact that the message has been mass-produced. Ordinarily this involves some mechanical conversion of the message to a new form that is amenable to mass reproduction and delivery. This mechanical conversion, reproduction, and delivery system is called a "medium" because it lies between people in the chain of communication. For example, writing consists of the conversion of spoken words into a new form of the same message, one that considerably facilitates transmission of that message to another person. Print, in turn, is a conversion of writing that allows mass reproduction as well. Radio permits mass delivery of the spoken word by converting it into electronic impulses that can be reconverted to sound by a receiver set.

Message storage capacity is not quite so obviously critical to the social importance of a medium as message flow. But in this age of computer-stored information "banks," we have come to appreciate anew the storage properties of precomputer media. The main elements of storage are the ease with which a message can be put into a system to be stored, the ease with which another person can "retrieve" that message from the system, and the degree to which the message can faithfully be preserved while it is being stored in the system. For example, the notes a student takes at a lecture are fairly easy to jot down at the time, but later retrieval may be difficult because they are not complete. For faithfulness of transmission, a tape recording of the lecture might be preferable, although it is slower and more cumbersome than notes. If someone other than the person attending the lecture is to learn the material, the tape recording is clearly preferable to scribbled notes, since the latter are notoriously difficult for anyone other than the note-taker to decipher.

Storage is closely linked to flow in many systems: the message is converted to a stored form that can then be transported across space and time to diverse audiences. Live broadcasting is an extreme case which sends the message across vast spaces (in some instances, between the earth and the moon) but does not store the message for later times. Such a system is called "real time" transmission in the vernacular of the computer world. Aside from spot news and sports, it is rarely used nowadays in the mass media.

Let us turn now to an analysis of nonmediated communication, the kind we engage in every day with the people around us. Flow is a simple matter in person-to-person discussion; each individual takes his turn formulating messages and transmitting them to the other. Storage of information is not a problem since each person is immediately available for elaboration, recapitulation, or explanation of points that the other does not understand.

A message often dies after a single telling in a purely interpersonal communication system. Flow can be achieved only via retelling, from someone who has heard it to someone who hasn't. Storage is limited to the capacity of human memory. A culture built on this kind of communication system is called an *oral tradition.*

Anthropologists generally agree that the most distinctive difference between human behavior and that of other animals is the transmission and storage of information by means of symbols—in a word, communication. For perhaps a million years, human beings lived in Africa and Eurasia, developing cultures that were stored and transmitted purely by oral tradition. Many of these were rich and diversified civilizations, in terms of literary and religious content as well as the technologies of agriculture, mining, manufacturing, and other economic functions.

Oral traditions today store and transmit all those categories of our culture's content that are *not* carried by the mass media. A few examples should suffice to convince the reader that we still utilize the "primitive" technology of oral tradition. Rumors and gossip, dirty jokes, and claims about quack medicines are usually omitted from the media—but they often flow through society at an astonishing rate.

The ancient literary epics, such as *Beowulf,* and the tales that account for the founding of the world's great religions share several characteristics with these modern oral traditions. For one thing, they tend to be filled with statements of dubious credibility. This is a natural outcome of a system that lacks sufficient storage capacity to permit independent "truth checks" on the validity of any claim. This is not to say that mass communication ensures truth, but only that it makes accounts of miracles and superhuman powers much easier to test. Modern science, which consists at heart of independent empirical tests of hypotheses and theories, is the most advanced system so far devised for checking the validity of a truth claim. It is practically impossible to conceive of science within the limited flow and storage capacities of oral tradition.

A second characteristic common to ancient and modern oral traditions is that they tend to be localized—in details, if not in general form. Many religions, including such very different ones as Taoism and Christianity, are believed by their adherents to have been founded by men whose births were quite miraculous. But the miracles differ substantially. Lao-Tze (the name means "old boy") is said to have been born white-haired and already very wise at the advanced age of sixty-two, while his mother (who had conceived him as a consequence of contemplating a falling star) leaned against a plum tree. It is difficult to argue that this belief is inherently less credible than the several accounts of the birth of Jesus in the synoptic Gospels of the Bible. Many scholars have suggested that miraculous birth is necessary to the establishment of a great religion, or that at least it is a most helpful ingredient. It has also been pointed out that Lao-Tze's advanced age at birth coincides nicely with traditional Chinese cultural values that venerate age.

This is not to deny the possible truth of these or any other stories that come to us from ancient oral traditions. A number of sources, including the Book of Genesis and the Indian epic of Gilgamesh, for example, tell of a great flood. Archaeological evidence seems to corroborate the story of the flood. The religious meanings drawn from this event, however, are quite different in the two traditions, reflecting the different cultures which the flood threatened.

Today's oral traditions may be less uplifting to the human spirit, but they exhibit these same qualities of untested validity and adaptation to localized values and needs. Gossip, for instance, is looked on as socially pernicious because the victim has no opportunity to test the truth of claims about him. Among the protections in the Bill of Rights is the guarantee that a defendant in court shall have the opportunity to confront his accusers—a form of truth-test not available to the object of rumor or gossip. (Not surprisingly, this constitutional guarantee has come into open conflict with the provision of freedom of speech and press in the First Amendment.)

Localization can be illustrated by the oral tradition of today's joke that carries an ethnic slur. An attentive barroom or barbershop listener can hear a "Polish joke" from Chicago translated into an "Italian joke" in San Francisco, where a different ethnic minority is the object of derision. Often the same tale can be traced to an "Irish joke" from New York a generation ago—and perhaps even back in the Middle Ages to a "Saxon joke" in Plantagenet England, for all anyone knows.

Revolutions in Writing and Print

Obviously it is impossible to trace local variations from a common oral tradition back very far, unless some method of storage was available at that earlier time. The introduction of writing was a revolution (the word is by no means too strong) in human history; it began the decline of reliance on the pure oral tradition. Writing made the flow of communication much more complex and permitted extrahuman storage for the first time. Once a person had written something down, many others could read it, and it could be saved as long as the tablet or papyrus on which it was written lasted. Ideas that formerly could be diffused and stored only through oral tradition and human memory were now amenable to much more efficient flow through a society. It is easy to imagine that written communication was the critical social innovation that made it possible for the civilizations in Egypt and the Fertile Crescent to combine elaborate political systems with carefully stored theological documents, and thus to produce what are sometimes characterized as Sacred Monarchies. At any rate, the earliest evidence we have in Western civilization of writing comes from the autocratic early nations of Sumer, Assyria, Babylon, and their neighbors in what is today called the Middle East.

For several thousand years this was the general model of social organization in the nation-states of Western civilization, as they rose and fell through the ages of Greece and Rome, the Middle Ages, and the early Renaissance. Storage became a major industry of the medieval monks copying ecclesiastical documents by hand in their scriptoria, and it permitted the construction of massive religious institutions (and the derivative political doctrine of the divine right of kings).

The next communication revolution, and the one of which the media pundit Marshall McLuhan has made so much in his communication-technology theory of history, was the beginning of the printing industry. The invention of movable type in mid-fifteenth-century Germany by Johann Gutenberg made production of written materials less laborious, and even economically profitable. Printing vastly increased the possibilities for the flow of messages within a society, with no sacrifice in the capacity to store the messages. If one is inclined to attribute all things to communication, it is possible to see printing as responsible for the rise of Protestantism and the fall of the Holy Roman Empire, the blooming of commerce and literacy, the emergence of city-states (and later nations), and the discovery of the New World. Printing certainly had a role in all these things, and they surely would have occurred more slowly without it.

The next four centuries brought enormous change to the Western world, and many improvements in print technology occurred. By 1900, the United States had one or more daily newspapers in every town of any size, national magazines, worldwide news-gathering agencies, a lively commerce in popular books, and a predominantly literate public to consume all these products. Photoengraving, rotary presses, the telegraph and teletype, linotype, and most of the other machinery of modern printing had been provided in the Industrial Revolution of the nineteenth century. As far as print was concerned, it seemed that only minor improvements in communication methods remained to be developed.

The Media Explosion

The twentieth century has, to be sure, brought further innovations in the printing industry. But they have been vastly overshadowed by the introduction of new media technologies, which have greatly extended the storage and flow capacities of modern society. Radio and films came first.

Radio had an enormous impact on flow, since a person did not even have to be literate to listen to it, and since the cost of a home receiver has never been very high. On the other hand, there were few provisions for storage of radio communication for some time, despite the prior availability of the phonograph record. Many of the delightful network radio shows of even the 1940s were broadcast live and never stored.

Film, on the other hand, was the storage technique *par excellence.* Prints of some of the very earliest movies, such as *The Great Train Robbery,* are still being shown today. Unfortunately, little content of any import for public affairs was recorded on early film. This medium has never been used very effectively for transmitting words; it seems to get across feelings better than ideas or concepts. Indeed, many critics consider some of the early silent films to be superior to the sound movies of the 1930s and later. In recent years, it has been the visual-emotional aspect of film that has been explored by the most creative talents in the field, and the explicit "message" movie is in serious disrepute.

Television, the *Wunderkind* of the field in the 1950s, has worked its way into a comfortable (and highly remunerative) niche as a compromise among the main features of print, radio, and film. Television provides the most extensive communication flow of any medium in history, and with the advent of videotape and cassette recordings it is beginning to lick the storage problem too—although not yet on a scale that involves most of its audience. The "white monster" in the living room brings us a continuous supply of light entertainment and capsule news (watered-down digests of the depth reporting of newspapers and magazines) and the visual impact of film, all at the ridiculously cheap price of our being exposed to a string of inane commercial advertisements for about one-fifth of our viewing time. McLuhan argues that television in the process also teaches us to receive information through several senses simultaneously, thus freeing us from the "linear" modes of thought that print forced on earlier generations.

We can, of course, expect continued expansion and innovation in media flow and storage capabilities. But even as they exist today, the mass media offer an amazingly versatile set of techniques for communicating. As new technologies (such as cable and satellite transmission and computerized information systems) are introduced, the student of the field will be best prepared to anticipate their social consequences if he thinks in terms of (1) their effect on flow and storage capacity and (2) their relationships to interpersonal communication.

INTERPERSONAL COMMUNICATION: THE FUNDAMENTAL FORM

The mass media should be looked on as products of the Industrial Revolution that primarily enable us to do more economically something people have "always" done—communicate with one another. Once they become available, new media gradually lead us into doing things we might not have considered before. But for the most part, we can analyze the potential uses of our modern media by considering their role in extending and modifying basic interpersonal communication.

It is usual to look on communication as a means of bringing about two kinds of changes: gains in information and modifications of opinions. In practice, however, it is often quite difficult to distinguish between the two. Information much of the time involves a mixture of data that we would all agree are "facts," plus the interpretations that people give to those facts in order to give them meaning in a social context. For instance, consider the fact that "Columbus discovered America in 1492." The exact details are rather less sweeping. Columbus had apparently been preceded to America by Leif Ericson, and the American continents were at the time inhabited by some millions of residents, of apparently Asian origin. Columbus was accompanied by a number of other sailors on his three ships, and they landed on a minor piece of land that is called today Watling's Island, not on an American continent. But in the context of Western history, and in terms of clearly demonstrating to European eyes of the 1490s the existence of hitherto unverified lands in the western Atlantic Ocean, these are technical quibbles. We teach our children that Columbus discovered America, secure in the assumption that this piece of information will be received in the context of a social interpretation that gives it the historical significance we intend it to have.

A second example is the fact that "Lincoln freed the slaves." Practically everyone who reads the Emancipation Proclamation is disappointed to find that Lincoln specifically exempted from freedom those slaves who happened to be unlucky enough to live in those border areas of the South that had remained loyal to the Union during the Civil War. To be more exact, it was the restoration of the Union following the military defeat of the Confederacy, and a legislative act—the Fifteenth Amendment to the Constitution (following Lincoln's death)—that rendered slavery illegal in the United States. Still, it is sensible to look at Lincoln in a broad social-political sense and give him credit (as do descendants of American slaves) or blame (as do some who might be characterized as the spiritual descendants of American slaveholders) for the abolition of slavery.

And so it is with almost any set of "facts" that people are likely to make any serious effort at communicating. Information, however objective at its core, requires some social context and line of argument to give it meaning for other people. In science, the philosopher Charles Darwin observed, no piece of evidence is significant except to the extent that it is "for or against some view." We tend much of the time to coalesce pieces of information into opinions and generalized beliefs about the world—and to pursue those opinions and beliefs by gathering and retaining information that supports them. When we communicate our ideas to other people, whatever line existed between "fact" and "opinion" has long since been blurred over.

We will certainly not abandon the distinction between informational and opinion content in communication. We consider the distinction important in judging the performance of the media, even though it is perhaps better characterized as an ideal goal to strive toward than as an absolute standard against which to assess media ethics. But in discussing interpersonal communication, we will not make so much of the fact-opinion distinction. It seems more reasonable to talk of people's "thoughts" and their sharing of them, without worrying too much for the moment about the exact nature of those thoughts.

When a person is communicating with someone else, he is not dealing strictly with his own thoughts. He also takes into account what he judges to be going on in the other person's head at the same time. Presumably he knows what he is talking about, and from the other person's conversation he gets some idea what that person is thinking about. We can distinguish, then, two quite different aspects of an interpersonal relationship. The first is usually called *agreement*. It refers to the degree of similarity between the thoughts of the two people who are interacting. The second is the degree of *accuracy* on the part of each person in understanding what the other is saying—and thinking.

To illustrate, suppose a new freeway has been proposed to connect the center of a large city to a residential suburb. The issue comes up in the conversation of a suburban matron and a friend who lives in the inner city. The city dweller guesses correctly that the suburbanite favors building the freeway, because it will make it easier for her to get to work. The suburban resident presumes that her inner-city acquaintance will oppose the freeway, because it will destroy part of her neighborhood; what she doesn't realize is that the city resident's feelings are much more mixed, because she sees the freeway as a means of getting unwanted commuter traffic off her local residential streets. We have here an instance of high accuracy on the part of the city dweller, low accuracy on the part of the suburbanite, and a moderate degree of agreement between the two people on the freeway issue.

Now what is communication likely to achieve between the two? The suburbanite's inaccurate perception of the other person's views can be corrected as they talk about the issue, so that both communicators become quite accurate in estimating one another's thoughts. There is some chance too that they will gradually develop a greater degree of commonality in their interpretation of the issue, so that they will come to agree somewhat more than they did at the beginning.

The concepts of interpersonal *agreement* and *accuracy*, then, define the two general notions of what most people mean when they speak of "effective communication." That is, these are the two kinds of social outcomes that communication (including mass communication) can achieve. Accuracy results from the expression of thoughts from one person to another. As a by-product, agreement also may occur, if more gradually. People's private values come from their entire individual lifetimes of experience and interaction. Such values are not easily changed. And so, while the world is happily arranged so that we come relatively often into contact with others whose values are similar to ours, we will almost never be in perfect agreement— and mere communication will not necessarily make us much more so. Whereas we might well imagine two people achieving perfect interpersonal accuracy, perfect agreement is a lot to ask of communication alone. Still, because of its importance in integrating and organizing society, agreement in some form turns out to be the goal most often set for the mass communication industry.

People do tend to strive for agreement, because some common values are necessary if they are to act as a social unit instead of going their individual ways. Social action has long since been established as more effective for most purposes than purely individualistic action.

Consequently there is a great deal of effort directed at achieving greater interpersonal agreement in society. Much of the time the results are discouraging, especially when messages regarding important and change-resistant values are mass-produced by the media and discharged into society on a wholesale basis. Certainly a high degree of accuracy is a more attainable goal for communication than agreement is, most of the time. Looking at it in a slightly different way, accuracy is purely a communication problem, whereas agreement can rarely be achieved simply by means of communication.

Interpersonal communication does not, of course, inevitably lead to a high degree of agreement. Two people may believe that they agree when in fact they do not, and may thus not bother to communicate their thoughts and feelings to one another. Or they may disagree so sharply on some aspects of a situation that they avoid the unpleasantness of discussing it. Marriage counselors have used this approach to diagnose various kinds of communication breakdowns between husbands and wives who come for counseling because each senses that the other "doesn't understand me." Sociologists have long noted the phenomenon of "pluralistic ignorance," as demonstrated in the small town where all the residents drank secretly, with the result that each believed himself (or herself) to be the only drinker in town.

When interpersonal networks are supplanted by mass media, there are necessarily some losses. A principal one is the restriction of flow to one direction. It is difficult to "talk back" to a mass medium, and thus to get your own personal feelings across. This is particularly true with television, which has become our most pervasive mechanism for message distribution. The result is probably a loss of accuracy, or at least a failure to improve on the level of accuracy afforded by oral culture. Modern mass communication stresses the engineering of a high level of agreement within society, rather than a high degree of accuracy between constituent subgroups, partly because the new technologies are not appreciably better at achieving accuracy than were the older methods of communication.

The media provide us with tools to communicate (in limited ways) as a society, rather than in small groups of geographically close individuals. This is an ambitious undertaking, but is seems reasonable to assess it by asking the same questions we would ask of oral tradition, writ large: How can the mass media be used to facilitate accuracy in mutual understanding within society and agreement on the goals and values of society as a whole? Or, on the other hand, how do the media *constrain* commmunication, causing us to *fail* to achieve between-group accuracy or societal agreement?

Clearly no single answer will suffice for all topics of communication. The later chapters of this book take up a variety of problems and indicate some differences in the effectiveness with which mass communication can be used to deal with them in American society.

RESEARCH ON COMMUNICATION

The most concise outline for the study of communication was proposed in this form by Harold Lasswell:

Who?
Says what?
In which channel?
To whom?
With what effect?[1]

Each of these simple questions defines an area of study in communication research. The question "who?" is often called *control analysis* or *source analysis*. It includes the study of communicators or "sources" such as reporters, speakers, broadcast networks, advertisers. The term "control" implies study of all the constraints that limit the behavior of communicators, such as laws governing freedom of expression, economic factors governing the mass media, physical and technical limitations on communication, and so forth.

[1]Harold D. Lasswell, "The Structure and Function of Communication in Society," in Wilbur Schramm (es.), *Mass Communications,* University of Illinois Press, Urbana, Ill., 1960, p. 117.

The question "says what?" is usually called *content analysis*. We will use the term "content" to refer to any material that might be communicated—names, values, commands for action—by words or other symbols.

The next question—"in which channel?"—refers to what specialists in mass communication call *channel analysis*. The mass media provide a set of technological and organizational channels for communicating from a source to an audience. Of course, there are many other channels, including interpersonal discussion, formal organizations and meetings, special-audience publications, and such esoteric channels as computerized information storage and retrieval systems. Picking the right one for a specific purpose has developed into an elaborate science.

The question "to whom?" points to the important field of *audience analysis* in mass communication research. This often means describing the people who "attend" to a message in terms of their demographic characteristics, such as age, sex, and income and education levels. But audience analysis also extends to study of the needs and wants people hold before a message reaches them, and the values that will guide their reactions to it.

Finally, the question "with what effect?" opens up the key field called *effects analysis*. Many people tend to think of "the effect of communication" as some form of persuasion, such as changing a person's values toward greater agreement with the communicator. But people are not so easily malleable. As we have suggested earlier, we would not want to say that communication is "effective" *only* if it succeeds in carrying out a communicator's attempt to elicit agreement from the audience. A great deal of media content, as we have noted, has as its first purpose that of information. Despite the close linkage between what we know and how we feel about the things we know, it is conceivable to inform without persuading and also to persuade without informing; communication can be "effective" in either respect. One of the major tasks of research has been to develop tools for measuring the relative effectiveness of different attempts at communicating information or persuasive messages.

There has been a strong trend in the past few decades toward adopting the research tools of social psychology for the study of mass communication. For effects analysis, and to an extent for channel analysis, controlled laboratory experimentation has been quite useful. In an experiment, one group is exposed to a message while another is not, and the effect of the message is inferred from subsequent differences between the two groups in the information or opinions they hold. Sample surveys, such as public opinion polls, have the advantage of measuring natural variation between people in the "real world." The survey is the principal tool for audience analysis. But experimentation, despite its apparent artificiality in many cases, is preferred by many on the grounds that is provides more conclusive scientific evidence. In a field survey, the researcher cannot be certain that people did not expose themselves to a message because of opinions they held, rather than developing those opinions as a consequence of exposure to the message.

Many questions regarding mass communication cannot be addressed by either experimental or sample survey techniques. Content analysis, for instance, is mostly a matter of documentary evidence, without direct assessment of the message's effects on audiences. There has been a strong emphasis since World War II on quantitative analysis of media content. Too often this degenerates into a pseudo-scientific counting of trivial items, at the expense of the highly significant statement that might occur only once, or that might be too complex to lend itself to easy quantification.

The more holistic ethnographic field methods of anthropology and descriptive sociology have been applied to control analysis, by careful observation and intensive interviewing of media "gatekeepers." Here too, the sample survey has been of some use, to develop generalizations that apply broadly to many media decision makers. But generally speaking, the research literature on control analysis is much too thin, considering the importance of the people in the mass media industry to the functioning of our society.

In this book, we will be making liberal use of the full range of evidence on mass communication, from historical and legal studies to field studies and laboratory experiments. To the greatest extent possible, we will try to limit ourselves to statements for which there is solid empirical grounding. But as we take on major problems of American society, we will inevitably find areas in which research simply does not (and is some cases cannot) provide answers. We will try throughout to make clear the kinds of evidence we are relying on and to indicate those statements that we cannot back up except intuitively or from our own professional experiences.

INSTITUTIONAL AND CONSUMER ORIENTATIONS

When we speak of communication about a given topic within society, it is not sensible to put all citizens on an equal footing. It does make some sense, however, to look at the process from two key perspectives: *institutions* and *consumers*. These can be considered analogous to the two persons who might be interacting in basic interpersonal communication. In the context of societal communication about such topics as war, politics, and race relations, various institutions involved communicate to consumers on the basis of their own structures, values, and goals.

The term "institution" has never been defined to universal satisfaction, although we offered an introductory description of mass media institutions in Chapter 2. We will use the concept fairly freely, to indicate a relatively enduring social organization that is internally structured to provide rules and rewards for its members and to achieve some broad goal in society at large. Thus, marriage is an institution, and so is Sears, Roebuck and Co.; so too are the medical profession and *The New York Times*. We will spend a good portion of this book analyzing the communication problems and solutions of some important national institutions in American society.

All members of society are *consumers* to the extent that an institution might serve their personal needs. Universal institutions such as medicine and government presumably include everyone as at least a potential consumer. Particular institutions, such as Los Angeles City Schools, Oscar Mayer Meat Packing Co., or (despite its name) All Souls Church are relevant only to limited sets of consumers.

Communication between institutions and their potential consumers can run in either direction, although it often does not. The institution (which is really a complex organization of persons, but which we will for the moment discuss as a monolithic whole) needs to know what its consumers think and needs to get across certain information to them. Conversely, consumers need to understand the institutions that serve them, and to get across to those institutions the nature of the services they need and want. Almost all institutions have organized themselves internally for communication with their consumers, but consumers have rarely been similarly organized until very recently. To speak of *the* consumer is much more of a fiction than to speak of *the* institution. But in this book we will give some attention to the internal problems of coordination and communication *within* each of these two parties, as well as to problems of communication *between* them.

Our choice of these two orientations, institution and consumer, as underlying viewpoints for this book is based primarily on our assumption that these are the two perspectives most likely to be useful to most of our readers. In the case of the "consumer" role, this is fairly obvious; all of us are consumers of various institutional services, and we need to know how to interact with them in a society where simple interpersonal channels are inadequate to handle the load.

But many of us will also eventually find ourselves in some institutional role as well, in connection with an occupation, voluntary organization, or special interest group. So we need to be sensitized to the communication problems we are likely to encounter in one institutional setting or another. In this book we will consider some American institutions that seem particularly important—either because of the number of people involved or because the use of mass communication is central to the institution's operation. While no one reader is likely to find all of these institutions critical in his or her life, we are confident that many of the principles that we develop in these chapters will be applicable to other institutional communication problems as well.

The consumer-institution framework may seem rather obvious. Surprisingly, though, it is not the usual approach to analyzing mass communication. Many introductory textbooks in mass communication adopt the perspective of media institutions themselves. assuming that the student is planning a career as a professional communicator. Another popular perspective is that of control of the media by those government (and private) agencies that coerce the media into performing their social functions responsibly. Those are worthwhile approaches to the analysis of mass communication, but they will be remote from the future day-to-day lives of many students; the number of professional communicators in society is small, and the number of decision makers who wield power over the media is still smaller.

Most of the content that is transmitted by the mass media originates with some institutional or consumer source. And most of the pressure on the media to provide better service comes from consumers and institutions. The media themselves do not generate much of their content spontaneously. Moreover, the agencies set up to control the media are forced to assume a minimal role (as in the case of government agencies) or find that they have little real power unless backed by heavy consumer or institutional support on a specific topic (as in "truth in advertising" campaigns or community efforts to control obscenity).

The mass media can be thought of as a general societal resource that is "there," potentially open to any of us for many purposes. The concepts introduced in this chapter should help the student begin to develop an understanding of the ways in which the media function regarding a variety of institutions and societal problems. Indirectly, these concepts could provide a "primer" for applying mass communication to new institutions and problems as they arise in the future.

THE LIMITATIONS OF COMMUNICATION

Before entering the "problem" sections of this book, we should emphasize that communication is not a cure-all for whatever ails American society. There is a serious danger in the popular inclination to treat real problems as if they were no more than a matter of "communicating better." What *can* be achieved through communication is a clear definition for society of what its problems are, plus perhaps the recognition that some seeming problems are more apparent than real.

Communication is a tool, and only that. Like other tools, it is useful only in relation to some material or substance, just as a hammer is a useful tool in relation to wood and nails, but meaningless in and of itself. In commercial marketing it is often remarked that "the best advertisement is a good product." Similarly, in politics the most effective campaign is one that is waged for a sound candidate, not the one that produces the catchiest slogan.

Generalizations about "communication" are not likely to mean too much, unless they refer to specific topics. The same is true of "mass communication." Statements of the form, "The mass media can do this, but they cannot do that," have to be tied to the specifics of a problem, including its context, its content, and some notion of the goals that it impedes. The sections that follow are founded on that assumption.

REFERENCES

Steven H. Chaffee and Jack McLeod (eds.), "Interpersonal Perception and Communication," special issue of *American Behavioral Scientist,* March/April 1973.

Harold D. Lasswell, "The Structure and Function of Communication in Society," in Lyman Bryson (ed.), *The Communication of Ideas* (New York: Institute for Religious and Social Studies, 1948); reprinted in Wilbur Schramm (ed.), *Mass Communications* (Urbana: University of Illinois Press, 1960).

Marshall McLuhan, *Understanding Media: The Extensions of Man* (New York: McGraw-Hill, 1964).

Theodore M. Newcomb, "An Approach to the Study of Communicative Acts," *Psychological Review,* November 1953, pp. 393–404; reprinted in Alfred G. Smith (ed.), *Communication and Culture* (New York: Holt, 1966).

The quotation from Charles Darwin is taken from Claire Selltiz et al., *Research Methods in Social Relations* (New York: Henry Holt, 1959), p. 200.

SUGGESTED STUDY PROJECT

Select a current news topic that is somewhat controversial, and make up a questionnaire that covers the main opinion issues on this topic. Make eight copies of your questionnaire. Give one copy each to two people who know one another, but who have not discussed the topic. After each person has filled out the questionnaire giving his own opinions, give him a second copy of it and ask him to fill it out as he *guesses* the other person has responded to the same questions. Next, ask the two people to discuss the issue for about fifteen minutes. When they have finished, give each of them another copy of the questionnaire to indicate their own opinions. Finally give each a questionnaire to fill out the way he thinks the other has answered it. Comparing the different questionnaires, do you find that the two people have changed their opinions after discussing the topic? Have they changed in the direction of agreeing more than they did originally? Are the issues they agree on those that they discussed? Have they become more accurate in judging one another's opinions?

Part Two

Public Information

Chapter 5

The Importance of Public Information

In a democracy such as ours, in which the people are to be sovereign, citizens can exercise their prerogative to make many key decisions about public affairs. Obviously enough, intelligent decision making by citizens rests upon the quality of information the public has at its disposal and sees fit to use. Few of us would want to entrust decision making to a mass of "know nothing and care less" citizens, and the country couldn't afford to do so.

From the founding of the Republic, American political theorists have assigned a key role to the news media as the source of information on which the citizenry is to base its democratic decisions. It was this public information function that led Thomas Jefferson in 1787 to write: "Were it left to us to decide whether we should have a government without newspapers, or newspapers without a government, I should not hesitate a moment to prefer the latter." To underscore the point, Jefferson added: "But I should mean that every man should receive those papers, and be capable of reading them." It was not enough that all citizens should be allowed to vote; they had to have ways of learning enough so that they could vote wisely, or democracy would not work.

The American press of Jefferson's time scarcely gave a hint of the vast system of mass communication that would eventually grow out of it. A leading historian of journalism, Edwin Emery, states that there were only about thirty-five newspapers in the thirteen colonies during the Revolutionary War, and that they reached only some 40,000 homes. (He adds, though, that each copy had many readers, and "every word was read.") Reporting was casual, sloppy, and slow; it took six weeks for news of the battle of Lexington and Concord to reach Savannah, Georgia. The papers were small weeklies, produced by local printers, and given far more to gossip and partisan politics than to news or information in our modern sense. The first daily newspaper, the bland and short-lived *Pennsylvania Evening Post,* did not appear until 1783. By 1800, however, there were six dailies in Philadelphia, five in New York, three in Baltimore, and two in Charleston, South Carolina.

Considering the shabby state of the newspapers of the time, it is testimony to a widespread faith in their potential for informing the public that James Madison was able to win adoption of what seemed to be an absolute guarantee of press freedom in the Bill of Rights. The first of the ten amendments that were adopted with the Constitution of 1787 provides in part that "Congress shall make no law . . . abridging the freedom of speech, or of the press." Most of the thirteen states had already enacted similar laws, and the question did not occasion much debate. But the amendment was quite helpful in winning ratification of the Constitution in some reluctant Northern and Southern states.

One must suspect that Jefferson and Madison would be, on the whole, quite pleased with the spectacular expansion and development of the American news media over the past two centuries. While opinion-mongering still exists, it has gradually given way to an emphasis on providing true public information. The overwhelming majority of citizens can read newspapers, and they do so daily. Television and radio supplement this with immediate transmission of capsule news, and both allow millions to witness "live" such events as presidential speeches, moon landings, and distant athletic contests. Vast news-gathering networks such as the Associated Press and the United Press International service even the smallest communities. Excellent newsmagazines such as *Time* and *Newsweek* reach large audiences. And diverse interpretations of the resultant glut of information are available, with syndicated columnists and commentators and "opinion" magazines representing many political persuasions. The American media system is far from perfect, to be sure. But it has come a long way.

Government for many years extended to the press the principle of laissez faire ("let it alone") known to free-enterprise commerce. The press was left "free" to produce such information as it might. Individual media enterprises were free to succeed or to fail and vanish.

But very little of a positive nature has been done by government to foster the growth or survival of informational media. A current example is educational or "public" television, which has developed very slowly and feebly in the United States, although it is a thriving public operation in many less developed nations. A few governmental attempts to protect informational media from extinction in the economic marketplace, such as the Newspaper Preservation Act of 1970 (the "failing newspaper law"), have met with strong ideological opposition, even from the media themselves. *Saturday Review,* an upper-middlebrow magazine struggling with rising postal rates and stiff competition, has editorialized that newspapers which cannot make money should stop publishing because a free press has "no right to expect the Constitution also to guarantee its profits through monopoly."

But while government was content more or less to keep "hands off" the informational mass media, massive private corporations began what might be considered a "positive effort" to encourage dissemination of information about their activities. The corporations were, of course, acting more out of a desire to further their own economic interests than to aid the news media or to increase the information levels of the public. Nevertheless, the primitive notion of corporations, where an industrial tycoon could snort, "The public be damned," gave way in the "progressive era" to corporate sensitivity and the need to maintain a respectable "public image." One of the first to recognize that he could manipulate the public by means of a news-hungry press was John D. Rockefeller, who in making himself the most visibly rich American had also become one of the most heartily despised. Rockefeller hired a media specialist, Ivy Lee, whose express duties were to render the aging billionaire's public image more "human." Lee, who since the turn of the century had been expounding the virtues of publicity and corporate openness, succeeded well enough with Rockefeller and other clients to inspire a host of imitators, and thereby founded one of the most controversial of American industries: public relations.

Today there is a public relations office in every corporation and organization of any appreciable size and ambition. PR has never lived down its early image, embodied in the sly publicity agent who would pull any stunt and tell any lie to gain notoriety for his well-heeled but otherwise undeserving client. The view of the PR man as a devious manipulator and subverter of social values was projected as early as the 1920s by John Dos Passos, in his novel *The Forty-second Parallel.* He created a fictional character named J. Ward Morehouse, who started out as a poverty-stricken newspaperman and created for himself a key role in the interface among business interests, labor organizations, and public opinion. In a speech to a Rotary Club luncheon, Morehouse pointed out that "American business has been slow to take advantage of the possibilities of modern publicity" and went on to describe in vague terms how public relations could be used to avoid "the grave dangers of socialism and demogoguery and worse." The fictional Mr. Morehouse also stressed the personal touch that could be added by the public relations counsel, who "can step in in a quite manly way and say, Look here, man, let's talk this over eye to eye. . . ." Dos Passos's implication that this kind of wheeler-dealer role was already developing within large corporations has obviously been borne out by the emergence in the past half-century of public relations as a specialization that is looked on as essential within all sorts of economic, political and administrative institutions. To be sure, PR is inherently a self-serving activity, and the industry still has its seamy side. And yet today it also provides a great deal of real information to the public. That has been the rationale on which government agencies have established skilled corps of "public information officers" to feed material to the press. No longer does American government stand aloof and count on journalists to generate news about public agencies. The laissez faire approach is dead in that respect. Governmental offices are in the "news"-producing business up to their bureaucratic necks. Indeed, the press has come to rely heavily on the government to provide it with information.

This shift has occurred quietly, largely unnoticed by the public until recent years. There is understandably a deep sense of unease on the part of citizens who look to journalists for an accounting of governmental activities, and find that the journalists in turn often merely pass along the government's own account of its own actions. It has been shown often enough that public agencies, like private corporations, strive to place in the media only those kinds of information that will reflect favorably on them— and thereby to obscure facts that might embarrass them in the public eye. In recent years, cynical and deceptive governmental information practices have given rise to the notion of a "credibility gap," in that many Americans feel they cannot believe what government spokesmen tell them. This was intensified by instances of duplicity in the build-up of the American military effort in Vietnam in the 1960s, when heavy criticism focused on the administration of President Lyndon Johnson. (One popular joke, circa 1967, hypothesized how one could tell whether the President was telling the truth: "When he tugs at his ear, he's not lying; when he wrinkles up his nose under his glasses, he's not lying; but when he moves his lips—that's when he's lying.")

What most citizens only vaguely understood was that *most* of their accounts of the war—and of all governmental operations— originated in public information offices, not with the press. Reporters are simply too few, too harried, and too inexpert to come anywhere near covering our vast governmental complex. While the press has, as we noted, expanded greatly since Jefferson's day, the growth of government at all levels has been many times greater.

Perhaps it is inevitable, then, that the press has accepted a massive indirect government subsidy in the form of this "news gathering" by public information offices. The price the press must pay in return is that of public relations, in the most manipulative sense of the term. And since the press presumably represents the public interest as a "watchdog" on government, this price is being paid by the public as well. Although public information programs are politically unpopular, the voters have acquiesced to officials' insistence that information is a necessary function for a public agency. The people are, in effect, paying taxes to be informed and hoping that they are not deceived in the process.

From the viewpoint of the corporation and the government agency, PR is indeed necessary. Public support, including willingness to provide taxes and personnel for each governmental operation, is essential. And the more closely an agency's survival depends on public support, the more necessary it finds a public relations program. The same is true of private corporations; those that deal directly with the general public must pay the greatest attention to public relations. The news media, advertising aside for the moment, traffic mainly in information. So public information, carefully selected, has become the common currency of both the PR industry and the press. It is the "coin" paid by public and private institutions to the news media, in exchange for the privilege of reaching the public with a message that will reflect favorably on them.

Whether all this is seen as underhanded and nefarious, as a necessary evil, or as a laudable enterprise, depends entirely on one's point of view. Some citizens see all public relations efforts as scurrilous attempts at "brainwashing." The industry also has its defenders (enemies call them apologists), who accept the entire marriage of convenience between PR and the press. But most people would say that their reaction to a PR operation is directly conditioned by their opinion of the agency involved. While one citizen might applaud public relations activities of a public university and deplore those of a military command, someone of an opposing political persuasion (anti-university and pro-military) might have precisely opposite reactions.

To analyze public information programs involving government and private organizations, we must look at them specifically in relation to the institutions that such programs serve, and we have to look at the special relationships that these institutions have with the public. In addition, we have to consider the role of the news media, since both government institutions and private corporations depend on these media to transmit the desired information to the public.

In the four chapters that follow, we examine public information problems facing four kinds of institutions. We start with the court system, as an example of a government institution that deeply affects the citizenry and therefore has a great responsibility to inform the public about its activities, but has not recognized that obligation satisfactorily. Then we move to the institutions of public education—the schools—which desperately need public support, and have tried to attain it through public information programs that don't seem to have worked too effectively. Then we examine the military, an institution that eats up massive amounts of tax money and too often sees its public information mission as one of gung-ho puffery rather than candid and open discussion of military affairs. Finally we consider private corporations, which have no direct need for taxpayer support and no inherent duty to inform the citizenry about their activities, but which nevertheless expend immense resources providing information to the public.

Throughout these chapters, we try to stress two themes. One is that any institution which affects citizens has a responsibility to inform the public about what it is doing. The second is that some institutions, even though they have a responsibility to provide public information, have not translated that responsibility into effective communication programs.

We selected the four institutions because they illustrate particular types of problems confronting citizens who want more and better information about public affairs. Each chapter is treated mostly in its own terms, but the chapters together invite discussion and comparison by readers. The overall lesson, and concern, of this section is that while high-quality public information is clearly desirable in today's America, we still have quite a way to go to reach that goal.

REFERENCES

John Dos Passos, "The Forty-second Parallel," in *U. S. A.* (New York: Harcourt, Brace & Company, 1937).

Edwin Emery and Henry Ladd Smith, *The Press and America* (Englewood Cliffs, N. J.: Prentice-Hall, 1954).

R. L. Tobin, "Antitrust Immunity and the Press," *Saturday Review,* Sept. 9, 1967, pp. 47–48.

SUGGESTED STUDY PROJECTS

1 Make your own estimate of the percentage of material in your local or campus newspaper that originated in a public information office's "news release." (To do

this, you need to keep track of the incoming mail to the editor's desk, so that you can identify stories later as either the work of a reporter on the staff, or the result of a release.) Compare the reporter-generated stories with those based on releases. Do you see any major differences between them in the way the elements of the story are handled? Can you detect any special advantages that the source of a news release gets in the news coverage?

2 Explore the public information system of a college or university. How many outside reporters cover the institution, and are they assigned full time or only part time? How many people on the university staff provide news releases or press information, aside from the actual news sources such as scientists or top administrators? What are the main factors that determine whether an activity at the university will get covered by the press? What advantages to the university are there in press coverage? What dangers, or disadvantages?

Chapter 6

The Courts and Public Information

It's sadly ironic how little most American citizens seem to know—or even care—about courts and judges. That fact that a single previously unknown federal district judge named John Sirica could "crack" a major part of the Watergate scandal through technical courtroom procedures hints at the immense importance the judiciary plays in a democracy. Less spectacular workings of the court system make the same point. A local trial judge can decide to impose the maximum jail penalty on persons convicted of possessing marijuana, or he can give them a suspended sentence; either way, the court is forging a policy on a controversial issue of wide public concern.

Courts are important for all of us, sometimes directly and sometimes indirectly. The court system, called the "third branch of government," was established by the founders of our constitutional system to act as an independent "umpire" of disputes between citizens, between other parts of government, and between citizens and government agencies. In some respects, the judicial branch is the "super branch" of government. It was the Supreme Court of the United States, after all, that ordered President Harry

Truman to withdraw the troops he had sent to seize the steel mills in 1952. It was the Supreme Court that ordered school boards to dismantle racially segregated school systems in 1954. It was the Supreme Court that ruled in 1970 that *The New York Times* and the *Washington Post* could continue publishing the "Pentagon papers," even though those documents had been officially classified as secret by the executive branch. We could go on with examples of what some scholars have called, somewhat alarmingly, "judicial supremacy." The important point is that an institution with such authority has a responsibility to explain its procedures and its decisions to the citizenry in ways that people can comprehend. For the most part, however, the court system of this country has not actively done so.

The reasons for such a state of affairs are interesting, if bewildering. Generally, they boil down to an overall notion on the part of judges that their station in American life sets them above and beyond any need for direct contact with, or support from, citizens. Traditionally, communication between courts and ordinary citizens has been analogous to that between Indian "sacred cows" and their worshipers. The courts, like the cows, have been happy enough to be praised but otherwise left alone; and the citizens, like the worshipers, have shown deference and respect, largely because of the awe and fear that accompanies such a tradition.

It appears that the constitutional framers planned it that way. When they established the American court system, they took care to convince the citizens that the judiciary deserved respect and confidence. The words of a high British judicial official in the Gilbert and Sullivan operetta *Iolanthe* would have made a good slogan for the early "educational campaign:"

> The law is the true embodiment
> Of everything that's excellent.
> It has no kind of fault or flaw,
> And I my Lords, embody the Law.

The theme has persisted: courts embody—that is, "discover" and "announce"—that overpowering set of precepts called "the law"; and "the law" discovers and announces excellence. The problem is that excellence has a way of dissipating under the realities of power. Courts, to be blunt about it, have no power of their own to enforce their decisions. They must rely on the cooperation of other government branches for that. Judges don't command troops. If left strictly to their own resources, courts would be mere "paper tigers." That is why it's crucial to the survival of the judiciary that it maintain a broad base of public support.

On what grounds is such support sustained? So far, the "sacred cow" image of the courts has held sway. Court pronouncements are obeyed out of deference, and a court's authority to make decisions is accepted as a "given." As citizens we learn—from parents, in civics classes in the schools,

The courts have no advertiser, they have no one to publicize the extent of their industry; they work quietly, their work cannot be understood by many, and the reasons for decisions in many cases are beyond public comprehension.

—1938 statement by Chief Justice of
the United States Charles Evans Hughes

and through the mass media—that we should accept and support this institution even though it is both a "sacred cow" and a "paper tiger." Our acceptance and support, we are told, are necessary in a society based upon orderliness. We're reminded that such a society needs to respect wise umpires who are trained to "discover" what "the law" is, who can insulate themselves from petty political squabbles, and who have the expertise to sort through, comprehend, and apply the quagmire of legal principles found in constitutions, statutes, and previous court opinions.

And so public support for the courts has relied mostly on messages that inspire awe and promote respect. More frequently than not, the messages are framed as euphemisms or in symbolic trappings. Since judges are supposed to be learned arbiters who merely discover what the law says, we hear that "ours is a government of law, not of men," and that "justice is blindfolded." (That impression is strengthened further by the symbolic messages of the judge's robes and the balanced scales of justice that adorn courtroom walls.) Since judges are supposed to be insulated from politics, we tend to accept the secrecy that shrouds certain judicial proceedings and records. We seldom ponder why judges do not hold news conferences, or give press interviews to explain their decisions, or hire public relations staffs to explain their work; those are the sorts of things "politicians" do. Since judges are deemed *the* experts in a terribly complicated field, we're more likely than not to accept the view that only they can comprehend the complexities and perplexities of court procedures and court decisions.

Such information about our courts might generate some respect for the judiciary from citizens. They seem to have worked well enough in the past. It's important to note, however, that none of those types of communication has better public information as its goal. It may be that in future years, as never before, the court system will find its "sacred cow" image insufficient. Groups of conservative citizens, even in the 1950s, launched a national campaign to impeach Chief Justice Earl Warren because they felt he was leading the Supreme Court into making too many "liberal" interpretations of the Constitution. Several years later, Gerald Ford, who was then Republican leader in the House of Representatives, spearheaded a drive to impeach Justice William O. Douglas; Ford declared that, in effect, a judge could be impeached for any reason whatsoever, as long as a majority of House members agreed. Still later, Richard Nixon stated that he might disobey a future Supreme Court order to release tape recordings of some of his presidential conversations concerning the Watergate scandals—unless he considered the Court's order to be "definitive." These three incidents suggest why courts might need increased public understanding and greater public support in years to come if they are to maintain their vital place in our society. One of the court system's greatest roles should be to educate the public—not only about the courts, but about the great and basic issues of our time that come before the courts for settlement. But unless citizens are given an opportunity to understand the full impact and meaning of the work of the courts, the judicial system might become a weak institution, subservient to the same political turmoil that it has tried so hard to transcend.

That suggests the need for more effective and deliberate communication programs to link courts and the public. Obstacles steeped in traditional practices and values will have to be overcome, and better cooperation by courts, the legal profession, and the news media will be necessary. Such cooperation is the key to improving public information about the judiciary. Unfortunately, relationships between courts and the news media have generally been tainted with suspicion of one another, sometimes by downright hostility. Courts, on the one hand, frequently view media reporting as a threat to what judges consider their prime mandate: the administration of justice, including the guarantee of defendants to a fair trial. The judges consider irresponsibly sensational and prejudicial news stories about court cases (particularly criminal cases) to be a threat to impartial courtroom proceedings. Frequently, the judges are right. Journalists, on the other hand, consider certain judicial attempts to restrict prejudicial news stories— such as excessive court secrecy, contempt citations against reporters, and court "gag" orders prohibiting certain news reports about a case—to violate their First Amendment rights of freedom of the press. More restraint, and mutual respect for each other's obligations, are needed on both sides if the necessary spirit of cooperation is to take root. American society will benefit if this happens, for both the courts and the public will have to rely largely on the media for better public information and public understanding about the judiciary.

PUBLIC INFORMATION AND PUBLIC UNDERSTANDING

America's courts have not organized themselves well for purposes of effective public communication. Traditionally, the courts have viewed lawyers and litigants (those persons involved in lawsuits) as their all-important clientele. A broader view is needed. Courts *deserve* to be understood by all

citizens, if only because courts play such a vital role in American life. And
all citizens *deserve* to be adequately and accurately informed about all aspects of the courts, if only because the courts define and defend the rights
of all citizens. Better public information, then, is both a deserved right and
a responsibility of both courts and citizens. To achieve it, we need more
effective communication policies aimed at:

1 Giving citizens a more realistic picture of how judges, and to some
extent other lawyers, view the court system
2 Letting judges and other lawyers know how citizens actually perceive the role of the judiciary
3 Helping citizens understand and evaluate courts, court procedures,
and court decisions

To help attain the first goal, judges would have to make deliberate
efforts to spell out candidly and publicly their own evaluations of the legal
process. They might give their views, for example, on why courts are important; on the shortcomings of probate; on the apparent need for more legal
aid for the poor. The key would be to gear such communications to the lay
citizen; lawyers have been talking among themselves about such topics for
a long time. Judges could be more willing to use the mass media for public
communication—by writing books and articles about the courts, by making
more public appearances, or by granting more interviews with journalists.
Organizations such as the American Bar Association could intensify their
efforts to help make education about the law more candid in the elementary
and secondary schools.

To find out how citizens evaluate the court system, scientific opinion
polls might be commissioned, perhaps by the legal profession itself. Such
studies could help find out whether citizens view courts as legitimate governmental agencies; why they think courts are important; how they think
lawyers feel about the legal system; and what things, if any, about they
legal system thay would like to know more about. Another approach would
be to encourage citizens to communicate their feelings to the legal profession, either directly by letters or visits, or indirectly through the mass media.
There is no legal or logical barrier to writing letters to judges, yet citizens
seldom do it. Perhaps they consider it improper or sacrilegious. That notion
could be dispelled through a public information program. Courts might
even hire "ombudsmen" to seek out citizens' praises and complaints about
how the court system operates.

For the third goal, the news media will need to play a central role in
giving citizens clearer, more accurate pictures of how courts really work
and of the legal significance of court decisions. Both the media and the
courts would first have to change some of their time-honored practices,

however. And there would have to be better cooperation between the courts and the news media than now exists.

Journalists usually have taken a shotgun approach to court news; they dutifully (though often inaccurately) report a court decision, and what it might mean, in conventional newswriting style. Mass communication flow, with its emphasis on speed and competitiveness, encourages such an approach. So do courtroom procedures. Since many courts announce their decisions in fairly large bundles, journalists often are forced to sift, digest, and report several court decisions rapidly; the result has been oversimplified, misleading, and erneous public information.

When the Supreme Court handed down its decision on prayer in the public schools in 1962, newspaper stories and headlines conveyed the impression that all praying had been banned from all public schools. Professor Chester Newland found such misleading headlines as: "Possible End To Christian, Jewish Holy Day Activity In Public Schools" and "No Praying In Schools, Court Rules." But all the Court had done in fact was hold that a prayer *composed by public officials as part of a government-sponsored religious education program* violated the Constitution. More recently, many newspapers used headlines such as "Supreme Court Orders Newsman To Testify" over stories about a 1972 decision regarding the right of reporters to withhold from grand juries the names of confidential news sources. Contrary to popular impression, the Court did not say that reporters had no legal right to keep such sources confidential; what the Court did say was that it found no *First Amendment grounds* for refusing to testify, but that legislatures could (and about twenty did) pass statutes protecting reporters and their sources.

The media could improve this situation by not being trapped into the view that "court news" means only quick "spot news" of court decisions. Legal institutions are more complex than that, and to adequately report and interpret the significance of their work, more and better journalistic resources should be committed to the judicial branch of government. More interpretative reporting about the courts and their decisions would be a step in the right direction. The media also need to employ more journalists who can competently specialize in judicial news.

Legal institutions could help by initiating public information programs in which "public relations" officers with legal training could help explain to reporters the legal significance of a court decision. Advance transcripts of major court opinions could be made available to journalists (they are not now), which would allow more time to write thoughtful and accurate news accounts. Less secrecy on the part of the courts and greater access to court personnel by the press could also contribute to more complete public information.

Some progress on these fronts has been made in recent years. The

American Bar Association (ABA) has published a booklet *Law and the Courts* to help journalists understand and better translate to the public some of the more technical aspects of court procedure; the ABA also has established "Gavel Awards" to honor and encourage outstanding coverage of legal affairs in the press. The Association of American Law Schools, with financial backing of the American Bar Foundation, has attempted to provide the news media with memoranda in which law professors decipher the legal issues involved in cases pending before the Supreme Court. The late Supreme Court Justice Hugo Black shattered precedent in 1968 when he answered questions about his views and the Court's work during an hourlong televised interview on *CBS Reports*. Justice Thurgood Marshall in 1972 agreed to submit to news interviews in order to respond to rumors that he had charged certain other justices with racial bigotry. A new Supreme Court procedure announced by Chief Justice Warren Burger in 1971, that important decisions would be released four days a week (instead of one or two), gives reporters more time to study and report individual Supreme Court opinions.

The news media, too, have recently shown greater willingness to help improve communication between courts and citizens. *The New York Times* set an example in 1955, when it hired Anthony Lewis as its Supreme Court correspondent, then sent him to Harvard University for a year to study law. Lewis's distinguished performances in covering the Court won him a Pulitzer Prize in 1963, during some of the most controversial years the Supreme Court ever experienced. Lewis's successor as court reporter for the *Times,* Fred Graham, was hired in 1972 by CBS as that network's first correspondent assigned full time to legal affairs. Hopefully other news media agencies will start devoting more resources to expert court coverage; but as of this writing only a handful—including also the Washington *Post,* the Washington *Star-News,* the Associated Press, and United Press International—even maintain specialized reporters at the Supreme Court building. And when it comes to covering the lower federal courts and the state court systems, media performance is even more haphazard. One step toward improving the quality of judicial news was undertaken in 1972 by a group called the Council on Law and Journalism. That cooperative venture (between the Association of American Law Schools and the Association for Education in Journalism) attempts to encourage interdisciplinary programs in which journalism students take law school courses as part of their college training; the stated purpose of the program is to demystify the law for the future journalists upon whom citizens will depend for legal information. Another example of media progress is the emergence of law-related columns and special legal news features. An example of the former is "Legal Briefs," a syndicated newspaper column co-authored by a University of Miami law professor and a former newspaper reporter. An example of the latter is the regular section in *Time* magazine devoted to the law.

More work is needed. Despite the hopeful developments discussed above, the American judicial system remains too much a closed society, an undercommunicated topic on the public agenda, and a considerably misunderstood phenomenon.

SUGGESTED STUDY PROJECTS

1 Examine the court and court-related news in an issue of a daily newspaper. How many of the stories are treated as "spot news"—that is, as news of a particular event such as a trial or arraignment? Can you find any stories which, in whole or in part, communicate how a court operates, or why it operates the way it does?
2 Try to find a news or feature article that explains the way a court system operates. Try to find one that explains the significance of an important court decision.
3 Anaylze an account from a wire service of a decision announced by the United States Supreme Court. To what extent, if any, does the news item explain the reason given by the Court for its decision? To what extent, if any, does the story discuss the probable impact the decision will have on American society? Then compare the wire service account with a newsmagazine story about the same decision. What differences can you notice that might be explained by the fact that newsmagazines have more time to reflect on and analyze a story?

REFERENCES

The following works provide useful source material on some of the problems and issues discussed in this chapter:

David L. Grey, *The Supreme Court and the News Media* (Evanston: Northwestern University Press, 1968.)

Chester A. Newland, "Press Coverage of the U. S. Supreme Court," *Western Political Quarterly*, March 1964, pp. 15–56.

Michael J. Petrick, "The Supreme Court and Authority Acceptance." *Western Political Quarterly*, March 1968, pp. 5–19.

Henry J. Schmandt, *Courts in the American Political System* (Belmont, Calif. Dickerson Publishing Company, 1968).

Chapter 7

Schools and Their Communities

If we were to select any one institution with which the readers of this book would be sure to have extensive contact, it would be schools. To begin with, of course, all of us have attended schools for many years, and we know them as physical and cultural presences in our local communities. Secondly, many readers will eventually find themselves involved with schools in various roles in later life, most likely as parents and teachers. Finally, schools represent the major single form of public expenditure in the United States, a clear sign of the high premium American society places on these institutions. To the extent that we are taxpayers—which we become to a constantly greater extent throughout most of our lives—we have a stake in schools even beyond any we might have as student, teacher, parent, or employer.

Education, as one of the least federalized public programs in the United States, is supposedly quite amenable to local decision making and design in terms of local needs. But, whether we are talking about the neighborhood grammar school or the state university, this image of educational programs as "the last bastion of local democracy" does not square very well with reality. Most citizens do not feel their programs are very well understood by the public. Such a situation is, of course, prima facie evidence of "a failure to communicate"; but as we have been suggesting throughout this book, that is too simple a description of the problem to be helpful in its solution.

Consider the channels that exist for communication between schools and citizens. First, there is the vote. In most school districts, school finance measures must be approved by the voters, or by legislators who have to run for reelection every few years. Boards of control (such as school boards of trustees and university boards of regents) are either elected, or appointed by elected authorities (e.g. mayors and governors). Thus, both the people who run public schools and the money they work with (for programs, equipment, and buildings) are directly or indirectly controlled by the citizenry by way of that basic communicatory link of the democratic process, the election—and the all-important campaign that precedes it.

Secondly, there are formal organizations through which citizens might communicate with schools somewhat more precisely than they can with the simplified mechanism of the vote. The school board is one, of course. Then there are parent-teacher organizations associated with almost every school in the country. Further, many school district administrators have established "lay advisory groups" in their communities to bring them into contact with the views of people who are neither parents nor school board members. Beyond that, there are many community service organizations like businessmen's clubs and the League of Women Voters which take a strong interest in education and can provide their members formal channels for input to school policy making.

Somewhat further removed from the school sphere there are our old friends, the mass media and casual interpersonal contact. Education is, of course, a standard (if seemingly rather dull) news topic for the media. And school matters are likely to come up in conversations that include teachers, students, or their parents, at the least.

What is most surprising about citizen-school communication is that it turns out to be conducted mainly in the mass media. The vote is simply an inadequate vehicle for communicating about something as complicated as education. Formal organizations reach only a very limited range of people, and only a few citizens have direct contact with school personnel. Each of these statements requires some documentation and elaboration here, because they contradict what most people assume to be the case. In particular, the central role of mass communication channels is likely to take many media people by surprise.

EDUCATION AND SOCIAL VALUE

As an indicator of a person's social prestige in American society, education ranks near the top, along with wealth, beauty, style, and a few other favored attributes. Of the most admired occupations in national surveys, almost all require many years of study—doctor, judge, nuclear physicist, etc. Most Americans have from a very young age struggled to succeed in the educational system. Strangely, almost all feel that to some extent they have failed. That is, most people can describe a higher plane of living that is introduced by the phrase, "If I'd gone on in school, I could have been a . . ." Some blame themselves, others blame the schools, and still others blame factors in their life situations ("I got married too young" or "my folks couldn't afford it"). But the main point here is that they associate lack of education with failure to achieve what they might have achieved. Implicit in this is the belief that many things can be achieved through education. That is at once a source of political strength for American educational institutions and a source of danger.

Up until the 1960s, a large majority of Americans held the belief that "more education" was the solution to many national problems, including poverty, crime, racial strife, immorality, and so forth. There was, in a rough way, correlational evidence to support this faith. Highly educated people tended not to be poor, involved in crime, deeply prejudiced, or particularly immoral. And so public policies were adopted to ensure that students would remain in secondary schools as long as they could take them, and to encourage them to go on to higher education as practiced at low-cost public junior colleges, state colleges, and universities.

A number of events conspired to burst this bubble in the 1960s. For one thing, the children of the "baby boom" that had followed World War II were filling the nation's schools and colleges in unprecedented numbers. The public bill for education accordingly inflated much faster than did the nation's overall wealth, and so the tax rate went up pretty sharply. Another factor was that the students themselves, having been to an extent pushed by anxious parents and pulled by a beaming society into advanced education, found things in their schools that they did not like. So they rebelled, with demonstrations and manifestos that evolved into a wave of student radicalism that eventually reached from its elite spawning places (such as the University of California's Berkeley campus) to many local high schools and even junior highs.

But probably the most telling argument against education was that it had "failed" to solve the problems that had been assigned to it. Poverty, crime, racial strife, and immorality are still with us. In some ways, educational institutions and policies seem to many to have added to these problems, but in any event they have not "solved" them. In retrospect, it was patently absurd to expect them to be solved totally, whether by education or any other panacea. Overly high expectations were set, as much by educational salesmen zealously peddling their product on a mass scale as by any other group.

A major revolt by taxpayers against public education began in the early 1960s, with the emergence on the political right of such spokesmen as Maxwell Rafferty, a small-town California school superintendent who argued for a return to "basic" education, composed largely of the three R's and heavy doses of patriotic indoctrination. Rafferty was elected state superintendent of public instruction, and he became a major theoretician of the movement that swept the conservative former actor Ronald Reagan into the governorship on a platform aimed mostly at reversing the growth to eminence of the University of California.

The political success of Rafferty and Reagan did not go unnoticed around the nation. As demonstrations against racial injustice and the involvement of the United States in Vietnam spread, so did campaigns against school funding. Although the demonstrations were largely limited to university campuses, the political reaction against education was not. Local district superintendents found themselves called on to defend, or otherwise explain, what was going on at the university; unable to account for things they had no contact with, they began to see needed bond issues, tax overrides, and budget measures voted down by their local citizens. In some districts where school bonds had routinely passed in earlier years, they went down to defeat in half a dozen (or more) consecutive elections.

We would not argue here that all requests by educators for public funding are justified, any more than all are unjustified. What is needed is public discussion and consideration of these proposals, so that the expenditures that are wise can be separated from those that are not.

Discussion of educational questions, however, is rare indeed in American society. One reason for this comes from the very importance of educational attainment as a mark of social prestige, and consequent de facto segregation of society along lines of educational stratification. Let us review the potential channels for school-citizen communication. After beginning with interpersonal networks, we will work successively through the mass media and formal organizations to the vote.

INTERPERSONAL DISCUSSION OF EDUCATION

Frank Sinatra, the singer, has been one of the most talented, successful, popular, and wealthy Americans of the past quarter-century. Yet people who have known him have said that he is notoriously ill at ease with educated people, because he was himself a high school dropout while growing up in Hoboken, New Jersey, during the Depression.

This is not a special failing in Frank Sinatra, but rather a genuine feeling in almost all of us. Those who "have more education" than we do seem to carry a special aura about them. Dropouts typically have a special respect, not justifiable on other grounds, for those who hold diplomas. This is true at every level in the educational hierarchy: high school dropouts feel that something sets them apart from holders of bachelor's degrees; people with master's degrees are somewhat awed by Ph.Ds.

This tendency is doubtless reinforced by a certain snobbery in the other direction. Those who have spent years attaining a high level of education often express some contempt for those who have not. Objectively speaking, we (as educators) see little to justify this; but it is quite obviously a fact of social life. Whatever the other merits of the people involved, the educated seem bound to look down on the uneducated, just as the wealthy look down on the poor, the beautiful look down on the ugly, the tall look down on the short, and so on.

This is not the place to go into the knotty problems of social inequality. We are concerned here with only a small question, that of interpersonal discussion of education. The fact is that there is not very much of it. Research into the social stratification of conversation tells us why.

The general principle governing interpersonal communication is, to put in homely terms, "likes talk to likes." A more pedantic expression would be to say that almost all personal communication is between peers. In the sphere of education this means, for instance, that parents of schoolchildren talk to other parents about schools; they do not talk with nonparents. But far more importantly, it means that people discuss education almost exclusively with others who have very nearly exactly the same "amount" of education.

American society is not the great "melting pot" of popular fable, but it does provide many opportunities for people of different backgrounds to interact now and then. When they do, the topic of conversation is usually drawn from what is called "popular culture"—such commonly understandable matters as sports, the weather, current movies and television programs, travel, cars, fashions, jokes, etc. The main source of popular culture information is the mass media, which thus perform the significant function of cementing together the different sectors of society.

But educational policy is, by and large, not a topic of popular culture. People do not talk about it casually, precisely because the opinions one holds on education are likely to be a badge of social status, and they will put one person in a conversation at a disadvantage vis-à-vis the other. Even during election campaigns involving school finances, when the local press is filled with education news, discussions of the issues are limited to persons who are within two or three years of one another in years of schooling completed. This conversational segregation cannot be explained by race, income, occupation, or other elements of general socioeconomic status. Even within the same families, husbands and wives (who are by definition of the same general social status) do not discuss educational matters if there is more than a few years' difference between them in education. (This holds true whether it is the husband or the wife who spent more years in school.) Since casual discussion is not a likely channel for the dissemination of educational ideas throughout society, let us consider some others.

MEDIA COVERAGE OF EDUCATION

Education, in the sense of the development of curriculum, new teaching methods, improved testing procedures, and the like, is considered interesting, but rarely really newsworthy, by the average editor. It lends itself nicely to use as "time copy" that can be kept around the city room until something is needed to fill up space, say a week from next Tuesday. Articles on educational matters tend to be long, bookish feature stories that are accompanied by staged photographs of well-scrubbed students and stiffly posed principals or teachers gathered around a table on which lies some new educational gimmick.

There are a few exceptions to this dull pattern, and these exceptions account for the great bulk of "education" news that lands on the front pages of major newspapers, in the education columns of national newsmagazines, and in network television newscasts. One, of course, is the continuing issue of segregation of school along racial lines. Another is the recurrent battle over the institution of religious exercises and indoctrination into public schools. A third is the "student power" movement, and a fourth is unionization (and occasional striking) among teachers. A fifth category might be called "student antics," which have enlivened news coverage from the days of goldfish swallowers through the era of panty raids down to the earthy day of the streaker.

For the most part, these types of "news" have little or no relationship to the internal processes of education. Either they are intertwined with larger sociopolitical cleavages in society (e.g. racial integration and religion in schools) or they can be seen as harmless elements of popular culture (e.g. panty raids and streaking). As such, they *do* get discussed by people whose educational backgrounds vary considerably, which is in itself a sign that they are not matters that are very central to the educational process.

During local school finance campaigns, of course, the media do try to explain what the schools are requesting funds for, and why. But this coverage tends to be obscured by the political aspects of the campaign, and it does not get digested by the public in interpersonal discussion as most information would. As a result, the citizenry's judgment as to whether funding should be approved or not is often made on the basis of aspects of education other than those that are at stake in the funding proposal.

FORMAL ORGANIZATIONS AS CHANNELS

What about the role of the school board, the parent-teacher organization, and the lay advisory board in school-citizen communication? In general, they reach overlapping groups of people: those who are interested in, support, and have benefited from public education. Communication tends, even in these formal settings, to be between peers. For instance, the more active parents in parent-teacher organizations tend to be those whose own education puts them on a par with educators—i.e. college-educated parents, especially those who are former teachers or other middle-level professionals. School board and lay advisory group members are drawn mainly from the professional and managerial strata of the community, and they are in touch with other citizens of similar standing. School administrators are often people who have been motivated in their career ambitions by the social prestige of high education and managerial status; they are no more drawn to interact with the "nobodies" in the community than other professionals.

The net result is that the formal organizations, which have been specifically designed as channels for citizen-school communication, provide mainly an extension of the highly segregated casual interpersonal channels. The main difference is that the formal channels are used by people whose interest and expertise in the educational area are extremely high. For rank-and-file citizens these channels are as remote as the people who control them. And yet they are the people who are periodically asked to vote funds for schools.

THE FINANCIAL VOTE AS COMMUNICATION

The question that faces the voter on the ballot follows this general form: "Should the (city/county/state/) appropriate —— million dollars for the construction of —— for the (school district/university system)?" There are two possible responses that can be uttered, by placing an appropriate mark: "yes" and "no." If more than one-half (or, for many financial measures, two-thirds) of the voters mark "yes," the appropriation goes forward, and the educational administrators are in business. If not, the same item will reappear on another ballot soon.

Even if we limit this simplified exchange to the narrow question posed on the ballot, it would be difficult to characterize it as communication. The million-dollar appropriations that get submitted to voters are almost invariably summaries of many discrete elements of the school program. Voters who clearly understand these different components of the proposal are not given the opportunity to vote for those they like and against those they disapprove of. Their vote must be an all-or-nothing gesture, on the total package. If enough people decide that a preponderance of meritorious elements exist in that total package, it will be approved.

Until the taxpayers' revolt of the 1960s, many educational administrators were fond of claiming that they "must be doing something right" in terms of communicating with their supporting communities. Their evidence was nothing more than the fact that they usually had their funding requests approved. When this approval ceased being granted by citizens, it was common to conclude that there had been "a breakdown in communication." But of course there never had been much serious communication between citizens and schools on educational matters. Only when it was needed—when unhappy results of noncommunication presented themselves to school personnel—was communication missed.

One ironic aspect of the vote as a communication mechanism is that the issues that are ordinarily on the ballot are for support of the aspects of schools in which citizens most often say they take pride—quality of facilities, teachers, and other things that cost money. Complaints about schools, which often get translated into "no" votes, usually have to do with matters that do not involve money in appreciable amounts. Examples are racial and religious issues, students' behavior, and movements for "student power." This means that the word "no" gets misdirected and often ends up curtailing the very programs that citizens most approve. They have no vote, and little voice, in policies that do not go on the ballot because they do not involve appropriating public money.

Studies of voting patterns across many elections involving school finances have uncovered a clear-cut trend that is surprising (and not a little embarrassing) to educators who feel that opposition to their funding requests is the work of a few tightfisted conservatives. As it happens, school financial measures stand their best chance of being approved when only a very small percentage of the eligible voters turn out to cast their ballots. As the percentage of voter turnout increases, the probability that a given funding proposal will be approved drops rapidly. It reaches its lowest point when a little more than one-third of the electorate shows up to cast a ballot; this happens also to be about the average level of turnout in school financial elections.

Dr. Richard Carter, who headed a major study group on school-community communication in the 1960s, points out that the relationship between turnout and approval of school financing is *curvilinear.* That is, the line representing the ratio of "yes" to "no" votes goes down from low to moderate turnout levels; then it begins to go up gradually, so that when turnout is very high (over 50 percent), the chances of approval become reasonably good again.

The key to this curvilinear pattern lies in the fact that different kinds of citizens are represented at different levels of turnout. When only a few voters bother to vote, they are mostly supporters of schools—parents and the well-educated. But only about one-third of all citizens have children in public schools, and most of those are also included in the better-educated sector of the population. Beyond them lies a group of citizens who have a strong economic interest in public spending, because they pay most of the taxes, but often have less close ties to the benefits of education. These people are predominantly middle-class, settled, somewhat older citizens. When a school election attracts them, turnout is increased, and the percentage of "no" votes increases.

Very high turnout in elections involving school finances is achieved only when an additional bloc of voters gets to the polls. These are the younger, poorer, less settled, and less educated citizens. Many of them have children in the preschool age range, or none at all. Ordinarily they do not feel they have a great stake in political issues, and so they tend often not to vote. When they do vote, the burdens of being a taxpayer often seem somewhat lighter to them than to their more affluent fellow citizens, so they are more likely to vote "yes" on school funding—perhaps on the odd chance that they might enjoy some benefits from an expanded educational operation.

It makes sense, of course, for citizens to vote their pocketbooks. But it is a sad comment on the state of public communication about education when purely demographic, parental, and economic factors govern so much of the voting pattern regarding important educational fiscal decisions. In any event, the time is long past when schools can count on a vague pro-education ideology of citizens to lead to a humble acquiescence to any funding request. More Americans are familiar with the processes of education than ever before, and thus more are willing to challenge the myth of education's omnipotence than ever before. Fortunately, this also means that more are capable of informed discussion and public debate of school policies and programs than ever before. What channels might they use?

THE MEDIA AS NONSEGREGATED CHANNELS

The "mass" media do not reach a single, huge, homogeneous "mass" audience. But they do reach many different audiences with the same message. And it is this property that makes the media the principal channel of communication between citizens and schools, despite the fact that the media do not consider this one of their major roles, whereas some formal organizations have been set up for this explicit purpose.

Let us begin with the evidence, and then consider the reasons that might lie behind it. National surveys of citizens show that most of them rely on the newspaper first and television second as a means of finding out what is going on in their schools. What is more, they also rank the newspaper first, and television again second, as channels through which they believe school personnel can find out what they, as citizens, think about education. In these ratings, other channels such as school boards and parent-teacher organizations were ranked substantially lower.

This is a particularly damning judgment by the public regarding formal organizations, when one considers how little educational news coverage is carried by television, and how little access citizens ordinarily have for getting their views on educational topics represented in the media. Aside from letters to the editor, which rather few people have the skill and inclination to write, general public inputs to the newspaper are decidedly limited. Many, probably most, Americans grow up, live and die without ever being quoted in a newspaper on any subject, let alone on educational policy.

Why do so many citizens rely on the mass media for their communication with schools, rather than take advantage of the various formal and personal channels that have been designed to permit more or less direct contact? One factor is undoubtedly convenience, since the media are available in one's home, whereas the other channels require some extra time and effort to use. But beyond that there is a clue in the social characteristics associated with media use. Surveys show that *the less educated citizen is more likely to communicate indirectly with schools, through the mass media.*

This fact runs counter to what we might expect on the basis of patterns of media use alone. It is, after all, the more educated person who pays more attention to the newspaper; on technical and complex educational issues, a citizen needs some background information and fairly sophisticated reading skills to follow the typical interpretative report. Those who dropped out of school when young are at an obvious disadvantage with such material, yet they are the persons most likely to say that newspapers (1) provide them with most of the information on schools and (2) give the schools the best idea of what they as citizens are thinking. Even television, which is often thought of as the medium of the "common man," occupies a greater share of the *available leisure time* of the more educated citizen. And to the extent that news and features regarding education appear on television, we can be certain that such programs are more attractive to viewers who are themselves at least fairly well educated.

To account for the reliance on the media by the less educated citizen, then, we must look at the alternatives open to him. He might attend meetings of the school board, the PTA, or a lay advisory group, or he might go directly to a teacher, principal, or superintendent. But, as we have noted earlier, such direct contacts are avoided because they put the less educated citizen in a situation where he is at a decided social disadvantage. Entanglement in a direct discussion or confrontation with educationally expert persons can be quite a threatening prospect to the more typical citizen, who is not college-trained and whose experience with schools is that of a sometime consumer—and often not a particularly successful one at that. Besides, consulting expert persons requires more effort than most people's interest in education would justify.

The mass media, by comparison, are not directly threatening to such a citizen, and they are available and easy to use. His ignorance of some of the niceties and the terminology of professional education cannot be exposed to others while he reads (or even writes to) his newspaper or watches his television set. His uncertainty in expressing himself clearly and grammatically is no great problem as long as he avoids direct contact with school personnel. And the newspaper and television set are already right there in his home. They belong to him, and he is comfortable with them.

The answer to the problem of noncommunication by citizens about education seems to lie, for better or for worse, with the mass media. Coverage of educational issues has not been defined by those who control the news as a glamor topic. Audiences, after all, do not get very excited about education except where it gets entangled with a political issue.

We see considerable hope over the long range, owing to two trends in professional communication. The first is the emergence in the past two decades of education reporters as recognized specialists within the newsrooms of our larger news media. To be sure, they still spend much of their time dealing with political issues that involve schools more than they do education. But specialized reporting in the area of education is being taught in journalism schools, and the products of these programs are being employed by the media in increasing numbers. They face a large challenge.

To help them meet it, many school districts and almost all universities and colleges have hired public information specialists to help get the message of educational administrators into the media.

It would be naïve to imagine that the information put out by these professional communicators of the educational establishment is pure and unvarnished truth. They serve the interests of the higher administrators who employ them. But skilled educational reporters will not be easily fooled, and it is by the product of a friendly-enemy clash between reporters and public information specialists that we can expect the general public to become better informed about its schools in future years.

REFERENCES

Richard F. Carter and William G. Savard, *Influence of Voter Turnout on School Bond and Tax Elections* (U. S. Government Printing Office, 1961).

Richard F. Carter, "Communication, Understanding and Support for Public Education," in Wilbur Schramm (ed.), *Paris-Stanford Studies in Communication* (Stanford Institute for Communication Research, 1962).

Richard F. Carter and Steven H. Chaffee, *Between Citizens and Schools* (Stanford Institute for Communication Research, 1966).

Richard F. Carter, W. Lee Ruggels, and Richard F. Olson, et al., *The Structure and Process of School-Community Relations* (Stanford University School of Education, 1966).

Richard F. Carter, Bradley Greenberg, and Alvin Haimson, *Informal Communication About Schools* (Stanford Institute for Communication Research, 1966).

Richard F. Carter and William R. Odell, *The Structure and Process of School-Community Relations: A Summary* (Stanford University School of Education and Institute for Communication Research, 1966).

Steven H. Chaffee and L. Scott Ward, *Channels of Communication in School-Community Relations (Journalism Monographs* No. 8, Association for Education in Journalism, 1968).

Scott M. Cutlip and Allen H. Center, *Effective Public Relations* (Englewood Cliffs, N. J.: Prentice-Hall, 1971).

Gordon McCloskey, *Education and Public Understanding* (New York: Harper & Row, 1967).

Philip K. Piele and J. S. Hall, *Budgets, Bonds, and Ballots* (Lexington, Mass.: Lexington Books, 1973).

SUGGESTED STUDY PROJECTS

1 Locate two school district superintendents, one of whom has suffered through a succession of defeats of bond issues or other funding proposals on the ballot, and one who has had little or no trouble getting funds approved. Interview them to find out what factors they think account for their relative success or lack of it. In particular, try to find out what communication mechanism they have used to make contact with citizens in their districts.

2 Look through back issues of your local newspaper for letters to the editor that have to do with local public schools. Separate those that are critical of the schools from those that are favorable. Does the pattern follow that of the public opinion poll data described in this chapter? At the time of a local election dealing with school funding, do you find that the letters have to do with different topics than at other times of the year?

Chapter 8

The Military and Its
Public

Eighty billion dollars is an impossible figure for most of us to comprehend. It happens to be approximately the amount of money that the United States had decided to spend in one year on its vast military establishment at the time this book was being written. Arguments over defense spending involve similarly incomprehensible figures. Should it be reduced, say to $60 billion, or increased to $100 billion? American citizens, with few exceptions, lack the slightest capacity to understand this awesome debate in terms of the money at stake—even though it is their money, and a great deal of it, that is being spent. The economics of militarism make no more sense to the typical lay ear than would a heated argument over the question "How high is up?"

What the larger public should be able to do, though, is to understand and evaluate what its military establishment *does,* even if it can't cope seriously with what that costs. Presumably if the nation's citizens are pleased with the actions of the military, they will provide the necessary funds. Unfortunately, the military viewpoint all too often seems to be that its services are a vital national necessity and therefore its funding should not be questioned. Accordingly, it sees no need to explain what it is doing; further, to tell what it is doing would be a "breach of security" that would impair its capacity to carry out its mission.

Still, the public has at least a hazy notion of what the military does. For instance, it offers secure employment at low wages for young men; if they fail to volunteer in sufficient numbers, it conscripts them. It operates spacious bases across the country (and abroad), providing local payroll boons that help solidify the political strengths of pro-military congressmen. It puts ships on the sea and planes in the air, and this swells the numbers of jobs in our hardware industries. From overseas bases it diffuses servicemen on liberty into distant countries, where they incidentally export such artifacts of American culture as chewing gum, materialism, raucous good humor, and draw poker.

And from time to time, in one place and another, it fights wars—or by a show of force prevents them. An ominous military presence around the globe is widely thought to be the hallmark of a great nation, and America's capacity to maintain such a far-flung establishment is envied in many other countries. Our purpose here is neither to condemn the American military operation nor to praise it. (Surely enough people are already busy at both those tasks.) Instead, we want to explain why most of us find it so hard to learn how it operates.

Considering the importance to society of its military effort, there has been surprisingly little study of it. Universities typically have departments and institutes to analyze all sorts of other major institutions: public health, agriculture, mass media, schools, labor relations, environmental pollution, government, etc. But few campuses offer any opportunity to study military affairs, beyond the elementary indoctrination of ROTC and here or there a course in military history. The result is that we do not have a great deal of hard or systematic data to go on. Instead, we will have to rely heavily on personal memoirs and anecdotes, plus the few studies that have sporadically been done, on the problem of communication between the military and the public.

PROBLEMS AND PEOPLE

As we shall make plain soon enough, there is abundant evidence that the American public is not getting the information it needs to evaluate its military operations. The result is that we are incapable as a society of stopping a decision such as the commitment of half a million American ground troops in Vietnam in the mid-1960s, now widely regarded as one of the great blunders in our nation's history.

What is *not* so clear is why we do not get the kinds of information that would enable us to avoid another Vietnam, or another Bay of Pigs. It would be easy enough to point to examples of individual lies, distortions, cover-ups, and self-delusions, on the part of various Presidents, generals, and others who are supposed to serve them at lower levels. But the very fact that there have been many individual failures suggests that it is somehow the system, not just the individuals in it, that is at fault. Indeed, we could just as easily cite a long list of commendable and even heroic attempts by individuals (including Presidents and generals) to get essential information and pass it on to the American people. This often turns out to be a very difficult thing for them to do, because of structural factors in the system by which these people operate. So that system deserves our careful scrutiny.

For simplicity, let us conceive of the military public information system as a transmission link-up of four entities. Information originates within the military establishment, in connection with some operation; it is then collated and packaged by military public information officers (PIOs), who in turn pass it on to the mass media; finally, the media disseminate it to the public at large.

As anyone knows who has ever played the parlor game "rumor," a message that passes from one person to another can get comically distorted in the process. So we should not be surprised that a lot of random error creeps into the transmission of military information during even the few steps in our simplified model of military-to-PIO-to-media-to-public. Such errors are unfortunate, and they can sometimes be disastrous, but they are understandable. They can be thought of as the product of human fallibility; to correct them, we need to recruit and train better PIOs and reporters. That is not so easily done, but at least the problem, and thus the solution, can be defined easily enough.

With other types of "errors," though, those that result from the structure of what we are calling the military information system, it is not so obvious what needs to be done to make the system work better.

In the sections that follow, we will examine structural as well as individual factors that impede the flow of military information at each stage. We will begin at the end, with the public itself, and then work back up the line to the media, the PIOs, and finally to the military establishment itself.

THE PASSIVE CONSUMER AND THE EXPERT

Most of us do not, truth to tell, make much of an attempt to find out what our massive military operation is doing. Perhaps in peacetime it isn't very interesting, and in wartime it is too complex or too painful. But even more, it is such a vast and technical business that we typically try to reduce it to the more manageable level of our own personal experience. Where the military is concerned, this leaves us with a choice between two general roles, which we will call here the *passive consumer* and the *expert*. Neither is especially helpful to the process of disseminating military information

The *passive consumer,* as his name would suggest, doesn't especially try to inform himself about the military. As a member of the media audience, he tacitly makes himself available to military information and accepts what happens to come his way, whether through the mass media, casual conversation, or possibly direct personal experience. Whatever information he has at any given time he can translate, if need be, into a loose structure of beliefs that is adequate for any "decisions" he might need to make. That is, he can decide whether to vote for an anti-war candidate, or one who has fought for new weapons programs, or a retired general; he can decide whether to encourage his son to join the Navy, or whether to pick up two Marines who are hitch-hiking, or whether to buy the wares of a disabled vet selling door to door, and so forth. There is not much emotional involvement in most of this, and so it doesn't matter terribly to him whether he has *all* the relevant information, or *accurate* information. So long as he has *some* information, he can make these decisions about as well as he makes many other decisions in his life. Military information takes its place in line with all the other inputs in his daily life; those messages that reach him are taken into account, and those that don't aren't. He can take comfort in the assumption that because he is tuned in to the media (especially television, on which most people say they rely for most of their news), he won't miss any intelligence that is really important.

The *expert* is quite a different animal. In most cases he has been in the service, in wartime. He knows how the military operates, or at least he thinks he does. He has army stories to tell in support of any viewpoint he might have. And this viewpoint conditions his interpretations of inputs he receives from the media regarding the military.

The United States today has millions of potential experts on military matters scattered throughout its population. To begin with, all of those in uniform at this moment are eligible participating citizens and ipso facto experts. Indeed, the political views of the military are a potent force, and politicians frequently play to them by way of the mass media.

In the civilian population, there are such conservative organizations as the American Legion and the Veterans of Foreign Wars, both dominated by men whose active military days are behind them but who seem determined that future generations shall have the same chances they had to enjoy a military experience. On the other side of the political coin have been "Veterans for Peace" organizations. These sprang up in great profusion during the period of military escalation in Vietnam, as former military personnel who opposed the war saw a chance to presume on their time spent in uniform as a claim to special expertise on matters military.

There is, in truth, little in the typical tour of duty in the armed services to qualify a person as an expert on larger policy questions. The memory of what it was once like for one person to spend, say, three or four (or even twenty or thirty) years in one branch of the service, typically within one limited job specialization, can provide the illusion of expertise. But true expertise is hard to come by, and few possess it on any question. Fewer still are willing to admit, or even able to recognize, that they lack it. It is easier to believe that one's own personal experience is universal, and that answers to any question involving the military can be derived from applying the lessons learned in that very limited contact with the total operation. This would be a very human tendency; to err, after all, is human.

Because the United States has fought so many extensive wars in the years when most of our present adult Americans were of an age to fight, there are rather few families in this country that have not had direct involvement with the military. Among adult men, some personal military experience is the rule rather than the exception. So the reservoir of potential experts in our society is massive. Never mind that the technology, strategy, and even the terminology of World War II are obsolete; those who fought that war will try to apply the models they learned when they were young to new, different wars that arise elsewhere as they grow older.

And Korea. The concepts of the "cold war" on which the Korean war was predicated worked, in the sense that they led to the establishment of a secure border between a Communistic and a pro-American government. And so of course those concepts could be transported elsewhere, and they would work again. At least in Asia.

But in Vietnam, as it turned out, they could not be transported whole and made to work again. This conclusion seems inescapable today, but it was accepted only very slowly and reluctantly by citizens whose personal experiences had been with one set of problems and one military solution to them. Our nationwide staff of lay experts on military issues makes American society peculiarly poor territory for the dissemination of new questions and new information. Old beliefs die hard, and they control the factors that might otherwise change them

We have, of course, exaggerated the picture to make a point here. And the important point is *not* that the American people, or even some small subset of them, are to blame for their failure to acquire information adequate to the military responsibilities they have assumed as a nation. Even if they were to blame, it is not a fact worth bemoaning here. There is, however, a good deal to be gained if the military hierarchy, its public information arm, and the press, recognize this.

What *is* important to realize is that whatever these agencies tell the public will be interpreted very selectively. Some citizens will try to fit new realities into obsolete models from another era. Others will accept it passively, along with their daily diet of toothpaste ads and weather forecasts. (Many will ignore it entirely, a fact that is universally frustrating to military information officers.)

Putting it another way, one price of involving the United States in a string of major wars has been to create a public for whom the military's scientific activities, its efforts to professionalize its personnel corps through liberal arts education, and even its public relations work, make little sense. "The Army is there to fight wars, damn it. Let's cut out all these frills."

Public opinion polls during the darkest years of the Vietnam war showed an ironic coalescence of anti-war sentiment from two very disparate ideological groups. One was the pacifistic "doves," predominantly young people who viewed the war as morally wrong and the draft as a direct personal threat. A second group, probably equally large, consisted of the other extreme—"superhawks" who joined the doves in deploring the *conduct* of the war. They demanded all-out prosecution of the war (including even the use of nuclear weapons) or nothing. As John Schmitz, a California Republican and John Birch Society stalwart who became the American Independent Party's 1972 presidential candidate, put it: "Never get into a war you don't intend to win."

President Nixon's "handling of the war" (as opinion pollsters were wont to put the question) was "approved" by only about one-third of the adult population until in 1972 he stepped up his offensive with heavy bombing and the mining of Haiphong harbor. From then on, about two-thirds of the nation regularly registered approval of his war policy. He was rewarded later that year with a landslide reelection, without having yet delivered on his 1968 pledge to end American involvement in Vietnam.

While President Nixon was able to get himself out of the political trap between these two contrasting sources of criticism, and finally out of the war itself, the Vietnam years have laid bare a serious division in American society over our military establishment. We doubt that this bitter cleavage will go away in peace. Younger people have been socialized to general anti-war and anti-military sentiments, just as their parents grew up in an era of wartime military necessity. However it communicates with the American people, the Pentagon will be addressing a divided audience for some years to come.

THE PRESS AS FRIEND AND FOE

When the ancient Greeks turned back the Persian invasion at the Plain of Marathon, the runner Pheidippides was sent back to Athens with the happy news. Although he reportedly died from the effort, he was thereafter considered a major state hero. Other messengers were not so fortunate, in that they had to carry home news of defeat. Their reward was to be slain, for the public offense of bearing bad tidings.

William Small, a television network news executive who grappled with the military in the Vietnam era, points out in his book *To Kill a Messenger* that something of this spirit survives today. A seemingly prevalent military view of the role of the press is that of the messenger who relays news of military success and consequently bears responsibility for military failure. When one reporter tried to ask politically embarrassing questions of an American general during a crisis in Vietnam, the general retorted: "When are you going to get on the team?"

Reporters, editors, and newscasters argue in return that they *do* operate as part of the team—if, and only if, they aggressively gather and interpret military information independently of official constraints. In their view, they should be free to question military activities and policies, and their questions should be answered fully and openly. They should have access to records and to controversial military personages, and they should be privy to military decision making insofar as security will reasonably permit. This, they maintain, serves the public interest, of which they are guardian.

Military officers may snort at this image the press corps paints of itself. And just as reporters can point to many examples of self-serving military cover-ups that have besmirched the good name of "security," so can military information specialists cite a long list of journalistic "goofs" in which facts were garbled, misread, or even consciously distorted for the sake of a "good story." It will do little good here to enter into this professional controversy. Let us, instead, examine the realities of journalistic military reporting in the United States, and then of the military's internal information operation, each from its own perspective.

The most striking fact about military reporters is that there are so few of them. Only the larger metropolitan newspapers and the wire services can afford to hire a full-time journalist to specialize in covering military affairs. To station one newsman in Vietnam to report on the war could cost $100,000 or more. Therefore few were sent; fewer still strayed far from Saigon during the war. In 1968, when there were more than half a million Americans in uniform in Vietnam, there were only a few dozen reporters there to cover their activities. (Although the comparison is not necessarily an apt one, in an American city of 500,000 residents one might find several hundred working journalists.)

At the Pentagon, the nation's military headquarters with some 25,000 personnel on duty, there are only two to three full-time reporters. They have approximately 2,500 separate offices to cover. At local military bases throughout the country, there are practically no full-time reporters to be found. Instead, the "military beat" is typically distributed across the duties of several different journalists on the staff. A rewrite specialist may process publicity releases from the Pentagon, while a photographer is occasionally dispatched to do a human interest feature on a serviceman. Any reporter who isn't doing much else at the moment might be tapped to "go see what's happening" when a news lead crops up that involves the local base. Even if military reporting is centralized in one person on the staff, this will rarely provide enough work to constitute a regular specialized assignment in itself.

This lack of numbers combines with other factors to prevent military reporting from becoming a professional specialty in American journalism. Usually a military beat is a way station in a reporter's career, not a permanent slot; he or she may "graduate" to it from the police beat, with early promotion to broader responsibilities almost certain for someone who does well. From the Pentagon, one might aspire to be Washington bureau chief; from covering a local base, to city hall or even to the city desk. An assignment as a war reporter is necessarily a temporary career interlude, an adventure that must end with the war, and more likely before. Schools of journalism, which teach many specialties including science and education reporting, and even literary and dramatic criticism, do not offer courses in military reporting, since there are few interested students and still fewer qualified faculty members. Only rarely does a person trained for a military career shift to one in journalism. (Hanson W. Baldwin of *The New York Times,* a graduate of the U. S. Naval Academy, is a notable exception.)

These structural factors may not seem terribly consequential in and of themselves, but they combine to prevent the development of a professionalized corps of military reporters. As we shall soon see, this situation contrasts dramatically with that of the military information officer.

The upshot is that the reporters who cover military affairs are generalists, not specialists, and they often find themselves at a loss to comprehend the complex events and operations they are covering. Their editors and those who write headlines for their stories are even less able to convert military information into news. Where expertise is low, random errors in reporting will naturally be high. But the relatively low expertise of the typical reporter, in comparison with the information officer, creates an imbalance in the transmission of military information that results in serious structural biases in the total package that eventually reaches the public. Before we can analyze that relationship, we need to examine the other party to it, the PIO.

THE INFORMATION OFFICER: A MARGINAL MAN

It is hard to imagine any two institutions in American society that have less in common than the journalistic and military professions. The one is devoted to public disclosure, while the other organizes its operations in the utmost secrecy. The one considers itself the natural antagonist of government, while the other exists strictly as a creation of government. The one competes in a fierce capitalistic arena for its economic survival, while the other is sustained entirely by public tax monies.

They do have a few points of similarity, however. Both have come under hard criticism from public and politicians in recent years. Neither has a well-defined code of ethics. And each exercises some claim over the professional responsibilities of that man-in-the-middle, the military information specialist.

Public information as a formal military activity was created in World War II. It now goes under various names, including *public affairs* and *public relations,* but we will stick to the designation that comes closest to our interest here, that of the public information officer (PIO).

The PIO is found literally everywhere there are American armed forces; each military command, including all the Navy ships at sea, designates a PIO. His role varies from one branch of the service to the next, but it almost invariably requires him to operate as what sociologists call a "marginal man"—on the fringe of both the military and the journalistic worlds, not quite trusted by either because he carries the taint of potentially conflicting loyalties.

The existence of the PIO does not necessarily grow out of a desire on the Pentagon's part to propagandize the American people so that they will submit to heavy taxation to support the massive Defense Department, although former Senator J. William Fulbright and other critics have made that charge. Both the press and the public put heavy demands on the military for access to information and installations. Reporters not only want to know about troop movements and casualties in wartime, they also have plenty of peacetime questions about military programs and plans. Even given the full run of the Pentagon, no reporter could begin to comprehend and explain all the activities in that building alone in a year. Local bases and ships constantly get requests for Cub Scout tours, Rotary Club speakers, news notes on local boys who have been promoted or earned medals, and the like. Television and film companies frequently ask permission to shoot on-location scenes in authentic military settings. Either the closing or the expansion of a local military installation is important economic news for a community and needs careful explanation to the public that is affected. All of these tasks have been centralized in the hands of PIOs.

Commanding officers, the admirals and generals, captains and colonels who head military units, are rarely interviewed by reporters. Instead, the military normally addresses its public through the voice of someone called a "spokesman"—the PIO. But despite the PIO's seeming importance (from the public viewpoint), he occupies a decidedly second-rate position in the military scheme of things.

The military hierarchy draws a clear distinction between "line" and "staff" officers. Line officers are preparing for (or hold) positions of command. That is, they fly planes, command ships, lead infantry units in battle, and so forth. Staff officers, by contrast, are specialists who serve special functions within these commands. Some, like lawyers, doctors, and dentists, might receive extra pay for their specialized skills, which helps to compensate for their limited career opportunities within the bureaucracy. But many, including the PIO, do not.

There are far more public information job slots in the military than there are trained career specialists to fill them. Nevertheless they are filled, often by someone for whom PIO work is a minor part-time activity, or "collateral duty." In smaller units, it is not uncommon to find, say, the communications officer doubling in brass as PIO, with no staff, no budget, and no professional background for the job. Larger units often entrust PIO work full time to a newly commissioned officer, but of course they would not "waste" a high-potential line officer on such peripheral duties. The most prized attribute a line officer can have is to be a graduate of one of the prestigious service academies; such an education, which opens up entry to the military's highly inbred "Old Boy" promotion process, increases one's chances of becoming a general or admiral greatly. For years the Navy used the PIO specialty as a dumping ground for Annapolis graduates whose sole qualification for information work was that they failed their physical examinations in mid-career and were thus no longer eligible to rise to a line command. Only on large and important staffs, such as a major base or a high administrative office in the Pentagon, is the PIO slot likely to be filled by an experienced officer who has been specifically trained for information work.

These isolated specialists (there are only a few hundred in the entire Defense Department) constitute a vital link between the military and its public. Many of them hold bachelor's or even master's degrees in journalism, and a few have worked on civilian newspapers. Most feel strong loyalties to the principles of *public* information. A few have even sacrificed their careers by ignoring orders from senior line officers to suppress information that the public had both a right and a need to know. They are not necessarily appreciated by more senior officers, and several branches of the service have periodically toyed with the idea of abolishing the PIO specialty entirely.

The infamous case of the My Lai massacre, which eventually resulted in the original conviction of Army Lieutenant William Calley for his part in the mass murder of Vietnamese villagers, points up both the sham and the heroism that the PIO can contribute. The Army originally covered up the My Lai story, to its eternal discredit; among those conspiring in this suppression were several officers whose duties consisted of "public information." But when tales from returned veterans eventually forced the story into the open, the Army itself conducted the thorough investigation that led to Calley's court-martial. PIOs played an equally important role in bringing the full story to light, however belatedly.

Needless to say, their efforts were not universally appreciated by the senior line officers who bore ultimate responsibility for the original suppression. A general does not want as his PIO "a reporter who happens to be in uniform." He wants a subordinate officer whose first loyalty is to that command and who will protect the general's name and career. The promotion prospects of a PIO who holds the public's right to know as a supreme professional value tend to be quite limited.

While the My Lai episode is unusual in degree, it is typical in kind. A study by Commander Robert Sims, a career Navy PIO, of flag officers (admirals and generals) stationed in Washington, D. C., shows clearly that they suspect PIOs generally of harboring extremely liberal sentiments toward the press—far more liberal than the views PIOs themselves actually expressed in the same study.

Senior line officers also misconstrue the function of the PIO, tending to view him as primarily a news manager rather than as a news source for the media. This notion was epitomized by an admiral at the U. S. Naval Base at Long Beach, California, on a morning after several sailors from a ship's party at a local country club had left the bar to engage in "drag races" in motorized golf carts, ruining a sizable portion of the course. After reading a vivid account of the damage in the morning paper, the admiral thundered to his PIO (who was also the base legal officer), "Don't you have any better control of your local newspapers than to let them publish this kind of stuff?"

The PIO stands with one foot in each of two contradictory worlds. Which way he should lean is never totally clear to him. Professional journalistic scruples call for full disclosure of information in which the public might have an interest. Yet his continuance in a military capacity demands that he bow to the wishes of the higher brass. Under a competent and principled commanding officer, there is little conflict, and the job can be a very rewarding one. But the *threat* of conflicting loyalties is always there, and few if any PIOs survive a career in the military without some scars from being torn between their two professional worlds.

MILITARY SECRECY

"Power tends to corrupt," according to Lord Acton, "and absolute power corrupts absolutely." Nowhere on earth is there a greater concentration of power than in the Pentagon. It might be considered a testimonial to the probity of American military men that there have been only a handful of documented cases of corruption within the Department of Defense over its many years. By and large, military personnel are dedicated and honest. For those who might not be, there is an intricate system of internal checks—routines and procedures, administrative inspections, audits, courts of inquiry—to encourage them to march a straight path.

But most of this is practically invisible to the public. It is the news media that provide what McLuhan calls "the extensions of man," or what other romantics have characterized as "the eyes and ears of the world." We do not feel comfortable granting a great public agency insulation from commensurately great public scrutiny. The military, on the other hand, asserts that it *must* have that insulation if it is to carry out the very purposes for which it is responsible to the American people.

The satirical novel *Catch-22* was so named because in the military every high-sounding principle seems to have a "catch" to it. A bomber pilot could ask to be relieved of his mission because he was crazy, and this would be a sufficient reason for grounding him. But "Catch-22" held that expressing concern for one's safety in the face of great danger was evidence that the pilot was quite sane—so he had to fly his mission after all. So it is with military secrecy in a libertarian society.

Military leaders believe in freedom of the press. It is one of the sacred Constitutional principles they work (and if need be fight) to defend. They generally concede that this freedom implies the people's right to know what the military is up to. The catch is that, to defend these rights and freedoms, it is necessary to prevent the people from knowing some things about military activities.

This may be fair enough in the abstract. Freedom of the press and the people's right to know are not absolutes. For all anyone knows, absolute freedom might tend to corrupt just as absolutely as Lord Acton claimed absolute power does. But two important questions must constantly be asked: Where is the line to be drawn? And who is to draw it?

The principle of military secrecy is established pretty solidly. Battle plans, strategic weapons development, defensive alignments, and other details of military activities often must be kept from the enemy, to be sure. Few critics of military secrecy argue otherwise. But once the principle of secrecy is admitted, it invites abuse. And the more the power to extend the cloak of secrecy from that which is vital to that which might be merely embarrassing is placed in military hands, the farther even good men will be inclined to stretch it.

Congressman John Moss of California has led the fight against excessive, dangerous, and even ludicrous military secrecy. During the Vietnam war he succeeded in securing legislation that forced the declassification of many long-secret military documents. One, it turned out, had to do with the care of Army mules—scarcely a vital piece of military intelligence in the late 1960s.

Obviously some sensible rules are needed. Lines need to be drawn that will limit secrecy to information which is truly essential to military operations and for which there is not an overriding public interest at stake. Beyond that, there is no more justification for secrecy in the Pentagon than there might be in your local animal shelter.

But we already have such sensible rules. Representative Moss's congressional committee has seen to that. The critical question, and one to which no satisfactory answer has yet been proposed, is that of enforcing these rules. So long as that is left in military hands, it constitutes an open invitation to abuse. Excessive secrecy can be protected by more secrecy, in an endless spiral. On the other hand, to remove the power to civilian hands, as by a commission of media representatives, would make these people privy to military information that should not be generally known. To substitute a civilian censor for a military one is not necessarily a net gain, any more than substituting a civilian reporter for a military PIO would be. Whoever crosses these lines becomes a marginal man.

THE FUTURE FOR MILITARY INFORMATION

The journalistic profession, it is hoped, holds the key to improved communication between the military and the public. After all, it is the job of journalists to collect and disseminate information. Those in the military (the PIOs) and those outside it (the military reporters) have been broadly neglected. Few of them have any special training for their work or any clear-cut ethical standards appropriate for the peculiarly paradoxical professional quandary their work places them in.

There are signs that this is changing. One by-product of the Vietnam war was that it demonstrated to many PIOs that excessive secrecy was in neither the public's best interest nor the military's. The war was conceived and expanded without public scrutiny, and the resulting shambles were left to the military to clean up and apologize for. On the media side, a goodly number of reporters gained experience that has made them wiser in the ways and limitations of the military.

The critical posture most reporters assumed toward that war was unprecedented in American history. While not an unmixed blessing, it is probably on balance a healthy attitude to carry into the future. Putting it succinctly, the war inadvertently brought the PIOs and the reporters closer together on the important aspects of military activities than they have ever been. If the PIOs are more defensive, they are also more likely to recognize that they themselves may be the objects of manipulation by their own superior officers. If the reporters are more cynical, they are also more attentive and informed regarding matters military.

REFERENCES

J. William Fulbright, *The Pentagon Propaganda Machine* (New York: Liveright, 1970).

Joseph Heller, *Catch-22* (New York: Dell, 1962).

Robert Sims, unpublished M. A. thesis (University of Wisconsin, 1970).

William J.Small, *To Kill a Messanger* (New York: Hastings House, 1970).

Chapter 9

Corporate Public Relations

To the casual observer it may seem somewhat puzzling that privately owned businesses should venture into the realm of public information. Venture they do. Public information programs constitute a lion's share of the mammoth undertaking called corporate public relations, which we reviewed briefly in Chapter 5.

Why, in a country that touts free enterprise as part of the democratic creed, do corporations inform other segments of society about their practices? In large part, the historical answer to that question was this: Private businesses believed that their economic well-being depended on a public policy of minimal government interference in corporation affairs; and they found out that many citizens would tolerate, if not demand, more government regulation of business.

It is not too surprising, then, that the first formal corporate public information programs were initiated by railroad and power companies in the 1880s, when popular sentiment toward those public service corporations was something less than enthusiastic. Those were the days when urbanization, the growth of big industry, and the emergence of labor unions shook Americans out of the pioneer spirit of individualistic independence. The many segments of society, it became quite clear, would continue to become increasingly *interdependent.* Growing friction between labor and management paralleled hostility toward big business on the part of working-class citizens.

Although most big business magnates of that era first responded to the challenge with invective along the lines of William H. Vanderbilt's "the public be damned," a few saw greater promise in a new approach. To stave off a swell of antagonism that they feared would lead to the demise of total laissez faire, they began to give employees and other citizens information about their positions and programs. John D. Rockefeller started one of the first such programs for his Standard Oil empire by hiring an agent to write responses to public criticism and by paying newspapers of the day to publish his agent's early efforts. Similar projects were tried by the Burlington and the Union Pacific railroads, and in 1889 George Westinghouse organized a department within his electric company to tell the public that his alternating-current electricity provided a social good because it was effective for electrocuting criminals.

The tactics of those early efforts were a bit sensational, if not sordid, and the messages often were more promotional than informational. Perhaps the first corporate publicists were taking cues from earlier promotional schemes. The adventures of Daniel Boone had been created by a Kentucky land speculator, John Filson, to promote settlement of that western region in the early 1800s. And in the 1840s, circus man P. T. Barnum had used his showmanship talents to exploit the public's taste for the sensational and bizarre. Still, the information programs of Rockefeller and his industrial contemporaries signaled an admission (though probably a reluctant one) that big business had a stake in supplying information and ideas to the public.

The stake became clearer in the first two decades of the twentieth century, when muckraking journalists delighted in exposing evils of big business. As Ida Tarbell took on Standard Oil, Samuel Hopkins Adams raked the patent medicine companies, and Upton Sinclair described the meat-packing industry as *The Jungle,* the political climate in the country looked favorable for government regulation of companies whose poor performance might jeopardize public welfare. President Theodore Roosevelt had made anti-monopoly crusades part of his political game. Big business was on the defensive.

In 1906, an organization called The Publicity Bureau was hired by a group of railroads to counter unfriendly public attitudes which by that time had generated into a full-blown drive for government regulation of rail transportation. The Bureau (which began operations in 1900 and was the first public relations firm in the country) was not able to stop what by then was probably inevitable government regulation. But other companies who dreaded the thought of being regulated as "public utilities" became Bureau clients—among them American Telephone and Telegraph and the Boston Elevated Railway. Still other corporations saw merit in some sort of public information program, and some of the larger ones started to do what Westinghouse had done: they established publicity departments within the company and began to hire reporters away from newspapers to serve as corporate publicity agents.

Among this new breed of corporate publicists was a former New York *World* reporter named Ivy Lee. When he went to work as the Pennsylvania Railroad's first publicity agent in 1908 (six years before he became a consultant to Rockefeller), he espoused a credo that has since been hailed as the philosophical foundation for respectable corporate public information policies. Don't ignore the citizenry, Ivy Lee counseled; a corporation benefits more by providing information than by hiding or disguising it. Lee's philosophy, and his skill at practicing it, set the tone for much of the practice of modern corporate public relations.

The Committee on Public Information, a government agency set up during World War I to mobilize support for the war effort, helped speed the pace of the growing PR industry. The CPI, headed and staffed by former newspapermen, was a training ground for journalists in the techniques of publicity. Among its members was Edward L. Bernays, who in 1923 wrote the first book about public relations *(Crystallizing Public Opinion)* and initiated the first college course in public relations. In 1930, Bernays formed a public relations firm which today is one of the country's largest.

Much of today's corporate PR still draws heavily from the traditions of the pre-1930 era. Publicity is viewed as a necessary and effective tool to soothe public hostility, either real or potential, toward business. Consequently, a large chunk of a corporation's public relations efforts continues to be devoted to giving out positive information about the firm. The "news release," a public statement about the company written in journalistic news style and submitted to the press for free publication, has become a staple product of PR operations. So has the news conference, which gives corporate executives a platform from which to address journalists and, they hope, the public. Company publications, including newspapers for employees and magazines for stockholders, seek to inform "publics" more intimately associated with the firm.

But in the consumer protection era of the 1970s, there is evidence that private business is again being put on the defensive in a major way. Complaints from consumer groups give an impression that corporations are not as concerned as they should be about product safety, environmental pollution, and inflationary prices. Politicians again have found that demands for more control on business will strike a favorable note with the electorate. Government regulatory agencies have increasingly banned unsafe products and have been more strict in enforcing government-imposed standards for safety and pollution. Even the White House has a consumer affairs adviser on its staff.

How should a corporation's public information program cope with these developments? In an age when citizens use mass media more than ever before and are consequently bombarded with claims and counterclaims from all sides, are traditional PR approaches adequate? Almost surely not. We will argue that a more sophisticated concept of public information is needed if corporations are to communicate effectively with today's citizenry, and in so doing are to be believed.

WHY PUBLIC INFORMATION?

The philosophy that corporations ought to provide (rather than hide) information is a necessary beginning for organizing an effective public information program. It is *only* a beginning because it leaves important questions begging: Who wants or needs information about a corporation's activities? What kinds of information are wanted or needed? How can information best be channeled? Why should a corporation try to provide information to the public, anyway?

That last question can be the key to answering all the others. Put another way, the general goals a corporation sets down for its public relations program, that is, the *reasons* the corporation has for communicating with the public, will determine how the company goes about informing citizens, or whether it tries to really communicate at all. One reason might be that the company is being threatened in some way by an "outside" force, such as government or a labor group or a neighborhood citizens association. Another possibility is that the firm wants to avoid some potential threat or crisis. Or, perhaps, a company simply feels it has an obligation, as a member of society, to communicate with other members. We'll elaborate briefly on these three common reasons for corporate public information programs.

Self-Defense

Like the old railroads and power companies, today's corporations often feel threatened by words and actions of "outsiders" and therefore use public relations to counteract the alien threats. Complaints need to be answered and unpopular company policies defended, often by means of a barrage of news releases and other public relations materials. Information is dispensed

as an antidote which, it is supposed, will cure (or at least control) the
nebulous disease of "bad image." The public relations goal is like the goal
of a hospital emergency room: Treat an injury that already has occurred.

Prevention of Crises

Part of Ivy Lee's public relations legacy is that an ongoing publicity program helps a corporation avoid serious problems with the public. Consequently, a lot of PR trade talk concerns "building a positive image" for the
organization. A basic assumption has been that giving out a lot of information about the merits of the company will lead to a "good corporate image."
A related premise is that a company perceived as "strong" and "good" will
be less vulnerable to whimsical demands by government and citizens. Information is considered preventive medicine, especially when sugar-coated. So
events which show the company's role as a concerned citizen are planned
and publicized, information indicating the firm's financial stability is given
out with fanfare, and potentially embarrassing situations are explained, perhaps explained away. The informational goal resembles that of political
diplomacy: Solve problems, with communication, before they reach a crisis
stage.

Social Responsibility

Because American society is more interdependent than ever before, many
corporate activities have become issues of widespread public interest. A
company's wage scale, hiring practices, smokestack emissions, and product
safety standards have entered the arena of legitimate societal concern. In
the future, still more matters formerly considered internal corporate affairs
will no doubt become public issues as their impact on society is recognized.
Corporations, then, have certain obligations to society. A seemingly obvious one is to communicate with persons affected by corporate policies.
Some persons (such as employees and stockholders) may be affected in a
direct, personal way by what a company does. And ultimately certain activities of a company can affect all of us, though indirectly. A corporation
which recognizes this may see a *responsibility*—not just a need—to help
citizens cope with the results of company decisions. Its public relations
program would attempt to find out what information about the company
will be useful to citizens, and attempt to provide it.

THE "TELL OUR SIDE" APPROACH

The "whys" of corporate public relations are probably of less concern to
the actual PR practitioner than are the nuts-and-bolts "hows" of communication strategy (although the "whys," we should point out, are likely to be
more important to the corporate executives, who pay the PR people to

come up with the "hows"). If there is a single time-honored guideline for a public information strategy, it probably is summed up best in the simple phrase: "Now let's tell *our* side of the story."

Few libertarians would quibble, from the philosophical viewpoint of free expression, with the desirability of providing opportunities for companies to explain and defend themselves. Indeed, some public relations advocates grandly proclaim that PR provides necessary input into the "marketplace of information and ideas" in which Anglo-American concepts of free expression are rooted.

Unfortunately for the cause of effective communication, however, the "tell our side" syndrome can become a set of blinders. For when the emphasis is to "tell," communication is considered as *giving* information and little more. The results of that strategy are obvious in a good many PR operations today; the goal of the operation is to tell everything the corporate executives think ought to be told ("our side"), in as many forms and through as many media as possible. PR offices become mills for grinding out announcements, news releases, and other publicity materials. And the measurement of "success" naïvely becomes one of quantity: How many materials have been produced, and how many have found their way through the intricate filtering processes of the mass media? The strategy is to create lots of messages, at least some of which are likely to be passed on to media audiences by hassled and skeptical media gatekeepers.

Even the early pioneers of publicity perceived a need to defer to the foibles of newspaper and magazine editors. The public relations materials most likely used in the news media, they found, were those which resembled in content and format the materials produced by journalists. So the publicity message came to be called a "news release," written in news style for the appropriate medium, and containing information likely to meet journalistic standards of "worthiness" (as described in Chapter 3). That formula continues to guide traditional corporate public information programs. And yet such an approach, standing on its own, hardly results in an effective public information program. There are several possible reasons, and we will mention three of them here briefly.

Perhaps the most important and obvious is that the "public" is taken into account only indirectly. A "tell our side" approach almost inevitably gears itself to corporate executives (who decide what "our side" is) and media gatekeepers (who are "told" in the form of publicity materials packaged as news and asked to pass the word along). For many executives, "our side" means bland, self-serving announcements about company officials getting new titles, the company earning record profits, and the vice president being honored by the board of directors—all in an attempt to forge a "good image" for the company. And to a good many media gatekeepers who daily face a deluge of such publicity announcements, the messages are propaganda produced by hacks for self-serving bosses, thus worthy only of newsroom wastepaper baskets.

Another reason is that "telling" is erroneously seen as the essence of effective communication. Early communication theorists viewed public information as a "hypodermic" process, in which messages, once injected into the public bloodstream, would have a predictable effect. But that view has been negated by three decades of communication research. As we suggested in Chapter 4, effective communication is more realistically viewed as a situation in which two persons or groups are able to clear up misconceptions and ambiguities. In order to achieve that sort of success, each party to communication has to co-orient with the other, which as a practical matter usually requires that each party *seek* information as well as give it. Merely "telling," without finding out what the other party wants or needs to be told, is a wasteful use of communication resources.

Finally, the "tell our side" strategy forces a public relations practitioner to become an advocate for the corporation's position rather than an intermediary who tries to facilitate understanding between the corporation and citizens. It is common, even among PR people, to view public relations as *persuasive* communication. We have deliberately chosen to deal with corporate public relations as public information rather than persuasion, not because that is how PR people usually view it, but because that is what it *needs to become.*

If a corporation is to have a more effective public information program, it will have to do more than advocate "our side"; it will need to communicate about things people consider *relevant to their own situations.* But first a corporation has to know what those things are, who the people are who want to know them, and the most effective media through which to communicate. That requires a different approach to corporate public information—one more attuned to the needs of an interdependent society in which corporations need to promote public awareness and understanding of their activities.

A "GO-BETWEEN" AND "PROBLEM-SOLVING" APPROACH

Let us take the luxury (and the hazard) of predicting a bit. Let's assume that the most commonly employed PR strategies were guided by the philosophy that effective communication involves more than one-way information peddling. Such an approach would considerably shatter the traditional view that the most effective public relations program is the one that bombards people with messages to create the mystical product called a "good corporate image." Instead, it would focus PR information programs toward help-ing *both* the corporation and its publics get more correct pictures of *one another;* it also would employ communication as a tool to help *both* corpo-rations and citizens solve problems. In such an approach, communication strategies are designed for the *sharing* (not just giving) of information, and for the *solving* (not just explaining away) of problems.

Some public relations organizations, but by no means a majority, have developed programs based at least in part on such an approach. What we describe below, then, is not entirely pie in the sky. Indeed, because we feel it is a more effective and socially responsible approach, we'd like to think of it as the basis for most public relations operations in the not too distant future. We'll describe it in terms of the two public information tasks that it assigns to public relations personnel: the go-between (or intermediary) and the problem solver.

The PR Intermediary: Facilitating Information

All public relations people need to concern themselves with such questions as: Which groups of citizens are we going to communicate with? What are we going to communicate about? What are the most appropriate channels for communicating with that group about that topic?

Guessing—or even dogmatically asserting—answers is a fairly simple, inexpensive, and common PR strategy, but it does not facilitate mutual understanding, unless by luck. To find the answers for sure, the public relations practitioner has to *seek* information. A professional PR program, then, should involve research as a preliminary step to providing public information.

Let's assume, for example, that a large electric power company plans to discontinue its coal-burning facility in town A and replace it with a nuclear energy plant in town B, twenty-five miles away. The company has, of course, a social responsibility to communicate with some fairly obvious groups of citizens: at a minimum, the townspeople of both villages and the employees of the original plant. But each of those groups is in fact a con-glomerate of smaller groups, and each smaller group has particular interests and anxieties about the change. In order to communicate effectively in that situation, the company's PR operation would seek information. It would try to answer certain basic questions, such as the ones that follow.

What specific groups, or publics, want or need information? PR research might show, for example, that local public officials in town A want to know whether the old plant will be available for prospective new industry, while officials in town B want to know whether the new plant will be annexed to the town limits and therefore subject to the local property tax. One citizen organization in town A might want to find out whether the company will still support local civic projects after it moves out of its plant, while another citizens committee in town B wants to know how the new plant will affect the water in the lake which borders the new plant site. Middle management in the town A plant might want to know whether the company will pay moving expenses for their families, while production workers wonder whether they'll have to find new jobs.

How do members of those groups relate the situation to their own lives? In other words, in what ways is the company's plan relevant to the persons concerned? We have suggested some possibilities above; for some persons, the impact on local taxes was particularly relevant, while for others ecology and family financial security were especially important. In a more general sense, some publics may view the situation as a problem while others look upon it as an opportunity.

What do members of the various publics think is the corporation's view of the situation? Do officials of town B, for example, expect the company to resist annexation? Do town B environmentalists think the company is unconcerned about water pollution? Do production workers at the old plant consider the company oblivious to their concern about their jobs?

How does the company, in fact, view the situation? What does it plan to do about the civic projects in town A, the moving expenses of its middle management, the possible pollution of the lake, and so forth?

How does the company think their publics view the situation? For example, does it think the environmentalists are hostile, the chamber of commerce apathetic, the employees disappointed but complacent?

When information about the above considerations is obtained, the question "What are we going to communicate about?" can be tackled in a professional, systematic way. Suppose, for example, the research showed that, while the company planned to utilize methods to prevent thermal pollution of the lake, the environmentalists in town B perceived the company as unconcerned about ecology. The public relations staff could then provide information to each party about the other's environmental concerns and thereby clear up an inaccurate picture.

The publics, of course, need to have the information they consider relevant made available to them through some appropriate information channel. As professional utilizers of mass communication, public relations personnel decide which media channels are most appropriate to a given communication effort. For management and workers, *internal* channels such as company newspapers or posters might be the most efficient media. Citizens' groups might be reached through *external* channels, such as the local newspaper or a special local news conference. Effective choice of medium depends both on the particular "public" and on the topic for communication.

An important point about the intermediary function of public relations needs to be underscored here: Public information takes a more or less neutral stance. Public information strategy means finding out what people are concerned about, then providing information relevant to those concerns. That involves a great deal more than trying only to persuade people by "telling our side."

Public Relations and Problem Solving

By acting as an information intermediary between a corporation and its publics, public relations can also help people solve problems. The wide range of problems that face a typical corporation, particularly in its relations with "outsiders," must be taken for granted. Earlier, we gave hypothetical examples of some problems stemming from a single decision to close down one plant and open another; corporations constantly grapple with multiples of such problems on a routine basis.

Communication can be a useful tool in problem solving, because a person (such as a corporate executive) faced with a problem (such as making a policy decision about spending money to reduce thermal pollution) usually will want information to help him weigh alternatives before choosing a course of action. Corporate public relations, then, needs (1) to search out *information about alternatives* and the pros and cons of each and (2) to pass the information along to the person who must solve the problem. The problem-solving approach, therefore, requires gathering information as well as dispensing it.

In contrast, a public information system built on the "tell our side" philosophy has disquieting implications for those faced with a problem. Since that traditional approach stresses information giving, or persuasion of corporate "publics," communication is used as a tool to maintain stability within the organization, and therefore it tends to be regulated by corporate management. If, then, a company policy causes a problem for someone, communication is used to bring the attitudes of the person "in line" or to convince him that no problem exists after all. Confronted with that kind of information strategy, a person may be forced to make decisions on the basis of routine habit or, even worse, to fatalistically accept the consequences of the company policy. That perverse version of "problem solving" is not compatible with a corporation's social responsibility to help cope with the problems its policies cause.

CORPORATIONS AND CITIZENS

We have just tried to thread together some guidlines for effective and responsible corporate public information. We ought to note, however, that private corporations have no direct obligation to set up any kind of public relations operation at all. Unlike courts, school systems, and the military, private businesses are not financed by public tax money and do not make official policies that bind citizens. But the simple fact is that corporations *have* gotten into the public information business, and in no small way. So they have obligations to themselves and their stockholders to establish effective programs. More important, they have obligations to their publics to communicate in a socially responsible way.

To many, the terms "corporate public relations" and "social responsibility" are inherently contradictory. Public relations has had a hard time living down its seamy beginnings, and its image continues to be somewhat tainted by the questionable practices of some contemporary publicists. Still, the ultimate success of any public relations effort rests in no small part on building and maintaining the confidence of the mass media and the citizenry—and mature PR practitioners know it. Organizations like the Public Relations Society of America and its affiliate chapters on many college campuses have in recent years done much to encourage socially responsible PR practices.

Public relations programs, of course, are almost always destined to be self-serving in one way or another; that, after all, is why they exist. However, this doesn't mean that they cannot be ethical. A program such as the one we described in this chapter, establishing PR as an intermediary and problem solver serving both the corporation and the public, might not make hostile citizens start admiring the corporation. It might, though, make them better understand the company. Ultimately, of course, a corporation's actual performance, rather than its public relations effort, will determine its future. A responsible company will want to ensure that citizens evaluate its performance on the basis of accurate information. But for a doggedly irresponsible corporation, a public information program would be a waste of money.

REFERENCES

Helpful texts which treat corporate public relations problems in detail are:

Scott M. Cutlip and Allen H. Center, *Effective Public Relations* (Englewood Cliffs, N. J.: Prentice-Hall, 1971).

Edward J. Robinson, *Communication and Public Relations* (Columbus, Ohio: Charles E. Merrill, 1966).

The authors thank Professor James E. Grunig of the University of Maryland, who made available materials from a 1972 project in which graduate students in journalism performed a communication audit of the Potomac Electric Power Company (PEPCO).

SUGGESTED STUDY PROJECT

Interview an official of an organization's public relations department to get a sense of the public information strategy the department employs. What relative emphasis does the operation place on simply grinding out information (the "tell our side" approach) in the form of news releases, brochures, etc.? What relative emphasis is given to seeking out information about the organization's publics and what those publics consider relevant? To what extent does the PR operation provide the organization's executives with information about alternatives needed to solve problems?

Part Three

Persuading Individuals

Chapter 10

The American Persuasion
Industry

In Part Two of this book, we shifted gradually from institutions whose function is supposed to be primarily *information* to those whose public information function is subordinate to *persuasion.* Now we are ready to look at persuasion in its more direct and unvarnished forms.

There exists in the United States today probably the most extensive and professionalized persuasion industry in world history. It includes many varieties of persuasive activity, and it goes under several names. When the goal is to influence consumer sales, it is called "advertising." When more general attitudinal goals are involved, we usually speak of "public relations," an industry we have already examined in some detail. When international political interests are at stake, the term "propaganda" is frequently used instead. These industries employ somewhat different technical skills, but there is a good deal of overlap among them in the concepts and practices they use. It is not unusual for a person to shift in his career from one to another of these fields, and many professional persuasion specialists could not tell you with any certainty which term best describes their work.

Instead of looking at these discrete professional industries as such, then, we will break the problem down according to the kinds of *goals* the public persuaders are trying to achieve. In particular, we will focus on the actual behavior of "consumers" that is to be influenced and try to construct the problem from the point of view of a consumer. Our focus on concrete behavior is, rather surprisingly perhaps, not the usual way of discussing persuasion in academic circles. Instead, there is a great tendency to talk in murky tones about "attitudes" and "values" and "images" and the like. We do not want to downplay the concept that persuasion proceeds by manipulating people's values. We only want to put "attitude" in its proper place, which is as a preliminary stage or step toward an eventual behavioral goal. That is, there is not much to be gained by changing the way people feel, unless it results in a corresponding change in what they actually do.

The psychologist B. F. Skinner, in his book *Beyond Freedom and Dignity,* argues that our feelings are the product, rather than the cause, of our behavior. It is external conditions of "reinforcement" in the social environment that determine what we will do. Having done something, we then experience emotional feelings about it, and these lead us into thinking that we have done the thing because we had these feelings. Skinner's conclusion is that we should be concerning ourselves directly with behavior, and the environmental reinforcements that control it, rather than with attitudes and feelings. This argument is quite controversial in academic circles, and Skinner has become the target of all sorts of critics—both radical and conservative—who intuitively "know" that *their* actions are the product of free will and fine intentions.

In the somewhat more "real" world of the persuasion industry, however, there is not much interest in merely influencing attitudes in and of themselves. It is not so much that most professional persuaders agree with Skinner's reasoning; in fact they do not. But they must agree with Skinner's conclusion, simply because hard-headed clients have real and concrete goals in mind. That is, the payoff for any campaign or program of persuasion comes from demonstrating that it has somehow got people to buy soap, or vote for a candidate, or give money, or not be litterbugs—regardless of how these people feel.

Social psychologists have gradually begun to discover that there is only a tenuous relationship between changes in attitudes toward a concept and subsequent changes in the way people behave toward that concept. This means that much of the voluminous research that has been done on methods of changing attitudes through mass communication may not apply very much at all to the more ultimate goal of producing changes in real behavior. In this section of the book, then, we will concentrate on fields in which *concrete acts,* rather than values and attitudes alone, are at stake.

We realize that this viewpoint, i.e. that behavior is largely independent of (and of more immediate importance than) values, flies in the face of conventional beliefs that are deeply ingrained in American culture. In many of our churches Sunday School teachers explain to children that it is not enough to *do* what is right; we must also feel in our hearts that we are doing it because it *is* right. The admission of black Americans into full participation in the cultural, social, and economic life of the nation has been delayed for more than a century by the argument that integration will come only gradually, as whites' feelings of racism are replaced by feelings of brotherhood. (When occasional fits and starts of integration have been tried, such as President Harry Truman's executive order in 1951 that integrated the armed services, or the appearance of Jackie Robinson in the lineup of the Brooklyn Dodgers, the feelings of most whites often have come into line with the new realities with remarkable speed.) The missionary movement in American churches, which in the nineteenth century sent emissaries around the world attempting to instill Christian beliefs, has been replaced in our time by commercial, political, and military efforts to export our secular belief structures (capitalism, democracy) to other societies. In this century we have fought two wars that our leaders have explained were for the purposes, respectively, of making the world safe for democracy and of changing the hearts and minds of men.

The more recent war in Vietnam—the longest in our nation's history—probably suffered most from the lack of a conception among our leaders of any realizable concrete goal. What they desired, apparently, was a strong, popular, honest, pro-American government in the southern portion of Vietnam; this would be bad for Communism, good for the United States, and supposedly very good for the Vietnamese people. So, of course, it was supposedly something that these people would want, and the United States would provide the military shield that would allow them to have it. There were many miscalculations in the evolution of the American commitment in Vietnam, but perhaps none was so fundamental as this assumption that the key to social and political change in Vietnam lay in changing the hearts and minds of its people.

The story of Vietnam is not a pleasant one, and we mention it here only to demonstrate that faith in changing psychological values can condition too much of our thinking. The commercial world employs quite a different model of human activity, one that Robert S. McNamara, incidentally, brought to the Vietnam war as Secretary of Defense. He called it, in the fashionable jargon of modern business schools and corporations, *cost-benefit analysis*. It has proved to be quite a useful tool in marketing and business administration, and it can probably be applied to most social problems that are governed primarily by rationality and that exist in limited contexts. It eventually did not work out in Vietnam because the enemy did not behave "rationally"—no cost was too great for victory—and because the enemy forces seemed to grow without limit, partly because the enemy population had never been realistically defined. The shattering experience of American involvement in Vietnam's war does not necessarily mean ipso facto that the cost-benefit approach is not a valid one—when its assumptions of rationality and defined limits hold true.

In this section of the book, we make use of the cost-benefit model as a way to analyze attempts of various institutions to persuade citizens to act in certain ways. To some extent, we'll be looking at the costs and benefits which those institutions have to consider when they try to formulate persuasive communication strategies. More important, though, is our attempt to use cost-benefit analysis as a point of departure for examining how the individual consumer-citizen can assess the institutions' attempts to persuade him. After all, the persuasion industry can't operate effectively by considering only what *it* does; instead it has to work on the basis of its understanding of the way things look to its target audience. We will assume here that this audience consists of people who organize their consumer behavior largely in terms of the costs to them and the benefits they might receive in return.

In taking this approach, we hope to help the reader as a consumer in two ways. First, we hope consumers will sharpen their own concepts of the costs and benefits available to them in the marketplace where the persuasion industry operates. Second, we try to help consumers better understand how the persuasion industry works (and how it tries to work on them) so that they can maximize their own benefits and minimize their own costs. Our approach should also be useful and interesting to readers who are interested in careers in the persuasion industry.

Chapter 11 considers that large portion of the industry that deals most explicitly with consumer costs and benefits in the normal sense of those terms. This is the field of marketing and the advertising of consumer goods. The costs include the obvious one of money plus such real factors as time and convenience. The benefits include not only the direct value of what is purchased but also some indirect ones—most particularly heavy subsidization of the mass communication system that we take so much for granted in this country.

Chapters 12 and 13 are about politics, especially about political campaigns, for that is when the persuasion industry goes to work on a double-time schedule. Because of the different cost-benefit orientations, we will deal separately with elections involving candidates and those where budgets and taxes are at stake. While there are certainly a lot of costs and benefits involved in electing good candidates or voting on a public policy issue, the campaigns on behalf of candidates do not focus nearly so explicitly on cost considerations as do financial elections.

Candidate elections are the most interesting to a majority of people, because candidacies are complex, based on coalitions of segments of society plus the individual (often colorful) personal attributes of the person running for office. Candidates have records and make promises, and these cut across many issues and interests. Rarely will a single voter be totally satisfied with the record and promises of a single candidate, across all issues and questions. Candidacies are compromises, and so are votes. But finally it becomes a consumer decision that is not so unlike buying a car or a tube of toothpaste, after all. The coming of our mass communication system, and the proliferation of the persuasion industry within it, has changed the way in which candidates campaign and even the kind of person who can campaign effectively. Have these changes in turn changed the political structure and process of American society? It is a problem that many thoughtful people have posed and one that we will want to deal with.

Elections without candidates constitute a special problem area. Early in this century, laws were adopted that made it possible to submit societal questions to public decisions, in the form of initiatives and referenda. Often voters are asked to decide for or against various mechanisms for racial integration; for or against fluoridation of their municipal water systems; for or against major public proposals, such as hosting the Olympic Games or instituting strict controls on pollution. Generally speaking, these campaigns tend to be fought over the benefits to the consumer, more than over costs. In this way they are more like candidate elections (where problems of cost tend to be submerged or ambiguous) than financial elections (where the public costs are usually put in very specific dollar terms but the benefits are often difficult for voters to understand). We will devote a separate chapter to these noncandidate elections, on the premise that they involve different cost-benefit orientations from the one the consumer (voter) is likely to develop in candidate elections.

Finally, we will spend a chapter (Chapter 14) on a remarkable persuasion industry that is almost wholly directed toward consumer cost, the institution of fund raising for charities and other worthy causes. As with politics, the media provide the main channel through which charitable fund-raising campaigns are articulated. From the charities' perspective, this has worked rather well. They usually get their money. But for the consumer, the form of fund raising that has evolved in this country has not been very helpful. The media do little to enlighten donors about the charities to which they give. Instead it has seemed enough to the media (and, understandably, to the charities) that people give, which they do. Now, few donors expect (or even want) to be "consumers" in the sense of benefiting personally from charities; but they might reasonably demand the interim benefit of being better informed about where their dollars are going.

These four chapters do not, of course, cover the entire persuasion industry. It is not our purpose here to be comprehensive. Instead, we try to give citizens a look at persuasion campaigns from a general perspective that can be applied to any topic which causes consumers to become targets of this ubiquitous industry.

REFERENCES

B. F. Skinner, *Beyond Freedom and Dignity* (New York: Knopf, 1971).

SUGGESTED STUDY PROJECTS

1 Ask at least twenty different people to give you a one-sentence definition of communication. How many of them define it as some form of persuasion? How many define it in terms of giving information of some sort, without persuasion? What would be your own definition, after analyzing those of other people? Would you include persuasion as a necessary element of communication, or not?
2 Make a list of at least ten different activities that people could do in their leisure time, such as going to a film or ball game, playing tennis, reading a book, playing cards, etc. Ask at least thirty people to rate each of these on two scales. The first scale is to indicate how much they like to do the activity: very much, pretty much, somewhat, not very much, not at all. The second scale is to indicate how often they actually do it: at least every day, every week, every month, every year, less than once a year, never. Across all these persons and all the activities, how strong is the statistical association between their feelings (liking it) and their behavior (doing it)? What other factors besides liking to do something seem to control how often a person does it?

Chapter 11

Commercial Advertising

Advertisements provide the lifeblood of the mass communications industry in the United States. Neither newspapers, magazines, radio, nor, especially, television as we know them could long survive without their income from commercial ads. This nation spends more money, and a greater share of its total productivity, on advertising than does any other country. Massive advertising revenues permit the mass media to operate without government support (and therefore without governmental control) and at greatly reduced cost to readers, listeners, and viewers. The difference in consumer cost can be easily demonstrated by comparing media. It costs several dollars to see a motion picture in a theater, where there is little or no advertising; on television the movie is free—although the viewer has to put up with periodic commercials. In print, such quality magazines as *The New Yorker* and *The Atlantic Monthly* often publish new works by major authors. Packaged with other articles (and ads), these are available at a considerably lower price than they will later command as books, even in paperbound editions.

One might, then, expect cost-conscious consumers to welcome advertising into the mass media. But of course they do not. Even though some ads are entertaining or informative, all too many seem to be tasteless slurs on the audience's intelligence and values. Further, most are at least somewhat misleading, and some contain downright lies.

What may be far worse than the content of advertisements is the apparent influence of advertisers. The very fact that ads pay the piper implies that advertisers can call the tune. To succeed, mass advertising requires a mass audience; so media content attracts advertising support only to the extent that it attracts an audience. And, it seems to many, the more mass the medium, the more crass its content. That is, the more a medium relies on advertising, the more it screens out material that might offend portions of its potential audience . The result is "lowest-common-demoninator" programing on television, boosterism in local newspapers, innocuous mixes of pop music and trivial news on the radio—inevitably a bland popular culture.

GOALS AND BENEFITS OF ADVERTISING

Whether advertising is solely to blame for this is arguable, but the general principles governing the relationship between media and advertiser are clear. (Advertising is part of the marketing industry, which has the task of delivering commercial products into the hands of consumers for a price. The ad itself is a persuasive message designed to increase the likelihood of product purchase. Media "news" and "program" content constitute tempting devices by which potential consumers are lured into exposure to advertisements. Advertisers assess nonadvertising content for its capacity to deliver to an ad large numbers of persons who might be persuaded to purchase the advertised product.

Consumers benefit from this arrangement in two ways. First, their use of the media is subsidized. And second, ads do provide some useful information—probably more than most people realize until they consider how often they consult them. But consumers also need to recognize that they are being "delivered" to these ads by the media. Not only should they be wary of misleading ads and "puffery," but they might also resolve to reward media content that they like by buying the sponsoring product.

It is commonplace (but rather pointless) to disparage advertising. The industry also has its apologists, some moved by pro-commercial ideologies, others well paid for their efforts. Rather than take sides, let us examine this remarkable institution from a variety of viewpoints and see what we can make of it. We will then consider in some detail the psychological and social processes that make it work.

The liberal economist John Kenneth Galbraith, in his book *The New Industrial State,* argues that advertising serves two economic functions which are not obvious. First, it is a means of *regulating demand* so that the market, in which huge corporations have invested enormous concentrations of capital, is *not* subject to the whims of individual consumers. The general effect, he says, "is to shift the locus of decision in the purchase of goods from the consumer where it is beyond control to the firm where it is subject to control." He notes that this is by no means an absolute control of consumer behavior. Superficially the process consists of a constant struggle among a few oligopolistic competitor firms, in which first one and then another gains a temporary advantage in a "zero-sum game." If one firm's sales begin to slip, it changes its advertising strategy (and perhaps its product) until things begin to improve; this in turn causes its competitors to lose sales, so they change too. Thus, there is little change over time in the comparative standings of the firms in a field; and consumers' purchasing patterns tend to be stable, habitual, and repetitive. Paradoxically, this tends to insulate the firm from the "marketplace" of romantic economic theory. It is worth noting that advertising can also be used to *discourage* consumer demand for a product. This is rare, of course, but it did happen during the fuel shortages of 1973 and 1974, when several major oil companies ran ads telling people how to conserve on gasoline use.

The second function Galbraith sees is that advertising sustains the prestige of the industrial system itself, by relentless propaganda on behalf of "goods in general." By implying that the endless pursuit (and therefore production) of things is inevitable, advertising has made industrial growth an end in itself. Only in very recent years, as the environmental impact of industrial society has become dramatically clear, have any serious numbers of Americans begun to consider the possibility that infinite economic growth may not necessarily be "progress." In all, Galbraith sees advertising as creating the kind of person needed in an industrial state—"one that reliably spends his income and works reliably because he is always in need of more."

Now let us shift from the perspective of the total society to that of individual consumers. Of what use is advertising to them, at the personal level of minimizing their expenditures and maximizing the benefits from their purchases? It is immediately obvious that some ads are a lot more helpful to us than others.

Perhaps the most informative consumer ads, as a group, are those to be found in newspapers. Classified "want ads" are consulted frequently by bargain hunters and job seekers, among others; shoppers rely on the full-page "display" ads to locate sales at department stores and supermarkets; theatergoers and film buffs would be seriously hampered without the daily entertainment page ads. When the New York newspaper *PM* was published as a cooperative venture by its staff in the late 1930s, it carried no advertising; after a while, however, reader demand led the paper to publish advertising information free—as a necessary public service.

At the other end of the scale lie the almost informationless musical "spot" jingles of radio in the 1930s and 1940s. About all the consumer learned was the name of a product, and lest anyone miss the message, that name was repeated endlessly. To make things even simpler, one-syllable names were devised to fit into meaningless slogans: "DUZ does everything"; "VEL's mar-*vel*-ous"; TIDE's in, dirt's out." It is of at least passing significance that the inventor of many of these easy-to-remember brand names was the psychologist John Watson, who in his academic days had been the author of *Behaviorism*, one of the most mechanistic views of human psychology ever set forth. The apparent commercial success of his advertising techniques suggests that Watson's simplified concept of the way people think and behave had at least some truth to it.

Television, despite the seeming advantage of an added dimension (the visual), is not much different from radio in its advertising methods. For easy-to-recall brand names, TV adds easy-to-recognize packages and emblems. To the music of radio it adds sensuous sights and symbols, tying products to them by sheer audiovisual contiguity. Thus the "Pepsi Generation," whoever that may be, has been invited to join something called the "Dodge Rebellion." All of this makes no sense, of course, but it isn't intended to; its purpose is to sell goods.

What goods are sold by advertising? In a sense almost all are, since unadvertised goods have little chance of being noticed and bought except in highly specialized markets. But if we look at the bulk of expensive national advertising, certain products dominate the picture. Soaps and dentrifices, beers and cigarettes typify one dominant group; these are products that are relatively low-cost and have high consumption, and for which it makes little difference—to either the economy or the consumer—which particular brand a person buys. The other dominant kind of advertiser is the public institution, for which a heavy advertising component is built into a guaranteed budget. This advertising practice, which requires acquiescence by public bodies (from the Defense Department to state public utilities commissions) provides us ubiquitous "institutional" ads for insurance companies, airlines, telephone companies, technological hardware manufacturers, and various branches of the military. This is perhaps the most direct public subsidy to the media. Public bodies establish rate structures for travel and utilities firms, they "farm out" enormous technical projects to a few contractors, they try to recruit volunteers—and in each case a healthy advertising budget is included in the planning. This money is eventually transferred to the media, for large (and typically decorative) ads. Unlike the highly competitive consumer ads, the institutional advertisements need not "sell" much of anything. Indeed, very few in the audience can exercise any choice for most of these products: public utilities are guaranteed monopolies, airlines are mostly patronized according to the timing and convenience of their flight schedules, and prime defense contractors are rarely patronized directly by anyone except other defense contractors. Instead, as a Galbraith might put it, these institutional ads serve the implicit function of convincing people that institutions of this general type are necessary: monopolistic utilities, oligopolistic travel services, military branches and contractors, etc. The media, needing the money, usually do not question these ads. Most citizens, needing the media in many ways, do not either. People seem to find institutional ads reasonably pleasant. Criticism focuses instead on the blatantly crass ads for low-cost, mass-distribution products.

Advertising serves another important function for the consumer. This is sometimes referred to as "added value." The mere fact that one brand is nationally advertised while another is unknown implies to a purchaser that the latter is more of a gamble than the former. This can be especially important when the product is very complex, or when it is the kind of thing that can vary greatly in quality. The notion of a "name brand" carries a kind of unwritten guarantee of (at least) minimal quality; if the firm has put a lot of money into advertising its name, it is perhaps less likely to endanger that name by marketing a low-quality product.

Or so it seems. Many consumers rely on the name-brand principle, which is one major reason why advertising works. But highly informed consumers can cite plenty of exceptions to this principle. For example, wines vary enormously in quality, and only a few brands advertise heavily. But it turns out that the advertised ones are mostly cheap, low-quality table wines, which rely on heavy sales volume for their profits. The best wines are in rather short supply, so there is sufficient demand from gourmets to assure a good market for them without advertising. The same principle holds true for many products that require a degree of connoisseurship to discern high quality: pipe tobacco, electronic equipment, colleges—the best are seldom advertised.

THE MEDIA MIX

The marketing industry looks on advertising as one of its principal methods of selling goods. And as with any other method of salesmanship, there is a constant effort to improve techniques and to get better access to potential customers. One of the key elements in this is the constant attempt to determine what is the best "media mix" for a given product. That is, what proportion of the advertising dollar should be invested in, say, television, instead of other media such as newspapers, magazines, or radio? As is so often the case in selling, there are no sure-fire rules. But some principles have been fairly well established.

The first principle has to do with the composition of a medium's audience. Television generally has the largest number of eyes and ears at its command. It is particularly the favored medium of children, old or isolated people, women at home, the less educated, and the poor. But it also attracts many millions of middle-aged, middle-income consumers. This makes television the ideal medium for selling products that are likely to be bought by just about anyone. It is hard to think of a better example than toothpaste, and no product has a more honored place in the history of broadcast advertising. Television is also a good way of reaching its specialized audiences, of course; it is particularly useful as a method of selling low-quality mass-produced toys to children, a practice that has understandably aroused the anger of parents and the opposition of consumer groups.

Radio once held the position occupied by television today. The use of afternoon serials designed to appeal to women doing their housework was such a hallmark of radio in the 1930s and 1940s that these programs have been known ever since for their prime product—"soap operas." Today radio's audience is much more limited and specialized: adolescents and young adults, with their strong taste for currently popular music, and people in cars, many of whom might be characterized as "between television sets" for the duration of their drive. During commuting rush hours in urban areas, many stations run "freeway hour" programs, with programing designed to attract listeners who might feel the need for certain products, including automobile engine additives, car stereo cassette systems, public transportation, or a good stiff drink. For the most part, radio is looked on as a minor but low-cost medium whose audience is growing and shifting, and therefore not an advertising channel that a sales campaign can afford to ignore. This is particularly obvious in political campaigns; few candidates dare to pass up radio advertising, since for relatively few dollars they can get their names and voices into the ears of . . . well, they are not quite sure who is reached, or how often, or with what effect. But why take the chance of missing someone?

The print media—newspapers and magazines—reach much more definable audiences. Most of them can provide a potential advertiser with rather detailed "demographic profiles" of their subscribers, who tend to be fairly well-educated and well-heeled. The problem is that subscribers are not necessarily all readers, and there is so much content in a typical newspaper or magazine that practically no one reads an entire edition. In particular, it is feared in the marketing industry that many readers will skip over advertisements altogether unless they offer some serious consumer information in an ad. This contrasts, of course, with broadcast media, which make it terribly difficult for a listener to avoid commercial messages. Fortunately, it is possible to cram a lot of information (or pseudo-information, such as grandiose and wordy general claims) into a large display advertisement in print. Supermarkets and department stores find the newspaper the ideal channel for attracting customers with special bargain prices; these are often "loss leaders," a few items offered at cut rates as a means of getting customers into the stores where they might then notice and buy other products at regular prices. The newspaper is also the prime medium for selling individual items, such as a used car or a house, by means of classified ads. The classified section of the daily newspaper has also become a major channel for both employers and job seekers, whose devotion to the "help wanted" section has become a twentieth-century tradition.

National advertising for major consumer products (e.g. new automobiles) has gravitated heavily toward magazines and away from newspapers. The general-circulation magazine seems to be a dying institution, but the surviving forms (such as the weekly newsmagazine) provide an optimal outlet for splashy, artistic, and fairly informative ads for many of the same products that are also advertised on television. As we mentioned earlier, television has taken over most of the job of selling low-cost products. But the secondary role of the magazine for such advertising is demonstrated by the fact that cheap consumer products that are no longer allowed to advertise on the air (for example, cigarettes and liquor) are still well represented in the pages of magazines.

Magazines have for some years tended toward more and more specialized topics and audiences. Consequently the specialized magazine offers the best method of delivering an advertisement for a particular product to a small number of persons of known interests. For example, it makes excellent sense to advertise automotive products in magazines devoted to auto racing, or women's personal wear and toiletries in magazines designed to attract female subscribers. This principle of audience selection goes a long way toward explaining why specialized magazines have replaced the once dominant general-interest magazine, typified by the late *Collier's, Look,* and *Life.* A small but coherent audience is a more valuable target for many advertisers than is the large but heterogeneous subscription list of the general magazine. The latter is in direct competition with television, which can deliver more eyes per dollar, and hence is a better buy from the sales viewpoint.

ADVERTISING AND THE CONSUMER

The consumer's viewpoint is quite different, of course, and it rarely gets much consideration by either the marketing industry or the media. They are locked in a tight economic game in which consumers are basically a common target; they are only secondarily (at most) considered to be people with their own economic needs and constraints. It would be foolish to suppose that industries designed to manipulate the transfer of consumer money to the producers of goods and services might also take care of the consumer's best interests, any more than we could expect consumers to keep the welfare of corporate advertisers at heart.

The media are caught in the middle, in a way. The advertisers need them, and the public wants them. But the various media are subject to control from both sides, since they are in competition with one another. Each newspaper, and each television station, is striving on the one hand to attract and hold an audience and on the other hand to sell that audience to advertisers. Generally speaking, media are more sensitive to the desires of a particular advertiser (of which they have relatively few) than to those of a particular listener or reader (of which they have thousands). One or two outraged advertisers can be a calamity, whereas three or four outraged subscribers can be laughed off. Only organized and concerted pressure by large numbers of consumers has much direct impact on a media unit.

Operating through governmental machinery, consumers have won some victories over misleading advertising. There are a number of "rules of the game" that limit the degree of deception that is permissible in advertisements. This works to the benefit of the more honest advertisers too, since they are protected from the threat of losing out to underhanded competitors. Within the limits prescribed by law and regulatory bodies, however, there is still some room for deceptive "puffery" and misleading advertising claims. This may be looked on as "legalized lying" from the consumer's perspective.

Since it is unlikely that even the most devoted consumer-oriented governmental administration could close all the loopholes that exist in the regulation of advertising, the old principle of *caveat emptor* ("let the buyer beware") will always hold to some extent in the American marketplace. Consequently the necessary "consumer skills" for modern society include the ability to see through advertising claims. Indeed, the solution to the problem of misleading advertising that is suggested most often by responsible marketing leaders is consumer education, rather than additional government regulation.

While we would not suggest that the Federal Trade Commission and governmental consumer affairs offices have by any means exhausted all possible and desirable areas of advertising regulation, it is worthwhile to consider consumer education as a separate, and equally desirable, alternative.

American schools have for many years taught certain kinds of consumer skills. Most notably, the use of "story problems" to teach arithmetic has focused children's attention on marketplace decisions. The institution of unit pricing in grocery stores in the 1960s was based on the premise that purchasers faced with two jars of, say, coffee would benefit from knowing whether the "large economy size" would in fact save them money. But unit pricing does not seem to have altered consumers' purchasing patterns much, and it is clear that more than simple arithmetic is involved.

Many consumers are simply incapable of judging quality among very similar brands of the same product. So they rely on other criteria to make their choices. One such surrogate is, paradoxically, price. For the most part, it is widely assumed that the more expensive brand is superior in quality; and if there is much danger from buying a low-quality brand (as in the case of medicine, for instance), the more costly brand stands an excellent chance of being purchased even if it is no better in quality than the less costly competing brands.

A second surrogate for quality is, as we have noted, advertising. There is a sense of safety in buying a "name brand" in preference to a cheaper brand of equal quality that bears an unknown label. This might seem like "irrational" behavior on the part of the consumer, but only if one makes the assumption that it would be possible (or at least practicable) for a customer to judge quality between brands. It would require a great deal of consumer education to instruct Americans in the fine points of judgment for each of the thousands of products that they buy every year. Needless to say, the schools have never attempted such a broad program of consumer education. Governmental agencies and the Consumers Union do make studies of certain products; their reports, in Government Printing Office brochures and the monthly *Consumer Reports,* go practically unread by the overwhelming majority of consumers. Apparently the information does not seem worth the effort to most people.

And yet most of us do seem to possess a certain healthy skepticism about advertising and other claims by salespeople. This skill is necessary to keep reputable producers and marketers in business. Where does it come from? To some extent, of course, it can be attributed to a cultural heritage from the open marketplace, the shrewdness of the Yankee traders, and the traditional bargaining between the canny farmer and the city slicker—to mention a few of our hallowed economic stereotypes. But in a time when most selling is done through the mass media, we should not be surprised that the critical consumer skill of skepticism is also a by-product of advertising itself. Professor Scott Ward of Harvard University's Marketing Science Institute has found that most grade-school children today are skilled consumers in many ways. They have disposable income (allowances), and they husband that resource rather carefully. In particular, they have learned—from intense exposure to advertising claims for toys and treats since they saw their first television programs as infants—to be wary of overblown descriptions of products. In effect, the penetration of advertising by means of modern media to the very young has produced some of the most market-wise children in human history. It is not at all difficult for a parent to explain the concept of a "gyp" to a youngster who begged for two months for a talking doll that turned out to be undersized, without batteries, and almost immediately breakable.

It would be too much to say that advertising itself creates the seeds of its own resistance. But early exposure of children to misleading ads is at least a cloud with a silver lining. If parents follow through and expose the falsities in an advertisement for a children's product, they can implant "antibodies" against advertising that will "immunize" people against its excesses at an earlier age than has been possible in the past.

This is a form of consumer education that can benefit both the individual budding consumer (who in a few years will be spending dollars instead of pennies) and the honest and reputable advertiser, who will be able to compete in a game where the consumers enforce many of the rules.

Sensitivity to advertisements is not limited to children, of course. All kinds of people are constantly exposed to advertisements, and it would be surprising if they did not learn from the experience. Professor Lawrence Bowen of the University of Washington has found interesting differences between the poor and middle-income groups, based on the media they use most often. In a controlled experiment, he selected from television and magazines examples of (1) highly informative advertisements and (2) other ads whose appeals were hardly sensible—such as an automobile ad featuring a beautiful woman in the seat, or a cigarette package in a bucolic woods-and-water setting. The middle-income group expressed a strong preference for the more informative advertisements, particularly those from magazines. The low-income persons in the study (who were of the same educational level as the middle-income group) exhibited a preference for the informative *television* ads. That is, each group made the distinction between informative and arbitrary ads primarily in the medium with which it had the most experience—print for the middle-income people and television for the poor.

The media, so long as they remain heavily dependent on advertising for their economic health, must continue to produce material that will attract salable audiences. Advertisers can hardly be expected to abandon their fundamental interest in selling products, institutions, and candidates. If anything in this equation is to change, it must be the audience. As consumers become wiser in their handling of advertising claims, their patterns of purchasing will shift, and the performance of the media will shift accordingly. The alternative method of providing new kinds of media fare is direct public subsidy of the media. Whether the indirect subsidy by way of advertising is preferable is a major decision facing the American public.

To date, the method of direct subsidy has been resisted by those who fear governmental control over media content, as well as by advertisers who of course fear loss of income. Direct subsidy has the advantage of accountability. It is possible to determine, more or less, where public money comes from and where it goes. The same cannot be said of funds in the "private sector," especially in such a complicated system as advertising, which eventually pays for the media by adding to the cost of advertised products. Since advertising affects the total economy in many substantial ways, it is difficult to assess what things would be like without it. Given the general health of the industry, and its long-standing entrenchment in American life as well as the media, we shall probably not have occasion to find out.

REFERENCES

Lawrence Bowen, "Advertising and the Poor: A Comparative Study of Patterns of Response to Television and Magazine Advertising between Middle and Low-Income Groups," Ph.D. dissertation (University of Wisconsin, 1973).

John Kenneth Galbraith, *The New Industrial State* (Boston: Houghton Mifflin, 1967).

L. Scott Ward, "Effects of Television Advertising on Children and Adolescents," and seven technical reports, all in E. A. Rubinstein, G. A. Comstock, and J. P. Murray (eds.), *Television and Social Behavior, Volume IV, Television in Day-to-Day Life: Patterns of Use,* U. S. Government Printing Office, 1972, pp. 432–567.

SUGGESTED STUDY PROJECTS

1 Compare the advertisements in a men's magazine with those in a women's magazine. What similarities, and what differences, do you find in *(a)* the products that are advertised and *(b)* the appeals that the ads use to try to sell these products?
2 Interview at least thirty people who are waiting in the checkout line at a store. Find out whether they considered any other store before coming to this one; whether they consulted the store's advertisements in advance; whether they bought any brands that they had not bought before; why they decided to buy the brands they had bought, rather than competing brands. What kinds of products do you conclude are most susceptible to "impulse buying" or "brand loyalty," and what ones seem to lead consumers to more careful information processing?

Chapter 12

Election Persuasion: Candidates and Issues

When professional political persuaders use communication skills to elect a particular candidate, they become players in an intricate "game" in which the stakes can be high, the likelihood of success unpredictable, and the rules murky.

The general problem facing such a persuader may seem simple enough to state: How can I convince citizens to behave in ways that will benefit the candidate I represent? As in most problem situations, however, finding an effective solution is harder than merely stating the problem. Political campaign communication—particularly through the mass media—is a powerful though controversial tool used by persuaders who must deal with the web of factors associated with a modern political campaign. Mass communication also can be vital for the citizen-voter who is asked to cope with the same web.

The web includes the activities of candidates, political parties, interest groups, increasingly independent and skeptical voters, and journalists. It includes the perceptions that each of those groups has of other groups. And it includes the stance each group takes toward campaign problems and events. Mass communication can be used to reveal those activities, perceptions, and stances, to help sort them out, and thus to make the campaign "game" a little easier to comprehend and win.

The benefits of using the mass media in political campaigns are not universally acknowledged, however. Over the years, critics have claimed that political persuaders use the mass media to degrade and even undermine the democratic electoral process. Others emphasize the unparalleled capacity of the mass media to provide communication with huge numbers of voters, thereby taking political power away from party "bosses" and spreading it throughout the citizenry. Still others acknowledge the tremendous benefits of mass political communication but stress a need for more specific rules to govern how the persuaders use the mass media.

The mass political persuader, of course, tries to use the media to the maximum benefit of his or her candidate. Trying to convince citizens to vote for the candidate is an obvious enough objective. Persuading persons to donate money, to help collect donations from others, or to help in canvassing are also important objectives of the political persuasion game.

The notion of benefits is a common denominator for those using the media in a campaign, and for obvious reasons. Given a choice, normal people inevitably prefer something they consider beneficial to something they perceive as costly. In the realm of political campaigns, persuaders and voters face several kinds of benefits and costs. An "effective" communication strategy usually means one which increases the benefits at the expense of the costs. That includes (1) seizing upon and reinforcing things considered beneficial to the candidate and (2) dealing with the aspects considered costly, either by downplaying them or by transforming them into benefits.

What kinds of beneficial and costly aspects must political persuaders face? Since a candidate can be elected only if enough people ultimately vote the "correct" way at the polls, the perceptions, orientations, and actions of voters might be considered most important; accordingly, we will consider those aspects first in our exploration of mass political persuasion.

VOTERS' PERCEPTIONS, ORIENTATIONS, AND ACTIONS

Professional persuaders need to "size up" voters' reaction to a candidacy before they can formulate and carry out effective campaign strategy. "Voters' reaction" includes:

1 How voters comprehend, or *perceive,* the candidacy
2 How voters *orient themselves to* the election
3 How voters are likely to *act* upon the candidacy—by voting, donating money, canvassing, or doing nothing

The political poll or survey plays an important part early in a campaign simply because it allows campaigners to get some preliminary information about some of the likely benefits and costs of a candidacy.

Voters' Perceptions

Suppose that surveys showed that a sizable proportion of registered Democrats did not accurately comprehend—in other words, misperceived—the stated policies of that party's presidential nominee on economics and foreign policy. Such a situation could be a benefit for the Republican candidate, whose professional campaigners would want to capitalize on it—perhaps by constructing campaign messages which further cloud the Democratic candidate's stated policies. On the other hand, the voter's misperceptions could be a serious cost for the Democrats; their campaigners would try to eliminate, or at least minimize, that cost—perhaps by switching their campaign messages to other issues, or perhaps by bombarding Democrats with communications designed to "set the record straight."

Communication is an enemy of inaccurate perception, in politics as well as any other arena. As we stated in Chapter 4, if people communicate enough about something, they should eventually be able to accurately comprehend each other. In the example above, if the Republicans remained silent and the Democrats communicated a lot with their party members, the costly misperception should diminish and at some point disappear. Political campaigns usually do not allow such a pure communication process, however. Nor do they often provide the time span necessary to clear up all misperceptions of voters. For the opposition to stay quiet would probably be as strategically unsound as it would be unlikely. So, even over an eight-month period, the chances of substantially clearing up a sizable misperception would be slight.

By trying to prevent voters' misperceptions from the beginning, a professional persuader could conceivably stop his candidate's cost from becoming the opposition's benefit. Clear, candid, consistent articulation of the candidate's attributes can go a long way in that respect.

Voters' Orientations

Students of politics have found that voters tend to "size up" a candidacy in three ways. One is to evaluate the candidacy in terms of the party affiliation of the candidate. Another is to assess the personal qualifications and characteristics of the candidate. The third involves examining the candidate's stated policies on issues that the voters consider important. These three ways of evaluating candidates are commonly called *party orientation, candidate orientation,* and *issue orientation.*

Voters who react to candidates primarily on the basis of party orientation are the party loyalists—those whose dedication to a particular party is so strong that they will support their party's candidate regardless of his personal qualities or his stand on issues. Most studies of voting behavior conducted in the 1940s, 1950s, and 1960s showed that party orientation was, overall, the strongest single influencing factor. In general, of course, this strength of party orientation has been a benefit for the Democrats (who for decades have had a larger number of registered party members nationwide than the Republicans). Republican campaign strategists, naturally, have tried to overcome this cost to them in national elections. They have done so by trying to develop stronger candidate and issue orientations among voters. The Republican Presidents Eisenhower and Nixon were elected only because the Republican campaigners cracked traditional party orientations of enough Democrats and Democrat-leaners. In traditionally Republican states and localities, on the other hand, party orientation is a benefit for the Republicans and a cost for the Democrats. In those situations, the Democrats can elect their candidates only by shifting the party orientation of enough Republicans over to candidate or issue orientations.

Much was written in the late 1960s and early 1970s about an emerging "independent" electorate which, in increasing numbers, appeared to be casting off the yoke of party orientation and evaluating candidacies instead on the basis of the candidate as a person, or on the basis of important issues. As more and more Republicans and Independents were elected in the Democrats' "solid South," and as Democrats gained victories in traditionally Republican states in the Midwest, analysts spoke of "the new politics" that seemed to be growing in America. This "new politics," when boiled down, meant that campaigners had found apparently successful communication strategies to tap the candidate and issue orientations of significantly larger numbers of voters.

Voters who respond to candidacies primarily on the basis of candidate orientation put a premium on such things as the candidate's demeanor, personal appearance, personality, age, and ethnic, religious, or family background. These and similar factors get blended together to form a general perception on the part of a voter that the candidate is, or is not, a person who can be trusted to do a competent job in the office being sought. It frequently gets expressed as that intangible "style" or "image" of the candidate. Many political observers, for example, claimed that the political successes of John, Robert, and Edward Kennedy came largely from favorable reaction by voters to such personal qualities.

Professional campaigners inevitably will claim that their greatest benefit is a "good candidate," one whom large numbers of voters consider trustworthy and competent as a person. The campaign problem, of course, is to get enough voters to react according to that orientation. "I vote for the man" is not a new claim among American voters. Yet many persons who made such claims actually were loyalists who usually voted "for the man" because of his party affiliation. A sizable chunk of "the new politics" involves communication strategies to capitalize on the benefit of a "good candidate" and to overcome the costs of a "weak" one.

Issue orientation has been an ideal in American politics. We like to think that voters set aside party affiliations and candidates' "style" and instead conscientiously study how well each candidate can deal with the great issues of the day. We might therefore bemoan the fact that only a relatively small proportion of citizens react that way in most elections. That is not to say that voters are completely unaware or unconcerned about candidates' positions on issues. Trying to deal with issues just requires more effort and sophistication than reacting to party labels or to personal characteristics of candidates. So a candidate's stance toward an issue is subject to more misperception by voters and often to superficial oversimplification by the political persuaders. Senator George McGovern's stand on welfare issues in 1972 proved to be a great cost to his candidacy, while President Nixon's position on law and order and peace turned out to be a benefit in his campaign. The campaign "platform" strives to identify important issues and spell out how candidates will, if elected, deal with them. But the "platform" seldom gets serious attention from voters, perhaps because they sense that the candidates themselves don't really take it that seriously. A candidate who takes a simplified, popular position on a salient issue can sometimes benefit to the extent of picking up enough additional votes to win a tight race. Likewise, a candidate who takes a complicated, unconventional approach to sensitive issues may add an additional cost to his candidacy. Communication strategies, then, tend to cast their candidate's positions as simple and popular and to tag the opponent's positions as incomprehensible and dangerous.

In the end, just about any candidacy is a compromise. Rarely will a candidate be fortunate enough to find voters' party orientations *and* candidate orientations *and* issue orientations all to his benefit. In most campaigns, a candidate will find at least one of those orientations to be a cost. Even though President Nixon won a landslide victory in 1972, the party orientation of Democratic voters started out as a major cost for his campaigners to overcome. The question becomes: How can campaign strategy be formulated to maintain and strengthen the benefits a candidacy possesses and to prevent the candidacy's costs from leading to a defeat on Election Day? The persuader's answer, in general terms, is to get enough voters to *agree* that the benefits of one candidacy far exceed the costs and that the costs of the opposition candidacy far exceed the benefits. Influencing voters' orientations, then, usually means achieving *agreement* (among sufficient numbers of citizens) that party loyalty is beneficial (or costly), that a candidate is a person who is competent (or incompetent), and that a candidate will handle pressing issues in a beneficial (or costly) way. All this contrasts with the problem of clearing up voters' misconceptions, where, as we suggested, the task is to present *accurate* pictures about the candidacy.

Voters' Actions

Influencing voters' orientations toward a candidacy is not enough. Favorable orientations are meaningless unless enough people *act* upon them. The real payoffs for an effective political campaign come from actual participation by citizens. Some persons favorably inclined toward a candidacy have to be transformed into fund raisers, canvassers, contributors, and—in the end—actual voters.

Inducing political action is no easy task in view of apparently increasing cynicism and apathy. America is notorious for its low rate of citizen participation in politics. A great challenge for campaigners is to transform apathy into interest and interest into action. Too many citizens consider political activity insufficiently rewarding, or even too costly. The most common form of electoral participation, casting a ballot, can hardly be considered costly in terms of the time or money it takes. Not enough people consider it very rewarding, though, and their reasons for this have to do with their feelings about parties, candidates, and issues. To influence citizens to act, professional persuaders try to emphasize the rewards that might come from acting in a certain way, as well as the costs that might result from *not* acting in that way. Bumper stickers proclaiming "Don't blame me; I voted for⎯⎯⎯⎯" provide an after-the-fact assessment of the cost of acting, or failing to act. The professional persuader, however, tries to induce action *during* the campaign and on Election Day.

The patronage system dangled direct, tangible rewards (in the form of jobs) before citizens as incentives to organize, canvass, donate money, and vote on behalf of a candidacy. The costs of not participating also were clear: If the candidate lost, patronage workers would be out of their jobs. Soliciting contributions of money and time in return for future favors is another obvious use of a cost-benefit strategy to induce political action. Though illegal, it apparently still contaminates American politics, as post-1972 investigations of campaign irregularities demonstrated.

Patronage and bribery, however, provide tangible rewards to only a minute fraction of potential political participants. With the growing use of mass communication by campaigners, the alleged benefits and costs are communicated to the huge majority of citizens through impersonal printed and electronic messages. Inducing voters to act has become largely a matter of cost versus benefit themes and slogans. With many specific variations, the messages usually run like this: "This candidate can do so many good things for you that you simply can't afford not to work and vote for him." Or: "That candidate will be so harmful to your interests that you simply will have to help keep him from getting elected." During the 1964 presidential race between incumbent President Lyndon Johnson and Senator Barry Goldwater, a television ad for Johnson showed a child licking an ice cream cone as a woman's voice in the background told of the dangers or radioactive fallout from nuclear testing. Then another voice said:

> They used to explode atomic weapons, but people from all over the world got together and signed a test ban treaty. There's a man who wants to be President who doesn't like this treaty. He wants to go on testing more bombs. If he's elected they might start testing all over again. Vote for President Johnson on November 3. The stakes are too high to stay at home.

Other action-inducing strategies commonly supplement media messages. Organizing "free rides to the polls" on Election Day can reduce the costs of voting for many citizens. The "check-off" system of connecting campaign donations to income tax returns was designed to make contributing seem rewarding and effortless.

Such tactics are similar to those used to get people to buy certain commercial products. The familiar, staged scenarios push products because they cost less or—more likely—because they allegedly confer rewards of social prestige, psychological peace of mind, and sexual gratification. These themes are found in political advertising, too. Candidacies being "sold" with much the same strategies as deodorants may seem peculiar and perhaps alarming. Joe McGinniss, who drew much public attention to the situation with his book *The Selling of the President 1968,* complained that citizens do not really *vote* for a candidate, but rather make a "psychological purchase" of him.

WHY USE THE MASS MEDIA?

The power of mass communication in shaping the political values and behaviors of citizens has been a much debated subject for decades, and it continues to be so. Into the 1940s, scholars more or less assumed that political mass communication was a major determinant of voting behavior. Central to that assumption was the "hypodermic" thesis that citizens often were helpless to resist persuasive messages found in the mass media. Newspaper endorsement of candidates was considered a crucial variable in determining election outcomes, and warnings about the disastrous effects of a "one-party press" were voiced by those who worried because the majority of newspapers consistently endorsed Republican candidates.

Later studies of voting behavior, notably the pioneer work of Bernard Berelson and Paul Lazarsfeld in the late 1940s and early 1950s, seemed to show otherwise, however. Citizens, according to the results of those studies, were not easily bamboozled or persuaded by mass political communication. Instead, the mass media were found to have little direct effect on voting behavior since citizens tended to get their political values from their families and other respected acquaintances, using the mass media primarily to reinforce their already acquired political leanings. More recently, however, the "selective exposure" notion of Berelson and his colleagues has been challenged as too simplistic. Studies of voters in the late 1960s and early 1970s indicate that, in some kinds of situations, voters do indeed use the mass media for political purposes other than reinforcement of previously held views. In short, mass communication can sometimes be an important and effective tool for political persuasion. A study of the 1968 presidential election by John Robinson strongly suggested that newspaper articles and editorials favoring then-President Richard Nixon may have been crucial in his close victory over Senator Hubert Humphrey. Other studies show that sometimes voters actually prefer messages that contradict their own previous position. Moreover, with the apparent decline of party orientation and the increase of "independent" voters and ticket splitters, there is reason to suspect that growing numbers of citizens no longer hold doggedly to previously established political orientations. In effect, more and more voters may be approaching campaigns with a sense of open-mindedness, or, if you will, a willingness to at least orient themselves more toward issues. All of this suggests that both professional campaigners and voters will continue to benefit from using the media as tools during elections.

Benefits for Professional Persuaders

Because the mass media are so pervasive in America, they provide channels for reaching nearly all prospective voters repeatedly and in a relatively short period of time. That fact alone explains why campaign strategists turned to the growing mass media system as a partial substitute for the more exhausting and less efficient schedule of personal appearances by candidates. Although personal appearances have not disappeared from the campaign scene, one of their primary functions is to provoke media news coverage which can then be relayed throughout the state or country. The great spread of mass communication, then, is an obvious but important benefit to those who orchestrate campaigns.

At least as important is the diversity of our mass media system. The huge variety of mass media enables campaigners to "target" specific messages to specific segments of voters. Joe McGinniss described how Nixon strategists in 1968 created special commercials for various ethnic and regional groups, then placed them in media aimed primarily at those groups. A Nixon campaign aide is quoted by McGinniss as saying:

> I started too late to do it properly this year, but by seventy-two I should have it broken down county by county across the whole country so we'll be able to zero in on a much more refined target.[1]

Diversity and specialization of media have other adaptations, too. Strategists apparently prefer to use certain kinds of print media for their "dirty politics" messages. Sam Archibald, the executive director of the Fair Campaign Practices Committee, reported in 1971 that unethical ads appeared most often in flyers, brochures, posters, and newspaper advertisements, in that order. The computer-written letter, a form of mass media disguised as personalized communication, has become the major channel for soliciting campaign contributions. The list of variations on the specialized media theme could go on and on. New media technology provides growing opportunities for political strategists to make mass communication adaptable to just about any special requirement, as we will see later.

Benefits for Citizens

American voters can, if they so choose, use the mass media to help them cope intelligently with an election campaign. Obtaining such benefits from the mass media, though, requires that citizens be judicious.

One potential benefit is that citizens use the media to help determine the important campaign issues. The media play an important role in that respect, one that is called "agenda setting." By reporting and emphasizing certain events and problems, journalists lay out a range of potential issues for both voters and politicians. The extent and quality of responses by politicians to these issues can depend largely on the earlier responses, or nonresponses, by citizens. Political polls, for example, regularly gauge voters' familarity with potential campaign issues. Rarely can the news media create a campaign issue unless sizable numbers of citizens consent. Once an issue is cast, citizens can use the media to familiarize themselves with it more thoroughly and to learn and evaluate the positions that candidates take toward it.

How seriously do contemporary voters study and react to issues? The election analyst Richard Scammon answers that question as follows.

Most Americans, he says, are middle-of-the-roaders politically and do not react strongly to most issues. Certain issues, however, jolt citizens out of their habitual voting patterns; Scammon calls these the "cutting issues," and he says they are not too common. Catholicism was such an issue in

[1]Joe McGinniss, *The Selling of the President 1968,* Pocket Books, New York, 1968, p. 125.

1960 because it caused large numbers of voters to move across traditional party lines. (Watergate undoubtedly was a "cutting issue" in several 1974 congressional elections, where districts with a long Republican history elected Democrats.) But, says Scammon, things like the Vietnam war and ecology did not jolt traditional voting habits sufficiently to be considered "cutting issues." Other researchers, including the political scientist Walter DeVries, see evidence of increased issue orientation among the electorate, particularly in state and local elections. DeVries cites the growing number of voters who defy party lines and "split" their ballot, voting for some Democrats and some Republicans. Issue-oriented voters may still be in a minority, but their ranks do show some signs of growing. The democratic ideal of voters intelligently judging candidates in terms of public issues implies rational and deliberate information seeking by those voters. For those who seek it, the mass media provide an inexpensive and nearly exhaustive supply of information.

Voters can also use the media to get a "feel" for the candidates. While many candidate appearances on the media are camouflaged by professional packaging techniques, others are not. Citizens can benefit from studying the more "uncontrolled" appearances by candidates on newscasts, news interview programs, and debates. By such deliberate attention, voters can make candidate orientation more than an emotional response to a superficial "image." Even the carefully packaged political advertisements can be useful to citizens. The commericals invite comparison with noncommercial messages about the candidate. Often, political ads contain information not readily available elsewhere. More often they do not. Campaign ads in the media can be used as morale boosters by loyal partisans, too. A study of a 1970 election by Sheinkopf, Atkin, and Bowen, for example, found that volunteer party workers in Wisconsin used their candidates' ads to bolster their confidence and to get information that they could later use in their campaign work.

Costs for Professional Persuaders

Using the mass media for political campaigning has certain drawbacks or costs. Professional persuaders weigh these costs against the benefits in determining the extent and nature of mass media campaigns. Naturally, they also attempt to minimize the costs wherever possible.

Take the financial costs of running an election campaign. Total spending in all 1972 elections by all candidates was about $400 million, a new record. About $100 million of that went to finance the presidential campaigns, and a considerable chunk of that went into mass media advertising. McGovern campaigners, for example, spent more than $100,000 to buy a half-hour of prime-time television over about 200 stations, and more than

$8.5 million altogether for radio and television ads. Those who would take greatest advantage of the pervasiveness and diversity of mass communication must be prepared to pay a pretty price for the benefits. Do candidates with huge campaign treasuries therefore automatically dominate media political advertising? "Of course," some say, although the 1971 Federal Election Campaign Act placed ceilings on the amount that a candidate can spend for ads. (The ceiling, incidentally, is calculated in each case by multiplying the number of eligible voters for an election by 10 cents. The law also stipulates that only 60 percent of that figure can be used for broadcast advertising.) Still, the soaring costs of buying media time—combined with post-1972 revelations about how campaign money is sometimes illegally acquired and disbursed—should cause continued concern.

Broadcast advertising can result in a special type of cost to professional campaigners. The "equal opportunity" doctrine enforced by the Federal Communications Commission requires that all bona fide candidates for public office be allowed comparable access to the airwaves. If a campaign strategist manages to get free air time for his candidate, he is in effect writing an invitation to free time for the opposition. The doctrine also applies to paid advertising time, so that a station which sells ad time to one candidate cannot turn down paid ads from his opponents.

Such costs can be minimized or even evaded. Campaign expenditure ceilings can be manipulated. If a presidential candidate spends his legal advertising limit, commercials on behalf of his running mate might be substituted. Financial figures can be juggled—or even hidden—in other ways. Moreover, candidates with less than adequate campaign funds might consider expenditure ceilings as a benefit rather than a cost, particularly if the opposition is well-to-do. In the case of the equal-opportunities rules, wealthy candidacies can get along quite well by relying on paid air time. That way, a less rich opponent can't claim free air time and can't afford to buy the amount of time which the doctrines would otherwise allow. Incumbents nearly always have an added advantage when it comes to using the media. A President running for reelection, gets more "free" exposure over the news media by merely conducting the business of the Presidency. Incumbents can make "official, nonpolitical" speeches during the campaign, sometimes even avoiding the requirements of the equal-opportunities doctrines by doing so. All in all, the benefits of using mass media for politicking continue to outweigh the costs, and so the media will continue to be the major channels for communicating with most voters.

Costs for Citizens

Energetic, conscientious voters do not find it costly to make use of mass communication during elections. Even with the inflation of the early 1970s, the mass media provided real financial bargains. Some citizens, however, do risk selling out the integrity of the electoral process—a disastrous cost—by their casual, undiscerning use of media.

SOME CAMPAIGN STRATEGIES IN THE MEDIA

In order to effectively evaluate political persuasion, citizens need to understand strategies the persuaders employ, particularly those involving the mass media. What follows is an analytical description of frequently used communication tactics.

Personalization

Voters like to feel that candidates have a personal interest in them, and the persuaders know it. Until quite recently, most mass communication, however, had to be quite impersonal. In some ways that has changed—thanks largely to the computer, of all things. Those highly "impersonal" machines make it possible to store, sort, and retrieve more information about the voter as a person than ever before. Computers supply campaign strategists with information about individuals' political leanings, motivations, fears, and (of course) their addresses and phone numbers. That information can then be used to communicate with the voters in a way that at least resembles a personal message. The computer can spew out a letter, with an individual's own name scattered through it, tapping that person's feelings. Strategists can also use computerized data to establish which of the many specialized magazines and radio stations certain types of individuals are likely to use; appropriate "personal" messages are then placed in those media. Other personalized forms of campaign communication, which may or may not be aided by computers, include door-to-door solicitations, phone calls, pamphlets, and voter "call-in" programs on radio and television.

"Market Strategy"

With the 1964 elections, political persuaders started wide use of a tactic long used to advertise commercial products. The idea was to abandon the traditional view that voting constituencies were grouped by traditional political boundaries such as precincts and counties. Instead, voters were to be considered in terms of the "media markets" of the advertising business. Campaign messages since then have been formulated and distributed according to the types of mass media that certain types of voters pay attention to. (As we noted in Chapter 11, marketing people call this the "media mix.") Just as it would be a considerable waste of money to advertise footballs in the *Ladies' Home Journal,* it would be inefficient to place many political ads for an avowedly segregationist candidate on a "soul" radio station. Incidentally, pre-1972 data showed that a national candidate wanting to appeal to *undecided* voters would reach more of them by buying ads on the "Dick Cavett Show" than on "Tonight."

Another aspect of "market strategy" involves the use of "top markets." Commercial advertising had developed a system in which the nation was divided into "market areas." The "top markets" were those with the largest numbers of media users—that is, the large cities. Thus, ads placed in fifty media within the top ten markets of the country might reach as many persons as would ads placed in a hundred media in smaller market areas. So for national political candidates who want maximum exposure to as many voters as possible for their money, "market strategy" provides an efficient method.

Polling

Most major campaigns spend a lot of time and money probing the feelings and intentions of prospective voters. Scientific procedures of sampling and querying voters can be invaluable as an aid to planning other campaign strategies, provided the research is competent and not self-deceptive. Polls designed and interpreted merely to boost optimism or cover up real problems are inevitably more costly than beneficial to a campaign. On the other hand, accurate assessments of voter reaction to a candidate, his party, and the issues of the day are now a staple of modern electioneering.

Data from polls can be analyzed and reanalyzed to suit many specific campaign requirements. The data could tell you, for example, how many Catholic male voters between eighteen and twenty-one years of age live in a certain election district. You could find out how many middle-aged black housewives know a candidate's proposals to stem the cost of living. You could discover how elderly Jewish voters reacted to a particular campaign statement or advertisement.

So-called "depth polling" is the technique of trying to find out *why* voters have certain political inclinations. Traditional political polling tries to discover *what* those inclinations are. "Depth polls" are interested in such things as why people vote or don't vote in the first place, why they don't like a candidate, why they might deviate from the party line, and so forth.

Results of polling can be put to unethical uses. Suppose a survey shows that most elderly people don't understand the complexities of a controversial tax issue. An unscrupulous campaign strategist could easily exploit that information; ads could be placed in appropriate media oversimplifying the issue and distorting the opposition's stance toward it.

"Blitz" and "Spurt"

Massive saturation of many media with political messages can be effective in getting a candidate large-scale exposure at the beginning of a campaign and in influencing uncommitted voters in the closing days. This "blitz" technique was popularized by Nixon campaign strategists in the 1968 election. An early blitz can be especially useful for a relatively unknown candidate who wants voters to know he's running for election. When predicted election results are close during the end of the campaign, late blitz tactics, such as political telethons and heavy advertising buying, are often used.

A variation is the "spurt" technique, in which persuaders launch a heavy advertising campaign before the opponents have even started. The campaign might last only two weeks, but the idea is to get voters to think that the candidate is on the media all the time. Then the persuaders lie low—perhaps even eliminating all mass media advertising—for a period. Late in the campaign, ads might again be placed in the media, depending on what the polls show.

The "Spot"

The short broadcast ad of thirty seconds or less has some real benefits, as political persuaders see it. For one thing, they can buy more short ads than long ones for the same money, and that means they can use more stations and more time periods. What matters to the persuaders is not so much the *length* of an ad as the *number* of ads that are placed. Besides, many viewers might "tune out" long political ads, buy they hardly have time to avoid the "spot." And what's more, the short spot ads lend themselves very nicely to superficial and emotional appeals and themes. After all, how much rationality and information can you deliver in fifteen seconds? Not much at all.

That disturbs thoughtful observers who worry about the spot ad becoming the dominant form of radio and television political persuasion. The preponderance of the spot could therefore signal increased attempts to win elections without paying much serious attention to issues and candidates' competence. The "spot," incidentally, is a natural for a "blitz" campaign.

Ads as "News"

The elections of 1970 and 1972 saw political advertising presented in a "news" format. When Senator Edmund Muskie announced his 1972 presidential candidacy, his media strategists took films of his arrival in Concord, New Hampshire, where the speech was to be made, of a talk he had with state legislators there, of the announcement itself, and of a press conference. They put the whole thing together into a "documentary" and paid television stations to run it that very night. Why this approach? Some strategists say their research indicates many voters are more persuaded by a news format than by the gimmickry of political "spots." Some say it's a realistic reaction to another research finding: "Undecided" voters tend to consider newslike messages as the most important way to find out about candidates. Other "news" formats were used with considerable frequency in the early 1970s. Ads guised as "man in the street" interviews with voters seemed quite popular. So did film clips of public officials praising a candidate. In addition, candidates seemed to be making more appearances on unrehearsed "talk shows." It all boils down to a serious effort by some strategists to make campaigns seem "newsworthy."

That approach, at least, provides voters with a change of pace from a tedious barrage of "spots." The news ads tend to be longer and to focus on issues. One danger, however, is that numbers of citizens might fail to distinguish between real news coverage and the news ads, particularly when those ads are placed adjacent to regular newscasts.

Conventional Strategies

Conventional campaign wisdom has not altogether been forced out by the newer communication tactics discussed above. Some politicians still win elections by largely shunning media advertising and by resorting to old-fashioned "personal contact" strategies, such as walking throughout an entire state or driving a campaign bus. Those candidates, however, could not but benefit from the coverage that their unusual campaign styles generated in the news media.

In *The Political Persuaders*, Dan Nimmo recounts three general rules of thumb of campaign strategy that have been around a long time. Still frequently used, they don't really contradict "new politics" tactics very much. First, if the voters are pretty well divided along party lines, the campaign should appeal primarily to party loyalty. Second, if there is little or no party orientation involved (as, for example, in a race between two Democrats in a state primary), the campaign strategy should appeal to special blocs of voters. Finally, if the electorate is largely indifferent to a candidacy, strategists should focus on candidate orientation by stressing personalities and on issue orientation by making some issues seem sensational.

CAMPAIGN ETHICS AND CITIZENS' RESPONSIBILITY

Many people who plan political communication tactics believe that there is no strategy which will, in itself, elect a candidate. Political persuasibility of citizens does have some limits, both practically and ethically.

Fortunately, most professional political persuaders realize their tremendous responsibility to be ethical, and they act accordingly. In political campaigning, it is not wrong to find out what voters want and why they want it, nor to provide them with information and a reasonable "sales pitch." The best political advertisement is one that provides good information about a good candidate.

In our system, it is more vital that voters be informed than that they be influenced. While it may be entirely proper for political persuaders to try to convince us, we all share a responsibility for making informed political judgments. In the past, not enough citizens took that responsibility, probably because they considered the costs greater than the benefits. The costs of *not* seeking and evaluating political information were graphically demonstrated by the staggering disclosures and events which followed the 1972 elections and ultimately led to the resignation of President Richard Nixon. Watergate notwithstanding, the claim that "everybody" engages in "dirty politics" is false. It is the task of the citizenry to make sure the claim doesn't become true.

REFERENCES

Sam Archibald, *The Pollution of Politics* (Washington: Public Affairs Press, 1971).

Bernard Berelson, Paul Lazarsfeld, and William McPhee, *Voting: A Study of Opinion Formation in a Presidential Campaign* (Chicago: University of Chicago Press, 1954).

Walter DeVries, *The Ticket-Splitter: A New Force in American Politics* (Grand Rapids, Mich.: Eerdmans, 1971).

Paul Lazarsfeld, Bernard Berelson, and Hazel Gaudet, *The People's Choice: How the Voter Makes Up His Mind in a Presidential Campaign* (New York: Columbia University Press, 1948).

Joe McGinniss, *The Selling of the President 1968* (New York: Pocket Books, 1968).

Dan Nimmo, *The Political Persuaders* (Englewood Cliffs, N.J.: Prentice-Hall, 1970).

John P. Robinson, "Perceived Media Bias and the 1968 Vote: Can The Media Affect Behavior After All?" *Journalism Quarterly*, Summer 1972, pp. 239–246.

Richard Scammon and Ben Wattenberg, *The Real Majority* (New York: Coward-McCann, 1970).

Kenneth Sheinkopf, Charles Atkin, and Lawrence Bowen, "The Functions of Political Advertising for Campaign Organizations," *Journal of Marketing Research*, November, 1972, pp. 401–405.

The following works are useful general references:

American Institute for Political Communication, *A Study of Political Strategy and Tactics* (Washington: American Institute for Political Communication, 1967).

Ray Hiebert et al. (eds.), *The Political Image Merchants: Strategies in the New Politics* (Washington: Acropolis Books, 1971).

SUGGESTED STUDY PROJECTS

1 Compare the newspaper, radio, and television ads of a single candidate in an election campaign. What differences show up in terms of whether the candidate is appealing to voters' party orientation, issue orientation, or candidate orientation? To what extent do these differences seem to be determined by the type of mass medium used (and therefore by the type of audience the candidate is trying to reach)?

2 During a campaign, collect documented examples of how political persuaders used the following strategies in their advertising campaigns: personalization, market strategy, "news"-format ads.

Chapter 13

Elections without Candidates

It is often claimed that a charismatic candidate, especially in the personalized politics of the television era, can be elected regardless of the policies he or she espouses. Perhaps it is fortunate, then, that our laws are made by many levels and branches of government, so that personal charisma—let us assume that it is randomly distributed across the political spectrum—tends to cancel itself out overall. Even more comforting is the thought that laws can be enacted by, or with the explicit approval of, a vote of all citizens rather than by politicians—comforting, that is, if the citizens who engage in the periodic practice of enacting laws through the ballot make their choices on the basis of rationality and adequate information. As we shall see, the ways in which campaigners, journalists, and citizens use the media during such elections can sometimes be *dis*comforting.

Two general kinds of bills appear on the ballot for direct popular vote. The one which we might call "lawmaking" includes initiatives, referenda, and plebescites on substantive laws. The second kind, which can be called "tax levying," would include issuance of bonds for public works, enactment of a governmental budget, imposition of new taxes, and other questions of public finance. Financial issues are not different from other lawmaking by ballot in a strictly legal sense, but they are different in the ways in which the media and public treat them.

PLEBISCITE, INITIATIVE, AND REFERENDUM

Through the nineteenth century, the United States was ruled by a strong Congress and (with a few notable exceptions) weak Presidents. Professor Woodrow Wilson of Princeton University summed up that system in his major work *Congressional Government*. Later, as President during World War I, Wilson was to be among those responsible for the twentieth-century shift toward strong Presidents and a comparatively weak Congress. The nineteenth-century House of Representatives was popularly elected as now, and it produced many leaders, such as Daniel Webster and Henry Clay, who were more powerful than their Presidents. The United States Senate, however, consisted of men appointed by the governors of their respective states—more often for patronage than for political skill or wisdom.

In the late 1880s there arose on the prairies of the Middle West a radical movement called populism, which in 1888 nominated William Jennings Bryan for President on the People's party ticket. Bryan never became President, despite being nominated twice subsequently by the Democratic party; and the People's party died out within a couple of decades. But its platform of 1892 included many populist political reforms that did become law. Among these were the direct popular election of United States senators and three experimental electoral mechanisms called initiative, referendum, and recall.

Direct election and the provision that an elected official can later be "recalled" from office in a special election do not concern us directly in this chapter, since we want to focus here on elections that do not involve individuals. We will concentrate on the institutions of initiative and referendum, which were looked on as dangerously radical developments at the time of their adoption, and which have been used much more widely than recall. Both are forms of a much older procedure known as the plebiscite.

Ancient Rome, to which the modern United States owes much as a model of republican government, was controlled largely by its Senate—literally the "elders" (the root *sen-* being also the base for our words "senior" and "senile"). The common people of Rome were known as *plebeians*. When a strong popular leader, such as Julius Caesar, attempted to pass laws that were opposed by the Senate, he was likely to appeal directly to the public for its endorsement of his policies. Caesar went so far as to keep his public informed of his views of the Senate's activities, by posting the *Acta*

Diurna ("daily acts") in public places in Rome. Caesar's *Acta* constituted the forerunner of our modern newspaper (he even included sports and gossip columns), and the term *diurna* survives in our word "journalism." The central notion in this interconnection of proto-journalism and republican politics was that the plebeians, who provided the ultimate financial and military support for the regime, should be able to review and choose between public policies. The term for this type of review thus became "plebiscite," which eventually came to refer to a popular balloting on a public issue as the most accurate method of representing "public opinion."

Initiative and referendum provisions were enacted in 1910 in Wisconsin, a state where radical populism had transformed itself into the Progressive movement within the dominant Republican party. By 1912, the year Wilson was elected President, these plebiscite mechanisms were law in many states and at the federal level as well. Initiative permits citizens to place on the ballot, by petition, a proposed law. State constitutions vary, so that in some cases a majority vote is enough to enact a law, whereas in others ratification or specific action by the legislature or executive is also required. For financial bills, it is common to require a two-thirds vote. Referendum operates after a law has been passed by the legislature and signed by the executive; a citizen petition may place it on the ballot for popular review, and if enough people (normally a majority) vote against it, the law is abolished.

Clearly, from their historical roots, these two methods of direct popular action on laws presuppose that the electorate will be informed on the issues at stake, so that an enlightened public decision will be made. We need not tackle the question of whether the *Acta Diurna* of Rome, or even the American press of 1912—which was approximately the peak year in the total number of daily papers in the country—provided an adequate system for informing the public on local issues of the moment. More than half a century of experience with citizen lawmaking has passed, and several new features—radio, magazines, television—have been added to society's repertoire of news media. How does the system seem to be working today, and what of the future?

Where any public issue is concerned, there can be distinguished at least three kinds of people: those who support the proposed law, those who oppose it, and the rest. The third group will decide who wins the argument, by voting "yes" or "no" on the initiative or referendum. Usually at least one of the first two groups is well organized and wages an active campaign. Organization and campaigning often mean more to their relative success than do the actual sizes of their groups. The third group, the "undecided" or "apathetic" sector of the electorate, is usually quite large and is not really a group in any serious sense of the word. It exists as a body only on Election

Day, and then only because its members either consider it their duty to vote, even if they don't care much about the issues, or are attracted to other races on the ballot, and once in the voting booth they vote on all the questions.

There are some issues, to be sure, in which most voters have a strong interest, either as supporters or as opponents of the proposed initiative or the law that is undergoing referendum. In such instances, of course, the preponderant numbers on one side versus the other make a great deal of difference, and no amount of highly organized campaigning or favorable media coverage can overcome a sizab.e opposition. But, considering the number of propositions that a single voter is asked to decide on in a given election year, it is doubtful that many ballot issues engage the deep interest of anywhere near a majority of the electorate.

We need to distinguish, then, between these *preponderant* issue elections, where most voters feel deeply committed to one side or the other, and *arbitrated* issues, in which the majority feels no direct stake in the outcome but casts a vote that decides which of the contending minority positions will win. In the case of a preponderant election, the mass media are probably relatively unimportant, functioning mainly to clear up who is on what side. Since demographic factors (race, income, education, locale, age, sex) are normally strong determinants of positions in a preponderant election situation, and since people tend mostly to talk with other people like themselves, we can also expect that interpersonal communication in such an election will consist mostly of agreement and mutual reinforcement of positions.

In an arbitrated election, though, interpersonal communication channels become more important, at least potentially. The typical arbitrated ballot issue begins with a small group of like-minded people who organize either to place an initiative on the ballot or to call a referendum on a law they dislike. Their petition drive, and the associated recruitment of workers for the campaign, concentrates mostly within those demographic sectors where their viewpoint will have a strong appeal on the basis of either class or ideology. For example, supporters of open-housing laws in the early 1960s gathered signatures, donations, and volunteers mostly in black neighborhoods and in university districts. End-the-war campaigns a few years later usually emanated from campuses, but they did relatively better in suburban areas—and less well among racial minorities—than did open-housing canvassers.

A campaign effort sometimes stimulates formation of an opposition group. Often, though, the opposition is so diffused and amorphous that it is unorganizable—but nevertheless preponderant on Election Day. This is particularly likely when the "supporters" are asking for change and the "opposition" represents the status quo, as in the case of both open-housing and end-the-war movements. Supporters of a position might fail to get their legislation approved by the voters in such situations either because they fail to convince the arbitrating majority of the need for the change they advocate, or because their strident campaigning "turns off" many voters who might otherwise have sided with them. Examples can be cited, but so can exceptions. For instance, militant student anti-war protesters probably set back the campaign against the Vietnam war in some cases during the mid-1960s. But equally militant white anti-busing protesters—who went so far as to burn a school bus in one Michigan district where white students were bused to predominantly black schools—won preponderant support for their position. Obviously it matters not only how the campaign is conducted, but what kind of people are conducting it. Or, more precisely, it matters what the media portray as the methods and personnel on each side of an issue.

The arbitrating majority in an electoral decision between two small, intensely organized interest groups tends to be quite sensitive to media images of the contending sides. Being uninterested as well as disinterested, these voters will make little effort to inform themselves on the issue. One or both interest groups may contact a given voter, but partisan information is usually held at least somewhat suspect by the undecided. Personal contact is usually not a feasible method of reaching every voter anyway, except in elections limited to rather small communities or in situations where an interest group has an abnormally large cadre of canvassers.

The news media offer an excellent potential source of information for the undecided voter in an arbitrated election. These voters are "open" to decisive media information on the issue in three important ways. First, they are regularly exposed to news from at least one medium—most often television, or the newspaper. Second, they have some need for information, since they will be voting on the issue, even if they feel no personal stake in it. Finally, having no precommitted position, they are amenable to arguments supporting either side: hence, they are unlikely to distort the information that reaches them in accordance with any preconceived notion about the question.

Nevertheless, the accumulated evidence of years of public opinion surveys and other sources indicates clearly that millions of Americans go to the polls each Election Day with no more than the haziest ideas about some of the issues they will be deciding there. One reason, undoubtedly, is that apathy can be fairly intense and unyielding. Voters do not care to know about many issues. Learning is work and not worth the effort—even when it is made as effortless as it can conceivably be, thanks to television's simplified news briefs.

But we should consider apathy an ever-present shortcoming of democratic decision making. There is no use wringing our hands over it; few if any among us would claim to be wholly informed on every issue. Instead we might look for ways of improving the situation. Having a more informed electorate should mean that arbitrated issues will be decided in favor of the side on which the greatest merit lies; any steps to increase nonselective information holding on the part of uncommitted voters will move the political process toward that goal.

Our analysis has to focus, as one might expect, on the news media. The other parties to an election are pretty much unchangeable in their behavior: the campaigners on each side do all they can, and the uncommitted voters will not do more unless it is, in effect, done for them. How do the news media deal with arbitrated elections?

First, in terms of news priorities, arbitrated ballot issues rank near the bottom of the "newsworthiness" list. Candidate elections nearly always get top billing. They involve real, interviewable and quotable individuals, vying for the same bloc of power. Issue elections without candidates ordinarily become newsworthy only if they excite the intense interest of many voters, that is, if they are preponderant elections. Arbitrated elections, where the *potential* power of the media to enlighten the public is probably greatest, tend to get the least coverage.

Secondly, traditional reporting techniques are poorly designed for arbitrated issues. Since higher news priority is given to candidate and preponderant-issue elections, it is not surprising that reporters have developed procedures and practices that serve these types of campaigns well. The primary methods of covering campaigns are the personal interview (with a candidate or a spokesman for an issue interest group); the article rehashing what was said in a speech; or a forum where several candidates often try to tie themselves to what they see as the popular side of a preponderant issue in hopes of gaining votes "on the issues," as it is put. There is little value to candidates in taking a side on an arbitrated issue, since by definition there are few votes to be had on either side. The upshot is that coverage of speeches and forums alike tends to draw attention *away from* arbitrated issues, in favor of the more glamorous items on the ballot.

A second feature of reporting that makes things difficult for voters' decision making on arbitrated issues is that it has long been conventional to report *who* is for or against a proposition, rather than to give their reasons in any detail. The habit of reporting on persons rather than issues is so ingrained that, given a forum of statements by each of five speakers on each of five issues, we might expect nine reporters out of ten to organize their stories speaker by speaker, rather than issue by issue. Television in particular relies on the technique of building campaign "features" around one person at a time. Film from several appearances in different places by the same person can be spliced together into a nice ninety-second package that purportedly shows "what Senator Blurp was up to on the campaign trail today." The same technique would be next to impossible in covering one side—much less both sides of an issue. Propositions do not photograph well, and they do not respond in vernacular or oracular tones to an interviewer or an audience. Their spokesmen do not tend to be very colorful, or otherwise newsworthy. So the only coverage they get ordinarily is in a bookish "wrap-up" article in the newspaper just before the election (when all other campaigning is at fever pitch), probably to be read only by those few dedicated partisans who have already committed themselves on the issue.

Uncommitted and apathetic voters do not care enough to rise up en masse and demand more coverage of issues or more news analyses that package the pros and cons of each proposition in a format that facilitates decision making by the voters. In fact, when most voters are asked how they voted on an arbitrated issue, those who can remember are usually able to give some sort of reason for their decision. In short, people will vote, and they will find a reason for voting the way they did, but not necessarily in that order. The point is, they will rarely complain that they were uninformed, much less misled, on an issue. That would constitute a personal failing and a deficiency of citizenship, and who wants to admit such a thing?

Still, by failing to address arbitrated issues in a way that would be more serviceable to the uncommitted (and mostly uninformed) voter, the news industry is missing a chance to make a significant contribution to democratic decision processes. It is often asserted that the mass media have little power to persuade people on political issues, since most voters have precommitted positions based on partisan identification and demographic subgroup ties. That may be so for some major candidate elections and proponderant issues; all the more reason, then, for the press to try to make its mark on the less glamorous—but often equally important—arbitrated issues. The effect would not be an obvious one, since it would simply be to facilitate decision making in *either* direction on an issue; it would show up only in the overall quality of the decisions made.

To demonstrate the need, let us consider in some detail one case from recent history. The state is California, and the year 1964. On the ballot is a seemingly monumental presidential election between Barry Goldwater and Lyndon Johnson; a race for U.S. senator that also pits a certified conservative (George Murphy) against a declared liberal (Pierre Salinger); and a bitterly contested referendum on the state's limited open-housing law. California, with an enormous number of people living outside urban centers in spacious suburbs, is perhaps the most media-dominated state in the union, as well as the most populous. Television in particular is thriving, especially in the Los Angeles and San Francisco markets, where a single transmitter can reach several million homes.

In this setting, an NBC vice president named Sylvanus (Pat) Weaver has quit his network job and set out to introduce cable television to California. Ordinarily this might be considered an act of public service, to enrich the lives of those who want to subscribe to cable by providing them extra channels on which they might see opera, ballet, plays, and other programs that do not earn sufficiently high Nielsen ratings for commercial broadcasting. Weaver is prepared to sink his total personal fortune, about a million dollars, into capitalizing this venture.

Broadcast televisors see Weaver as a competitor they do not need. What's more, they see a simple way of getting rid of him and his cable scheme: have it declared illegal. They place an initiative on the ballot, one of several dozen items on California ballots that year. It is no less than a constitutional amendment, since California law provides that the state's constitution can be amended on an initiative by a simple majority vote. The amendment is to prohibit the charging of any fee for television within the state.

This simple measure will, of course, destroy Weaver's plan, since cable television is supported mainly by fees from those who subscribe to the service. The campaign pitch is simple: "You don't want to have to pay for television, do you? If you vote for this initiative, you can continue to get your TV programs free." This is not untrue, only misleading. Weaver spends his million dollars trying to persuade voters that free broadcast television will not be imperiled by subscription cable systems (a claim that subsequent experience has proved correct). He tries to describe the additional kinds of programing that his plan will bring into those homes that want it and will pay for it.

Three out of every five voters decided to "save free TV" by voting for the initiative. This amendment was eventually declared unconstitutional, but not before Weaver's venture had run out of money. Although now legal, and thriving in some smaller California markets, cable television was not established successfully in either Los Angeles or San Francisco ten years later. The many local broadcast channels in these megalopolitan areas will probably withstand the cable challenge through the normal processes of open economic competition.

Here we have an instance of an arbitrated election, and one that resulted in a bad law—an unconstitutional law almost surely contrary to the public interest. Few voters had any real stake in opposing Weaver's cable plan, and many (especially in remote areas) might have subscribed to it. But the news media, with whom Weaver would have been in direct competition, made no special effort to explain the situation. Instead, the broadcast television industry ran ads appealing to the status quo ("free TV") that went essentially unchallenged except by Weaver himself. Much heavier news coverage went to the major candidates and the referendum to repeal the open-housing law (another initiative that passed, two to one, only to be declared unconstitutional later).

The Weaver case demonstrates the enormous appeal of the idea that something (in this case, broadcast television) can be got for nothing. We should turn next to financial elections, where many voters feel they are paying something and getting nothing.

CITIZENS TAXING CITIZENS

Even the most autocratic regime needs a certain degree of popular support, since the money to run a government comes from taxes that are paid by nearly every citizen. Practically no one objects to the principle of taxation in general, but practically all of us have some specific complaint about our own taxes—they are too high, they are unfair, they are unwisely spent, they are destroying incentive, etc. So when a financial measure goes on ballot, it faces an uphill battle. More often than not, it loses.

We can get some feel for the procedure of asking citizens themselves whether they are to be taxed by examining briefly how this institution developed historically. It is most obvious in the evolution of parliamentary rule in England. Today's British government retains the three units that were there more than 500 years ago: a monarch, the Lords, and the Commons. But their relative powers have gradually reversed, and taxation lies at the heart of that reversal. The first major erosion of the absolute power of the monarch was the Magna Charta of 1215, by which King John was forced to agree to recognize the power of the Lords on whom he was dependent for raising funds from their local feudal baronies. Gradually there developed a powerful House of Lords, but these noblemen themselves were unable to raise their local revenues without support from the rising middle class. The Commons split off as a "lower house," subordinate to the Lords in both title and power. But the House of Commons was delegated—necessarily—the "power of the purse," to levy taxes. Over time, this became the most essential power in the government, and the Commons was able to assert its dominance over both the Lords and the throne. Today members of Parliament (M.P.s) must be elected from local districts, and this gives them the constitutional standing to tax those districts as a parliament. The monarch does not rule in any serious sense, and the titled members of the Lords may enter into the government only if they are also elected M.P.s in the same manner as members of the Commons.

The United States adopted whole the English principle that the power of taxation should reside in the lower house of the Congress: its members are elected every two years from local districts of approximately equal population. All money bills must originate in the House of Representatives.

Facing reelection campaigns every other year, and being responsible for money bills, congressional representatives are notoriously tax-conscious in comparison with other members of the American government. The same is generally true at the state level, where in most states the lower house is more frequently elected and bears greater responsibility for financial measures. In local government—county, town, municipal—electoral districts are usually small enough, elections frequent enough, and the results of public spending observable enough that taxation and public works often become larger political issues even than the candidates themselves.

The basic principle is that public financing of government (which citizens always resist to some extent) is more likely to be tolerated by the taxpayers if they are closely involved in the decision to levy the tax or spend the money. This was the principle that eventually turned England's government upside down, and it also accounts for the widespread use of plebiscites to make decisions on state and local public expenditures in the present-day United States.

In this system the press plays the role of gadfly, which can be roughly described as "to print news and raise hell." When taxes and public expenses are concerned, it is very difficult to tell when the press is printing news and when it is simply raising hell.

When discussing public finance, the journalist often uses language that suggests chicanery at every turn. The laws defining income tax structures contain many exemptions and deductions; these become "loopholes," "dodges," and "shields" in news parlance. When new public buildings are constructed, they are described as "plush" and "ornate," and the people who work in them are said to be "feeding at the public trough," growing fat and comfortable and constituting the "establishment." Characterizations of politicians as "crooked," public contracts as "rigged," and taxes as "confiscatory" occur often enough in print—and get confirmed just often enough in fact—to keep these images very much alive in the public mind. Whether this builds a healthy skepticism or an unfortunate cynicism toward government finance depends largely on your point of view.

Many observers consider that the press achieves its finest hours when it exposes governmental graft, misspending of funds, and other financial peccadilloes. This "muckraking" tradition, which began in the 1890s with the work of Lincoln Steffens on municipal corruption, enjoyed a renaissance in recent years—especially in the collection of revelations of White House involvement in the Watergate scandals. Prizes for outstanding journalistic achievement tend strongly to go to neo-muckrakers, especially those who uncover financial frauds within government.

But public money must be spent, even occasionally misspent, if we are to build and operate courts, schools, city offices, bridges, medical and welfare facilities, fire stations, jails, and the like. Tighter controls and accountability are always needed as these large amounts of money change hands, and the press can serve a critically important "watchdog" function in this regard.

The question must be asked, however, whether the press is capable of reporting adequately on public fiscal needs so that a reasonable proportion of the electorate will be able to cast an informed vote on a fiscal plebiscite. These bills often reach ballot in a summary form, consisting of a very few sentences describing a large, complex program or public works project and an incomprehensible price tag that ordinarily runs into the millions of dollars.

Reporters and editors strive mightily to unravel the intricacies of such proposals. In the long run they have four kinds of tools with which to work. The most popular is the interview. A reporter can ask various proponents of a financial bill to explain why it is needed and how the exact dollar figure has been determined. The next task is to seek out the opposition (usually highly available in a local "taxpayers alliance" of some sort) and get their views. Chances are, of course, that the opposition's supporters will talk a different language, one focused on costs, from the proponents of the issue, who will stress public benefits. It takes a highly skilled reporter to elicit from these differing viewpoints comments on the same elements of the issue, so that citizens can judge whether they want to vote yes or no.

A second method is to read the total bill and the supporting financial documents that have gone into it, and try to develop an analysis of the proposal that is independent of both the proponents' and the opponents' views to some extent. Few reporters have the technical background for this kind of work, and those who do should probably win more prizes than they do. It is instructive to note that the Watergate story was finally uncovered not by political reporters, whose method might have been to interview various high-ranking politicians about the burglary of Democratic party headquarters, but by police and financial page reporters who knew something about checks, laundered money, bag men, and balance sheets.

A third method, more or less a compromise, is to take quantitative data handed out by proponents (or opponents) of the measure and publish these figures without substantive editing. This is particularly likely to be done when the interested parties have been so thoughtful as to provide the media with handy visual devices, such as "fiscal pies" that show graphically what percentage of the money will be spent on what, and what percentage is to come from each of several sources. Such simplified pictures get high priority from the media, but not necessarily because they are the best way of presenting the information. Rather they are favored by editors as a means of breaking up the dullness of a gray page of type in a newspaper, or of avoiding the monotony of seeing an announcer's face constantly on camera during a television newscast.

The other tool available to the media is out of the hands of the working reporter covering a fiscal issue. It is the editorial, a hallowed newspaper tradition that is being taken up more and more by radio and television stations. In an editorial, the operator of the media outlet decides whether he wants the citizenry to approve or reject a financial measure, then he carefully marshals evidence to support that conclusion. (There is also presumably some gathering of evidence before reaching an editorial conclusion, but it is much easier to select useful material from the wealth of information available when an editor knows what he is looking for.) Most media owners, being part of the local business community, tend to adopt the conservative view of public expenditures common among business people. Editorials, then, are not so likely to support a fiscal proposal that is on the ballot as the broader range of voters would be if they were simply informed (by any or all of the first three methods) about the issue and left to make their own decisions. No systematic assessment of the net impact of editorials on financial issue voting has ever been conducted; but the effect is thought by many media specialists to be fairly large—much more so than in more publicized and partisan elections where candidates for major offices are involved.

As communities spread and change, and as their governmental structures and facilities become more and more antiquated, the task of understanding public finance becomes progressively more difficult for citizen and press alike. The greater responsibility for decision lies with the citizen, who casts the votes that count in these arbitrated elections. The greater responsibility for gathering, sorting, and presenting relevant information lies with the media, and particularly with the reporter. It is difficult to prepare citizens better for their decisional responsibilities except through the news media. The challenge of preparing reporters better for their informational responsibilities has not yet been faced squarely by the news media, nor by the schools that train reporters. Methods of reporting by means of interview and handout, and the process of creating public conclusions through the use of editorials, still prevail over original, objective reporting in the local media.

REFERENCES

Woodrow Wilson, *Congressional Government* (Cleveland: Meridian Books, 1965).

SUGGESTED STUDY PROJECTS

1   During a local election campaign, identify one ballot issue on which most people have clearly taken sides (a "preponderant" issue) and one on which there are a

great number of undecided and apathetic voters (an "arbitrated" issue). Then keep track of *(a)* the amount and kind of coverage each issue receives in the local media and *(b)* the extent to which candidates take positions on each issue. Do your findings agree or disagree with the generalizations in this chapter?

2 Check back over a number of elections in which financial issues appeared on the ballot, and keep track of the percentages who voted "yes" and "no." Then examine the editorial recommendations of the local newspapers in each case. Do the editorials tend to be more conservative (that is, more often opposed to the appropriation) than are the voters in general?

Chapter 14

Charity and Persuasion

Philanthropy, once thought of as a special beneficence granted by the very rich, has become all but a civic duty for most Americans. Medical and social welfare causes that are indisputably worthwhile vie for the charity dollar, of which all citizens are constantly admonished to donate their "fair share." So many major employers have routinized charity donations by payroll check-off systems that the phrase "I gave at the office" has become a national cliché. Stimulated by yearly donation campaigns and eased by tax deduction laws, charity has grown into a multibillion-dollar industry.

The mass media provide the main channel for fund-raising efforts. Churches and voluntary community organizations can make some direct contact, but they are limited in the number of potential donors they can reach. A great many appeals are also made by telephone or direct mail addressed to every household. But all these channels are buttressed by heavy persuasive publicity and advertising. For the most part, the media donate their time and space for charity appeals. Newspapers, for example, readily accede to requests by charities for free "news" space. Television stations keep a variety of free "public service" advertisements on hand to fill air time that has not been bought by commercial advertisers; some of these are charitable appeals.

Donations are, for most citizens, just that and nothing more; in other words, the donors expect nothing in return. Some giving is tied to an indirect "consumer" role, as when the will of a cancer victim includes a bequest to the American Cancer Society, or his survivors send gifts to it. But the giver himself gets no direct benefits. He gives to help others.

There is obviously some personal reward in charity. The plea to "give until it hurts" has been replaced by the more positive "give until it feels good." The latter conception probably comes closer to the emotional feeling of most donors. Charities appeal to the best in people. It is not uncommon to find tax-conscious citizens, who are notable for their opposition to heavy public expenditures for welfare, working hard on a United Fund drive. In return for a donation, the charity has little to offer beyond personal satisfaction and social approval. One method of providing the latter is to offer donor tokens such as lapel badges, bumper strips, letter seals, or window stickers. Even so, there are many anonymous donors, and very few givers make any special show of their munificence. Although there have been some outright frauds in the name of charity, it would be hard to argue that the growth of fund raising has not had an overwhelmingly benign influence on the nation. It has become a method of expressing the national moral conscience through unselfish individual acts.

There are, nevertheless, problems of communication between charities and their donors that need to be addressed. For, despite the open welcome that the mass media give to charity campaigns, consumers do not get adequate information to guide their giving decisions. The questions "How much should I give?" and "To which charity should I give?" are not easily answered by the conscientious donor. Our capacity to give is not unlimited, and we sense that some causes are more worthwhile than others. How could the media come to our aid?

HOW MEDIA "COVER" CHARITIES

The typical local newspaper—and more recently broadcast news offices—is run by people who are stirred by the same philanthropic impulses as most other Americans when it comes to charity. They are willing to donate to charities, and like most employers they are equally willing to pressure their less affluent employees into donating. It has probably seemed only one small further step to donate space, or air time, to the promotion of the charity.

No other major piece of the "news hole" is so freely given. The rest of the news of the day, plus "human interest" items, must pass the editor's essential test: they must be deemed likely to attract readership. Not so with space or time that is given over to charity promotion. The editor fears, and pretty much knows, that few among his audience will have much interest in the charity. So he puts his journalistic skills to work to try to create some lame "news peg" for the charity item. This may involve treating a pseudo-event, such as the "official opening" of the annual fund drive, as serious news. Or perhaps an energetic press agent has hired a comely model or a well-known athlete to be photographed in aid of the campaign for donations. Local politicians are typically pleased to allow their newsworthy names and faces to be incorporated into the effort.

The result is not news, of course, but it does provide a body of verbal and pictorial material that can be treated in much the same fashion as the editor normally handles news. On a newspaper, for instance, a reporter will be assigned to write a "story," or a series of them, "covering" the charity drive. (Since it is typical to donate a fixed amount of space, usually large, to a charity drive, the reporter will have to strain to fill it; most reporters take pride in their ability to stretch out a minimal amount of information to a desired length when called on to do so.) The reporter's article is then given a headline, almost invariably one stretching across several columns of the paper. The mandatory photograph earns a caption below, and often a head-line above; the journalist assigned to write these items usually has to look at the article to find anything worth writing in the caption. This process may be repeated for several days, weeks, or even months—however long the official campaign for the charity lasts.

Not all charities get this royal treatment, of course, or there would be little room in the paper for anything else. The most extensive coverage is given to the oldest and best-known causes. These attributes of age and familiarity are not particularly related to the relative merits of the many charitable causes that vie for the donor's dollar. It is possible, for example, for a fund-raising campaign to become so prosperous that it actually suc-ceeds—for example, it may produce a cure for the ill that it was intended to attack. This happened to the March of Dimes, the anti-poliomyelitis drive that was given an enormous boost by the backing of President Franklin D. Roosevelt, himself a polio victim. After vaccines to prevent the disease were invented in the 1950s, the original reason for the March of Dimes would seem to have vanished. But the campaign had become such a fixture that it was able to attract funds anyway; this happy circumstance led its directors to shift their efforts to attacks on certain other diseases which had not by themselves been able to generate nearly the same level of donations. These were not less deserving diseases, in terms of medical severity, incidence, or research needs; they simply had not enjoyed polio's advantages, in terms of public awareness and willingness to donate directly for their eradication. In the age of media, even a disease must make its mark in terms of what people *perceive* it to be, rather than what it is.

To say this is certainly not to decry the practice of donating media space to certain well-established charities. What *is* unfortunate is that, having given away the space, the media make so little effort to fill it well. No other topic of extensive news coverage is given such uncritical treatment as is a charity—any charity. Criticism and controversy, which are certainly not unknown in charitable campaigns, rarely surface in the press and even less often on television. It is as if there were a vast "conspiracy of silence" surrounding the campaign, which is treated as a sacred cow. But in most cases this should be attributed to errors of omission, not commission. Having given away the space, the media take little further interest in it.

WHAT CONSUMERS NEED TO KNOW

Perhaps no two words in the American idiom are so inextricably joined as are the adjective "worthy" and the noun "charity." When someone threatens to give away his money, it is inevitably to a worthy charity. The same admirable fate awaits ill-gotten gains that fall into honest hands at last. But the concept of a "worthy charity" implies that there must also be some unworthy ones around, or at least some that are less worthy than others. Assuming that this is so, we might reasonably ask why we have not heard of any.

A few fund-raising scandals have in fact been identified in the past. One of these involved the Kenny Foundation, which in the era before polio vaccine promoted funds for Sister Kenny's treatment of polio victims. The foundation fell into the hands of operators who extracted huge profits from it and were eventually exposed—but not before it had reaped enormous donations spurred by uncritical media publicity, including a Hollywood "biopic" on Sister Kenny, portrayed by Rosalind Russell. Indeed, many people who had donated time and money to the Kenny campaign refused for some time to believe that they had been defrauded.

Few charities ever degenerate into outright frauds, of course. Nevertheless, there is enormous variance among them in their efficiency of operation. Professor Scott Cutlip, author of a detailed history of fund raising in the United States, suggests that this is one method by which donors could decide which charities are most "worthy"—if only the media would make the information available. Cutlip points out that the percentage of the donated dollar that goes toward administration of the fund, rather than to the purpose for which the fund exists, is a fairly good measure to use. Some administrative "overhead" is essential to any fund, of course, but it is difficult to understand why the administrative percentage is fives times as large in one fund as in another.

Administrative overhead is not by any means the only criterion by which a donor might choose between charities. Surely one would want to have some idea of the overall incidence and seriousness of the problem or disease the charity intends to alleviate; of the likelihood of success, given the method or approach the charity employs in dealing with the problem; and of the extent to which other organizations, private or governmental, are working in the same problem area. These are difficult, sometimes intangible, matters to evaluate. But the press does not shrink from assessing even more amorphous elements when it comes to politics, governmental budgets, or international diplomacy.

It is our guess that the media fail to conduct any comparative reporting on charities simply because the media have never done so. That is, the role of journalism regarding charity drives has long since become institutionalized, handed down from one editor to the next. That role is to cooperate with each charity that approaches the editor, to the extent of providing some free space and donating a bit of reportorial skill to try and put a good face on it.

Thus do editors discharge their civic duty toward one charity and then another. This is looked on as "public service" by the medium, and performing such a service is thought to be good for attracting audiences.

Only rarely does it occur to a journalist that there is also a "public interest" to be serviced here. Citizens are willing to give to charity; the promotional content on behalf of a particular fund no doubt strengthens and channels that general motivation. But beyond that, citizens need to be able to see the full range of alternative charitable causes to which they might donate, in a context that will allow them to make informed choices of the "worthiest."

Current journalistic practice is for the media, in effect, to make those choices for its audiences. That is, the editor allots more space to one cause than another, and none to a third. There is no "round up" story comparing the three in any objective (or even subjective) way. The audience is left with only generalized motivations toward one charity and then the next, as a guide to giving. Chances are, then, that the charity which receives the greatest publicity will get the heaviest donations, and the unpublicized fund will receive very little.

For editors to make choices for their audiences is a time-honored custom in American journalism. The editorial page of almost every newspaper makes evaluations regarding elections, public policy issues, and private enterprise developments that affect the community significantly. But ordinarily these matters are also the subject of more objective reporting in the news columns. The same cannot be said of charities. It is ironic that so little useful public information is asked or provided in this domain, which in so many other ways manifests what is best in American society.

The most basic reason why this lack of reporting persists is probably inherent in the nature of giving. One donates money to a worthy charity, asks no questions, and feels good about the whole thing. (The same is true of editors who donate a piece of their news product.) To raise questions, to compare or "shop" charities, to get picky about things would spoil this general aura of pleasantness. Perhaps people would give less overall to charity if they were better informed regarding comparative worthiness.

On the other hand, it is an old principle of the marketplace that the best products are most likely to sell when consumers are most informed about quality. The most worthy charities, then, should be the ones that would thrive if givers were better able to assess all fund drives on a systematic basis.

REFERENCES

Scott M. Cutlip, *Fund Raising in the United States* (New Brunswick, N. J.: Rutgers University Press, 1965).

SUGGESTED STUDY PROJECTS

1 Interview the promotion directors for several large charity drives. Find out how they plan their campaign, how they select media, how much they spend on different elements of the campaign, and what kinds of technical skills they need in their work.
2 Keep a clipping file of your local newspaper's coverage of a major charity drive. Analyze the information that is provided to the public through this channel, in terms of the criticisms made in this chapter. Are those criticisms justified in the case you have selected?

Part Four

Social Control

Chapter 15

Social Control through Mass Communication

In any society there are certain forms of social behavior that almost everyone defines as undesirable. Murder, theft, and incest are common examples. A particular society may also determine that some behavior that is perfectly permissible elsewhere cannot be tolerated. For example, some cultures allow nudity, while others may require that the face be kept covered. Some societies do not permit the taking of fish from water, and some have banned the dumping of refuse into it. Almost all societies exercise some controls over speech—but they differ enormously in their choices of which words are illegal.

In most cases, the reasons for social taboos and prohibitions are obvious. In many others, no particular reason can be discerned other than the desire to control per se. The enforcement of slightly dated fashions of dress and hair style, for example, seems to be a recurrent passion of secondary school educators that is based on a role-inherent need to demonstrate their control over students.

The most obvious method of exercising control over social behavior—

whatever the origin of the prohibition—is to enact a law against it, then to punish those who violate the rule. This mechanism is satisfactory enough where the principal reason for the prohibition is to demonstrate or exercise power, or to define which members of society are "good" and which ones are "bad" citizens. It is not such a useful technique when the type of behavior at issue is truly harmful and is therefore an act that needs to be prevented, rather than simply punished.

Whether punishment is an effective deterrent to unlawful behavior is an issue that does not admit an easy answer. Those who are in a position to administer punishments may find this rewarding enough that they are unwilling to surrender their power even if it serves no useful purpose. On the other hand, those who consider themselves potential punishees can scarcely be expected to render impartial judgments on the question either. Faced with conflicting claims about punishment by the two "involved" sides, the remainder of society tends instead to seek methods for the *prevention* of undesirable social behaviors. If they do not occur, the problem of whether and how to punish them will not arise.

Not suprisingly, the mass media have long been looked upon as a means of controlling social behavior. And as the media have grown in variety and in their penetration of American society, there has been a correlative intensification of the search for mass communication techniques of social control.

In this section we consider four general types of social behavior that have proved themselves continuing objects of attempts at societal control. To judge from the persistence with which these four have remained major public concerns, attempts to control them by means of communication have been no more resoundingly successful than controls through coercion and punishment.

In all four cases, the emphasis is on preventing something from occurring by persuading a would-be violator *not to act*. This is distinctly different from the topics taken up in our previous section, in which we discussed the uses of communication to persuade individuals *to do something*. The results of effective social control are harder, in a very real way, to assess, because they consist of the fact that nothing has happened—when something presumably might have. It is commonplace to lump together attempts to encourage socially beneficial acts and attempts to discourage socially harmful acts. But from the perspective of communication strategies, these two general goals call for very different approaches.

Chapter 16 focuses on crime—specifically, acts of violence against other persons. We will assume that the undesirability of such acts can be almost universally agreed on, since anyone might find himself the unwilling and undeserved victim of violent attack.

Next (Chapter 17) we will take up the problem of environmental pollution. Like violent crime, pollution is deplored by the vast majority of people in the United States—although widespread concern for the environment is a decidedly recent pheonomenon, and it is just beginning to be tested against politico-economic interests. The principal difference between pollution and physical violence is that the latter ordinarily consists of an identifiable act by one person against another, as individuals. A single example of pollution, by contrast, usually does not in itself constitute a major transgression, nor can a single victim be easily identified. The offense is instead societal in level, both in its commission and its consequences. A thousand instances of assault and battery yield a thousand clearly aggrieved individuals. A thousand days' discharge of poisons from an industrial plant into a city's air or water supply harms many thousand of citizens, but to an extent that is difficult to assess. So mass communication is faced with an added challenge in the case of pollution control: not only must individual violations be prevented, but the problem must be dealt with at a societal level. (Many would argue that this is also true of violent crime, but the societal nature of pollution problems is far less debatable; hence we will use that topic as a framework for discussing social control at the level of society, and violent crime for our analysis of social control at the level of the individual.)

Chapters 18 and 19 will address more controversial areas of social control, in that they consist of acts that only a certain segment of American society considers criminal or even undesirable. Again, one is essentially an individual transgression and the other a societal transgression. One key premise in these chapters is that the role of mass communication as a form of social control will be different where society is nowhere near unanimous in its desire to control the behavior.

Chapter 18 addresses the matter of sexual activity. Sexual intercourse is about as common a form of social behavior as one can imagine; a chapter in the previous section on individual persuasion might well have been devoted to the problem of encouraging it in those who are so unusual and unfortunate as not to have enjoyed this deeply human activity. (A fair amount of mass communication has attempted to do just that, which in turn has brought about controversial "anti-pornography" laws.) It is *deviance* from "normal" sexual behavior that arouses in some the urge to control. Deviance may take such forms as sexual crime (rape or pedophilia), homosexuality, or promiscuity. The bulk of responsible attempts at control of sexual deviance has, sensibly, centered on sexual crimes where the object of the sex act is unwilling, under-aged, or incompetent.

But sex is a funny thing. Discussion of one form seems inevitably to arouse discussion of all. Approaches to social control of sexual crimes tend to get bound up in the broader—and less agreed-upon—concepts of "undesirable" sexual acts. The mass media have become the point of crystallization for much of this perennial societal squabble. Here we will try to address the basic question "What can and should the media do to control sexual crimes?" It will be impossible, however, to limit the discussion to that narrow topic.

Finally, in Chapter 19 we will take up the issue of political radicalism, which is both controversial and societal (in contrast to violent crime, which is on the whole noncontroversial and individual as a problem in social control). Some few hundreds of years ago, this chapter might well have been devoted to heresy rather than radicalism. Marshall McLuhan has suggested that the religious heresies that broke up the European order of the Middle Ages resulted from the introduction of mass communication, in the form of printing. Whatever their origins, these heresies can be seen in retrospect to have been profoundly political in nature; the churches they challenged are still with us, albeit deeply altered, but the political arrangements of that time are not. Religious freedom is a relatively well-established principle in the United States today (although blasphemy, for example, is still a crime in four states). Political freedom is not nearly so firmly fixed in this nation, particularly where the mass media and the concept of "radicalism" are concerned. The cyclical history of attempts to control one sort of radicalism after another through mass communication in the United States has provided us with most of our practical definitions of "freedom of the press" and "freedom of speech."

Central to the pursuit of social control through communication is the doctrine of illegal words. Can undesirable acts be prevented by prohibitions against writing or uttering the verbal symbols that represent (and might evoke) those acts? Such an overly general question can be attacked only in relation to particular kinds of acts and words. In the four chapters that follow, we will give special attention to legal prohibitions that are directed against words per se.

And, although a picture may not be worth precisely one thousand words, visual displays in the mass media have been involved in as many attempts at social control in recent years as have verbal passages. Would-be censors have found that it is even more difficult to write effective laws against specific kinds of pictures than against words. The content and potential effects of pictures—still or moving—elude clean definition. The rising importance of nonverbal mass communication presents a growing challenge for social control both by and of the media.

Mass Communication and Violence

Probably the oldest social problem of all is how to prevent one person from physically attacking another. Long before the arrival of mass communication, social violence had been institutionalized in forms ranging from man-to-man combatives to total war. Control of violence has been sought through punishment ("An eye for an eye, a tooth for a tooth") and by outlawing it ("Thou shalt not kill"). Neither approach has been totally effective, although it is highly doubtful that we are "becoming a more violent people." The problem remains eternally with us. From the perspective of this book we can address it in two ways. First, do the mass media contribute to crime and violence in American society? And second, can the mass media help in minimizing or controlling crime and violence?

The first of these questions would probably never have been asked except for the fact that the media have traditionally made violence—on the part of both villains and heroes—a major theme of popular art (and of news for that matter). In fairness, this was an inherited trait, carried to the modern media via some impeccable bloodlines. Much of the greatest ancient literature was built around war; the works of Herodotus, Homer, and Caesar and the Old Testament are examples. Murder was a standard device of Greek myths and of Shakespeare's plays, partly because it was a highly efficient method of bringing about real-life political changes, as history's long list of beheaded queens and stabbed princes attests.

Public fascination with violence, on both the grand and the clandestine scale, is scarcely surprising. The mass media, being by definition public institutions, have recognized this appetite from the beginning and have developed several stylized methods for feeding it. On the broad motion picture screen, war has become the grand epic. Casts of thousands (of whom only hundreds survive the great battles) swirl around the private loves and public conquests of a semi-superhuman military hero. Such stars as John Wayne and Charlton Heston, two of the all-time box-office champions, are closely identified with this kind of role. More private forms of murder have been a major staple of popular novelists, from the classic Sherlock Holmes stories of A. Conan Doyle to the enormous volume of murder tales by such prolific twentieth-century authors as Agatha Christie and Erle Stanley Gardner. Mystery novels have sold billions of copies, most of them paperback editions, and have made household names of such fictional private detectives as Sam Spade, Nick Carter, Nero Wolfe, and their cold-war descendant Agent 007 (Ian Fleming's James Bond). Two other major themes that developed in radio and films in the first half of this century were the police or crime drama and the ubiquitous western. The first of these gradually evolved from criminal centered movies of the thirties (e.g. James Cagney in *Public Enemy* and Edward G. Robinson in *Little Caesar*) to radio shows dramatizing peace-keeping agents (such as "Gang Busters," "FBI in Peace and War," and Jack Webb's low-key "Dragnet"). The gallop on horseback and the dramatic shoot-out were ideally suited to the screen, where the western has flourished ever since the silent days of Bronco Bill Anderson and William S. Hart, and has furnished favorite roles for masculine heroes as diverse as Gary Cooper, Burt Lancaster, Gregory Peck, Alan Ladd, Lee Marvin, James Stewart, and even Marlon Brando. Although lacking the motion picture's ability to depict the stock action clichés of the western, both radio and comic books (and the newspaper "funnies") managed to put across the Lone Ranger and Red Ryder, each with his faithful (if unlikely) Indian companion.

The standard format for the plot of a western is worth some note here because of the central role of violence. The hero is a modest, resourceful, soft-spoken man faithful to the law and capable of outdrawing any gunman or outslugging anyone in a fair fist fight. Early in the story an underhanded criminal (more often, a gang of them) gains money, property, power, or other dominion by some unfair set of tactics such as ambush, theft, bribery, or deceit. Occasionally the hero is bested in a one-against-many fight, adding an element of revenge to his motivation. He then works methodically toward establishing a showdown in which he can finally resolve the problem by outdrawing or outpunching the leading "bad guy" in a climactic fair fight. Then he moves on to the next town, where, a few months (in the case of "B" movies) or evenings (in the case of radio) later, he is once again called on to restore law and order to the Old West.

Such an existence left little time for serious love affairs, which would have tied the hero to a home base. Of the major semi-serialized western heroes, only B-movie star Roy Rogers maintained a stable marital relationship (with his co-star and real-life wife Dale Evans), and even that was rivaled by his close attachment to his "wonder horse" Trigger—the fictional West's best-known mount aside from the Lone Ranger's trusty Silver.

When television burst forth as the "ultimate" mass medium in mid-century, it seized on all these sure-fire violent themes and transported them almost unchanged into the nation's living rooms. Early on, the old grade B westerns of Hopalong Cassidy were dug out of film studio libraries and enjoyed a thriving second life on the television screen of the early fifties. The weekly television western "Gunsmoke" soon moved to the top of the Nielsen ratings to stay, and it evoked a spate of other adventure western series in the late fifties. Gradually the western (again led by "Gunsmoke") evolved into a setting for "family problems" stories, as exemplified by the enormously popular "Bonanza" of the 1960s. But violence remained the ultimate mechanism for resolving serious conflicts, if the villain was so incorrigible as to refuse to listen to reason from the omniscient hero—who had evolved into the stolid marshal of "Gunsmoke," the upright father of "Bonanza," and the sage old wagonmaster of "Wagon Train." Meanwhile, the murder-mystery thriller was condensed into half-hour and one-hour television dramas, most successfully in the long-running "Perry Mason" series, a formula-written adaptation of Erle Stanley Gardner's clever lawyer who never lost a case. Private eyes such as Cannon and Mannix supplanted the vintage Sam Spade and the Thin Man. Modern law officers became more popular on television than in any other medium, led by the popularity of the televised version of "Dragnet." Among the Nielsen-rated leaders of this genre have been the policemen of "Ironside," "Hawaii Five-0," "Adam-12," "Racket Squad," "M-Squad," and "N.Y.P.D."; the youthful undercover cops of "Mod Squad"; federal agents on "The Untouchables" and "The FBI"; and international operatives devoted to freedom in such spoofs as "Get Smart," "I Spy," and "The Man From UNCLE." With so many criminals being brought to justice, a clutch of additional lawyers was needed to handle the caseload, and "The Defenders," "The Bold Ones," "Judd for the Defense," and "Owen Marshall" helped fill this gap. The grand sweep of war is more difficult to transfer to the small screen and shorter time span of television. But when the fine war film *The Bridge on the River Kwai* was first shown on home screens, it drew the largest audience in history.

Not all these programs depict violence on a regular basis; almost all of them punish vicious criminal acts in the end, and their heroes tend to use force with evident restraint. But the disquieting fact remains that violence is a core ingredient of many of the most popular films, books, and television programs—including those that are most often seen by children. A study of one week of viewing by tenth graders in 1970 showed "Mod Squad," "Bonanza," "Dragnet," "It Takes a Thief," "Then Came Bronson," "Mission: Impossible," and "Ironside" among the leaders, each attracting from 15 to 35 percent of the teenage audience. "Mod Squad" was the second-favorite show among a sample of sixth graders, and a sizable portion of first graders watched the daytime "Batman" and listed "Adam-12" among their favorites. Among the shows designed specifically for young children are many cartoon adventures that depict extreme violence in a manner that could not be duplicated by real actors.

Violence on television historically appears to ebb and flow, in tune with audience ratings. It crested in the late fifties as the westerns came to dominate the tube, subsided as these shows lost popularity and mostly vanished from the screen, then built to a new high in the late sixties. Motion picture violence, on the other hand, has built steadily since the 1930s. The film critic Joseph Morgenstern, of *Newsweek,* is among those who view this trend with growing alarm, charging that "Moviemakers have found ultra-violence ultra-profitable, the mass audience has found it enjoyable—and an influential majority of reviewers has found it intellectually attractive and artistically valid." He goes on to comment from an artistic standpoint:

> This kind of entertainment is seductive in more ways than one. With its obscurity, macho bravura or both, it puts you promptly on the defensive. You can't be much of a man if you don't dig it, or at least concede its underlying wisdom. Man is base (and woman is baser), say the pundit artists. How true, how true, respond the admiring critics, only too glad to get a secure ride on the hate-humanity bandwagon. . . .

> Purveyors of the new violence can tell themselves and their critics that they're involved in a program of character building, public service and ethical culture, but a few visits to neighborhood theaters suggest that a large part of the mass audience simply loves the violence as violence. The givens are not always the takens. Kids in the balcony at a recent Times Square showing of "Dirty Harry" were stomping their feet with glee at each shooting or beating. One boy was coming on strong as a munitions expert, giving his girl a run-down on the range and impact of each weapon as it appeared. When the massacres ended

and the house lights came up, he breathed a sigh of deep satisfaction and said quietly: "That was nice.". . .

There's a sense of imminent disaster when you're in an audience that's grooving on ultra-violence, and you're tempted to say that things can't go on this way too much longer. They can, of course, and probably will. Today's ultra-violent films will be tomorrow's "Wednesday Night at the Movies" on TV. . . .[1]

What Morgenstern is complaining about is a tendency for the media to depict scenes of gore and violence with a frequency and intensity far beyond the experiences of most people in real life. Unless checked by some external pressure, they will continue in this practice, because it has proved itself profitable many times over. In the face of audience popularity, critics will have little impact on the media, and self-regulation by the film and television industries does not seem to offer a likely path toward control. Governmental regulation of media content is generally barred by the First Amendment, although, as we have seen in other chapters of this book, government will step in and control the media where it presumes that a clear-cut public danger exists.

The central question becomes, then, not whether the media overemphasize violence (they clearly do), but whether this has an adverse influence on human social behavior. Media officials have long maintained that no conclusive case has been proved on that score, and that therefore there is no compelling reason to reduce the level of violent content in the media. Their "calm down" arguments have been effective in averting serious action by public bodies against violence. Since a great deal of research has been conducted on the issue of "effects" by social psychologists, we should examine the evidence and its political status in some detail.

EFFECTS OF VIOLENCE IN THE MEDIA

Studies of the behavioral impact of violence in the media have focused almost exclusively on violence in fictional films and on television, and on children in the audience. Youngsters are a major proportion of the television audience, the ages of eleven and twelve being about the peak viewing years in the typical American's life cycle; adolescents and young adults have come to be the main audience for films shown in American theaters. And youth is presumably a more impressionable state than in adulthood. Nevertheless it is unfortunate that practically nothing is known directly about the effects of violence in other media, the impact of depictions of

---

[1]Joseph Morgenstern, "The New Violence," *Newsweek,* Feb. 14, 1972, pp. 66 ff. Copyright Newsweek, Inc., 1972. Reprinted by permission.

violence in news and advertising, or the reactions of adults to this type of content. As is so often the case in social research, we must for now be satisfied to assess what *is* known, and then consider how it might be extrapolated to spheres that have not been studied directly.

There are three levels at which violence might be shown to have an adverse social impact. The first concerns *immediate, short-term effects,* which might be demonstrated in, for example, a carefully controlled experiment where some children are shown a violent film and others are not; if those who see the film subsequently exhibit substantially more aggressive behavior than the "control group," this can be taken as evidence of immediate adverse effects, although it does not necessarily demonstrate any lasting influence of the violent film. A second level is that of *long-term cumulative individual differences.* This might be demonstrated by following a large number of youngsters over a period of years and finding that those who had been exposed to more violent television programs when young tended to be the same ones who were most likely to start fights or to threaten to beat up other people in later years. Finally, one might approach the question in terms of *macro-societal variation,* as is implied in the suggestion that the United States may have fostered a national "culture of violence" by its emphasis on violence in the media; this level of analysis would require comparisons between countries where media violence is common and those where it is rare or absent (as in the case of nations that have not developed more than negligible mass media systems).

Most of the research to date has been designed to test for immediate short-term effects of media violence. In recent years there have been some studies of cumulative individual differences. Cross-cultural evidence of macro-societal variation is almost totally lacking. Since these levels represent a sort of "staircase" in which each level would presuppose the previous one, let us begin with the issue of short-term effects, which have been heavily studied in laboratory experiments.

A number of psychological theories have been offered to explain what might happen in a child's mind when he sees a brutal fight or killing on the screen. One is the simple process of *imitation;* the viewer might learn new ways of behaving from what he sees and might therefore be more likely to act in a similar manner if a reasonably appropriate occasion arises later. A second mechanism is the Freudian hypothesis of *identification* with an admired character; in the course of watching the story, the youngster might well begin to think of himself in that role and thus become more likely to act out whatever his "hero" does. When the hero achieves some goal by violence, the identifying child is thereby encouraged to do so as well. A third hypothetical condition is that of *linkage* of the fictional portrayal with real life. The distinction between fantasy and reality is not always clear-cut for a youngster, whose limited range of experience may not provide an adequate background for reality testing. (This may also be true of some adults; in studies of the urban poor, the most common reason given for watching television is that "it helps me to solve my everyday problems.")

On the other side of the coin is the suggestion, naturally much favored by television network executives and film producers, that exposure to violence in the media produces a sort of *catharsis,* in which the youngster's latent impulses toward aggressive behavior are satisfied by the substitute experience of viewing filmed violence. This notion is borrowed from Aristotle, who suggested that a socially beneficial result for the audience of a Greek tragedy might be to alleviate personal feelings of fear, as a result of experiencing the vicarious fear from the play. One would hardly suggest that this hypothetical "catharsis" process might be generalized to all types of theater, of course; neither Aristotle nor any modern media mogul has proposed that exposure to comedy would leave an audience less mirthful than it had been at the start. Does it apply to violence? Since catharsis is a wholly psycho-emotional concept, not directly observable in the way a scientist normally tries to observe things, researchers have had to content themselves with an indirect search. Because of the social importance of violent behavior, research has focused on this type of content and effect, rather than on Aristotle's original field of tragedy. If aggressive tendencies are cathartically relieved by viewing violent shows, this effect should show up in the form of lessened aggressive behavior among youngsters who have been deliberately exposed to media violence in an experiment.

Short-term Effects

Since the early 1960s, some twenty-five experiments have demonstrated that exposure to violence on film or television usually increases the likelihood that children will display aggressive behavioral tendencies immediately thereafter. The leading pioneers in this work have been Dr. Albert Bandura of Stanford University and Dr. Leonard Berkowitz of the University of Wisconsin, along with their students and colleagues at these two institutions. Various experiments indicate that this adverse effect of violence in the media is heightened under certain conditions—namely, when the violent acts portrayed have been justified or rewarded rather than punished; when the youngsters have been angered or insulted just before viewing the violent show; or when the audience consisted of youngsters who had a history of behaving somewhat more aggressively than the "average" child. The research record includes many studies of preschool and elementary school children, a few of high school–age youngsters, many of college students, and at least one of adult males. All told, about 90 percent of the experiments that have been reported would support the general conclusion that exposure to media violence *does* arouse aggressive behavioral tendencies. Various ingenious methods have been used to try to isolate the hypothetical intervening processes of imitation, identification, and linkage with reality; and there is evidence that each of those mechanisms plays some part in arousing aggression.

On the other side of the picture lie a small number of experiments conducted by Dr. Seymour Feshbach of the University of California at Los Angeles and his associates, which appear to provide some indirect support for the contradictory "catharsis" hypothesis. That is, teenage boys in an institutional setting who were limited to nonviolent television programs behaved *more* aggressively than another group that was limited to watching violent shows. Whether this was the result of an invisible process of catharsis is a moot point from a policy standpoint. If the same result were to be found in a more natural setting, such as the home, it would at least give one pause before demanding controls on violence in the media.

At this writing, however, the great preponderance of evidence indicates that there are indeed adverse short-term effects of violence in the media; only a small minority of studies suggest the opposite. As is common among behavioral scientists, each "side" has attacked the *methods* of the other. Since their methods are not greatly different, one example should suffice to demonstrate to the reader the kind of evidence available. The following summarizes an experiment conducted by Professor Feshbach; it is not one of those particularly supporting his catharsis hypothesis.

Sixty children, aged 9 through 11, were assigned at random to one of three conditions: 20 were shown a six-minute film depicting a college student demonstration, in which students and police clashed violently; before the film, they were told that it was "a newsreel of a student riot which was photographed by NBC news photographers who were right on the scene—you might have seen some of this news on televison before" *(reality condition).* Another 20 were shown the same film, but told, "We are going to show you a film that was made in a Hollywood studio. The story is about a student riot. You might have seen some of the actors on television before" *(fantasy condition).* (In fact, the film was a combination of news film and clips from a studio dramatic production.) The violent content included three uses of weapons; 13 displays of clubs; 19 instances of associated shouting and yelling; and 11 of running, including police moving in on demonstrators who were chanting, "Pigs off campus." Finally, to provide a "baseline" for comparison with these "fantasy condition" and "reality condition" groups, the remaining 20 youngsters were not shown the film at all ("control group").

Following this procedure, each of the 60 children was asked to help play a guessing game, using an "aggression machine." This apparatus consisted of a panel of four buttons by which the youngster could control the "noise level" of a signal to another person (actually an accomplice of the experimenter) who was ostensibly attempting to match a set of colored cards to a set of colored lights. Each time the accomplice made an error (which he purposely did 15 times in 22 attempts at matching colors), the child was instructed to signal to him that he was mistaken, by pressing one of the four buttons. Any of the four buttons would carry the signal, but they ranged in noise level from 1 ("soft") through 7 ("loud, painful"); the intermediate levels were labeled "3" and "5," and the child was given a demonstration via headphones of the progressive loudness of the "1," "3," and "5" buttons—being told by the experimenter that the "7" button was "so loud and painful that I am not even going to show it to you." The headphones were then placed on the accomplice (and the noise switch secretly turned off to spare him pain), who proceeded to make his scheduled 15 errors; the child correspondingly made 15 noise signals to him. The measure of "aggression" was the average noise level of the buttons pressed by each child, across the 15 trials.

The results were quite clear-cut. The mean noise level administered by the control children (no film) was 3.3; the "reality" condition increased this to 4.3, while the "fantasy" condition decreased it to 2.3. These differences are large enough that it is highly unlikely that they could be due to chance statistical fluctuations alone, even though the sample size may seem small. The author concluded that the effect of the violent film was to increase aggressive behavioral tendencies when it was presented as reality, and to decrease them when it was clearly labeled as fantasy. This overall pattern held up regardless of the age, sex, or socio-economic status of the child.[2]

There is something in this experiment and its conclusions for adherents of every point of view. It demonstrates a condition (reality) under which the witnessing of violence stimulates aggressiveness, and another (fantasy) in which there is an opposite result. The study is open to objections in terms of "reality" itself, of course. Children are rarely told so clearly that they are watching either real or fictional events on television—although the experiment suggests the latter might well be a worthwhile suggestion to parents. Further, they rarely watch only a six-minute film clip, and almost never in a school setting; more typically they view television (by the hour) at home, with a wide variety of programs and ads surrounding a particular sequence. And of course the "aggression machine" provided a bizarre opportunity to administer pain to another person (with whom they were entirely unfamiliar) without fear of any consequences. Controlled laboratory experiments are almost inherently open to challenge on such grounds. If children were allowed to watch as they "normally" would, the key elements of random assignment and careful specification of the "stimulus" film material would

[2]Summarized from Seymour Feshbach, "Reality and Fantasy in Filmed Violence," in John P. Murray, Eli A. Rubinstein, and George A. Comstock (eds.), *Television and Social Behavior*, vol. 2, *Television and Social Learning*, U.S. Government Printing Office, Washington, D.C., 1972.

be lost, and the result of the study would be equivocal. And if their subsequent aggressive behavior were measured by turning a number of stimulated youngsters loose on one another, to observe who hit whom first, the experimenters would deserve to be soundly condemned on ethical grounds.

But neither Feshbach's experiment described here nor any other single study need stand scrutiny alone. Different experiments have used different stimulus films, have shown them to children of different ages and backgrounds in a wide variety of settings, and have varied the conditions of operation in terms of preliminary instructions given by the experimenter. More importantly, many different measures of aggressiveness have been used. (Feshbach's study included several other measures that have not been mentioned here.) Each study has "flaws" in its particular methods, but they do not all have the same flaws by any means. Taken as a group, the experimental research demonstrates that *much more often than not* the immediate short-term effect of violence in the media is to induce increased aggressive behavior, not the reverse. Some of those who view violence are probably unaffected by it, and a few (under certain, perhaps most, conditions) react less aggressively than they normally would; but on the whole the social effect appears to be a decidedly adverse one.

Long-term Effects
Many barriers face the social scientist who wants to find out whether any single kind of experience, such as exposure to violence in the media, has any specific "effect" on a person, such as inducing him to behave more aggressively than he otherwise would. These particular activities tend to be smothered in a welter of other influences and personality traits in an individual's daily life. When the question is raised concerning a developing child, all the processes of maturation add to the confusion of social factors in the overall picture. It might, then, be considered a tribute to the perseverance and ingenuity of behavioral scientists that they have been able to come up with any answers to the "effects" question at all. But the reader should not be surprised that those answers are somewhat tentative, equivocal, and subject to several important qualifications.

Basically the answer turns out about the same as that indicated by the experimental studies of short-term effects. That is, heavy exposure to violence does appear to have long-term effects on children, rendering them more likely to behave aggressively toward their peers than youngsters who have experienced less cumulative exposure to violent portrayals. How are social scientists able to arrive at such a conclusion? The road has been a tortuous one, crossing several shaky logical bridges and guided by some signs that are not simple to read. Let us retrace several of the important steps.

First, the question has to be put in a relative way. Can it be shown that there is a statistical correlation, or association, between exposure to violence on television and aggressive behavior? If there were no such correlation, then we would have no basis for suspecting that there is any causal relationship between the two things. But the converse is not so clear. Even if there *is* such a correlation, there need not necessarily be any causal link, or it might be that causation runs in the reverse direction—i.e., that aggressive youngsters seek out violent programs to watch. To check these possibilities, researchers must seek out evidence of the *time order* of events; does exposure to violence precede aggressiveness, or follow it, in time? They must also eliminate "all other factors" from consideration. There might be some "factor X" that induces both violence viewing and aggressiveness; this would create a statistical association between these two behaviors, even though neither is causing the other. In short-term studies, "all other factors" are controlled by random assignment of children to the experimental and control conditions of the experiment; in long-term studies of natural variation this type of artificial control is not usually possible, and less "clean" methods of eliminating the possibility of factor X have to be devised. One obvious approach is to measure many of the other variables that might prove to be factor X and include them in the statistical package that is analyzed in the study. There are other, more subtle, techniques too.

To "measure" long-term exposure to violent programs, researchers have had to rely on statements by the child himself. A typical study used a list of sixty-five weekly "prime time" television shows, and asked each youngster in the survey to indicate how often he watched each program. These frequency scores were then multiplied by a coefficient of "violence ratings" for each program, based on assessments by critics and the general public of the amount of violence typically shown on each program. The sum of all these frequency-by-violence figures made up each child's overall measure of exposure to violence on television. Similarly, a youngster's preference level for violent programs was measured by asking him to list his four favorite programs; the sum of the violence rating scores for these four programs provide a single "violence preference" figure for each child.

Measuring aggressiveness is not so straightforward. There is a lot of disagreement about what is "agressive" behavior. For example, some people would classify swearing as undesirable aggression, while others would not. But some kinds of social behavior are clearly aggressive, and undesirable from the point of view of their victims. These include physical attacks on others, with or without weapons, and the use of threats of attack as a means of getting one's way. Since parents and peers all too often encourage these acts, many youngsters are not reluctant to admit them; self-reported aggressiveness scores yield results rather like those based on reports by

parents and teachers. But the best source of accurate "aggressiveness" ratings appears to be the peer group—the child's fellow students in school. The
most valid studies of youthful aggression are those that have measured
these behavioral tendencies by asking youngsters questions such as: "Who
in your class at school is most likely to hit, or threaten to hit, other children
to get his way?"

As we have indicated above, there is a statistical tendency for the
children who score high on measures of viewing violence also to be rated as
highly aggressive by their peers—and by themselves, for that matter. We
would not have bothered writing this chapter to this point, if this were not
the case. The correlation generally is found in all kinds of youngsters, regardless of age, sex, race, locale. The question that immediately arises is
whether this aggressiveness can be blamed on the heavy exposure to violence in the media. And the answer seems to be "yes," at least in some
measure.

Evidence of time order is unanimous in pointing to the conclusion that
viewing precedes aggressiveness, rather than the reverse. Several studies show
that viewing violence at an earlier time predicts later aggression more
strongly than the reverse pattern. Further, there is no correlation between
aggressiveness and a child's *preference* for programs characterized by violence; the aggressive youngsters seem to be those who "just happen" to
watch violence on television, without particularly seeking out this type of
show. And what about factor X? No one has been able to find a viable
candidate for this role, although many likely factors, such as intelligence,
social class, parental affection and punishment styles, and other communication influences have been tested. One study in New York showed that
viewing violence predicted aggressiveness in a sample of boys over a *ten-
year* period of their lives, even when all other factors that might have "predisposed" the youngsters to aggression were controlled statistically to remove any possible influence they might have. Taken together, these studies
of long-term effects point with a unanimity rare in social research to the
conclusion that continued heavy exposure to violence in the media does
tend to make youngsters more aggressive than they would otherwise be.
That is, of course, the same conclusion that has been reached from the great
majority of experimental short-term studies, which makes the two sets of
results even more impressive. It's always possible for improved scientific
techniques to produce a different conclusion at some time in the future, but
that seems unlikely considering that the many different types of studies to
date have produced mostly similar results.

The psychological mechanisms indicated in experimental studies also
seem to account for the long-term influences of violence in the media. A
survey of teenagers in Wisconsin and Maryland showed that learning and
imitation of aggressive behavior are an important intervening link in this

process. So is identification with violent characters, for boys at least; girls (and nonwhites) do not seem to identify much with the violent television and movie heroes—who are, of course, white males. Perception that a dramatic program is like real life is another key element to the process, as the Feshbach experiment described above would suggest. Unlike some of Feshbach's experiments, however, there is no evidence of "catharsis" having any long-term role in the relationship between violence in the media and youthful aggression. If that were the case, there would be negative correlations between viewing and aggressiveness among the children who are most "predisposed" to aggressive behavior; but that is not the case. If there are conditions under which catharsis of aggressiveness occurs as a result of watching violent shows, this hypothetical effect is probably no more than a temporary one. The great preponderance of evidence would suggest that it does not occur at all, although it is an intriguing, nonobvious proposition for psychologists.

CONTROLLING THE EFFECTS OF VIOLENCE IN THE MEDIA

If the mass media's proclivity for portraying violence has socially undesirable side effects, as research indicates, what can be done about it? One solution, which seems all too obvious to many observers, would be to pass a law prohibiting excessive violence in visual media. But that "cure"—even if such a law could be written and administered satisfactorily—would probably make more mischief than the problem it is aimed at. The First Amendment may not quite be "absolute," but exceptions to it are undertaken at great peril. Freedom of speech and of the press is as fundamental a precept as any underlying the American system of political and personal freedom. It extends to all forms of communication; as new technologies are introduced, they have a natural claim to the protection of the First Amendment. But the problem of violence is primarily one of artistic taste and originality, or the lack thereof, by the media; and such things are hard to legislate. Codes and restrictions tend to produce dull and slavishly plodding media performance. Cases in point are the heavily censored movies of the 1930s and 1940s, the "proletarian art" prescribed in the Soviet Union, German plays that were approved in the Nazi era—and present-day American commercial television, which is heavily constrained already by sponsor-sensitive programing executives. From a consumer's viewpoint, it would be hard to endorse any policy change that would make television programs even more bland and inane than so many of them already are. Certainly a law to that purpose, which would set a legal precedent for governmental control of media content, would not be worth its total cost to society.

Since television and film are already self-controlled to some extent anyway, perhaps this offers a potential road to social control of the violence that the media stimulate. We should encourage any efforts by scriptwriters and others in the entertainment media to break out of the straitjacket of violence and other clichés and seek fresh new dramatic themes. Because it appears to be sure-fire box-office material, violence is seized on far more often than it deserves by programers who hope to guarantee that their work will be a "success." This tendency is doubtless reinforced by the fact that vulgarity and sex, the other general themes with proven attractiveness to large media audiences, are de facto banned from television. Because television "comes into every living room," sex and vulgarity are censored from it to avoid complaints from the audience; violence is not, and it is thus one of the few "shock" devices left to television writers.

Whether the excessive violence of television drama (and comedy) is scaled down appreciably or not, there are other mechanisms that might reduce its effect. Dr. Jesse Steinfeld, Surgeon General of the United States, suggested to a Senate investigative committee in 1972 that television adopt a set of labels for its programs, similar to the "X," "R," "GP" system now used by the motion picture industry for self-regulation. Violent programs would be shown, but preceded by an announcement to this effect: "Warning: The Surgeon General has determined that watching the following program is dangerous to the mental health of children and, possibly, adults." This would probably not reduce the popularity of violent programs, any more than similar warnings have reduced cigarette smoking appreciably. But since the impact of violence on television viewers depends partly on the viewers' frame of mind (as in the Feshbach experiment described above, for example), providing "immunizing" contexts might well reduce the adverse behavioral impact of violent programs.

An alternative approach would be to institute controls "at the other end" of the viewing process, in the home. There are three general possibilities. One is for parents to regulate the child's viewing; to the extent that this has been tried, it does not seem to work very well, if only because youngsters who are deprived of programs they want to watch may well respond aggressively to the restriction itself. Another technique would be to counsel the child against aggressive behavior; this certainly meets the main problem head on, and it should be encouraged on general principles. A final possibility is for parents to help the child "interpret" what he sees on television, by explaining that dramatized violence is not "real" and pointing out instances where violence failed to achieve its goal or was used unnecessarily. Parental counseling of this sort could probably alleviate the problem to a great extent, because it would alter the mental "set" of the viewing child; unfortunately it would require an enormous change in behavior by parents, so many of whom exploit the television set as a cheap babysitter that diverts their children from other activities that might call for some special effort on the parents' part.

Parents, of course, are not totally responsible for the preparation of their children for the outside world. To a great extent, that job has been delegated to the schools. It is worth noting that there is no standardized school curriculum designed to prepare children to use the mass media, especially television, particularly with reference to the learning of social behavior or the interpretation of violence. By the time they graduate from high school, American children are likely to have spent more time in front of a television set than in class. During the remainder of their lives they will probably spend more time with television than with any other leisure-time pursuit; in an astonishingly large minority of cases, they will spend more time with television than in working for their livelihood. Yet, although there are curriculum modules covering many elements of life, our educational system has not developed a "preparation for television." Perhaps the topic does not seem "academic" enough; or perhaps the phenomenon of television has come upon our lives too suddenly. Whatever the reason, some sort of instruction or guided experience to help young people cope with the inputs they get from television seems a much needed innovation in American education.

USING THE MEDIA TO CONTROL VIOLENCE

While (as previous sections in this chapter indicate) the mass media contribute in some measure to the level of violence in our society, they are used more intentionally to control or reduce violence. In the very materials we have been discussing—detective novels, police dramas on television, western movies—the overriding theme is that of law enforcement and the supremacy of right and honesty. Probably no sector of our mass media industry has devoted itself so much to detailing the work of law officers as prime-time network television has in the past ten years.

This "law enforcement effort" has not been subjected to social or psychological research on a scale approaching that of the scientific assault on violence in these same, and other, programs. Yet it seems reasonable to assume that young people, and their elders, for that matter, learn law-abiding patterns of behavior from the media just as certainly as they learn aggressive and anti-social acts.

At least one study in the research on violence and children points in this direction. A study team headed by Dr. Aletha Huston Stein of Pennsylvania State University experimented with very young children in a preschool, by exposing some of them to an episode of "Misterogers' Neighborhood" that stressed efforts to help other people. After seeing this television program, the children were observed to be more helpful to one another than were similar children in a "control" group that had not seen the program. This finding provides strength for the conclusion that television is a school for all kinds of social learning, and it relieves us of the narrow notion that violence alone is learned from the media. It is probably more judicious to assume that *any media content is going to be "learned" to some extent by its audience*—the more so when that audience is young, or when the behavior is depicted as rewarded, or when it is tied to real life or to characters with whom the audience members feel an indentification or kinship.

It is possible, then, that the media could be used to control or minimize the level of violence in American society. This possibility has occurred to many people who have tried to deal with the problem of violence. In the Kerner Commission's report on civil disorders in 1968, it was suggested that in urban race riots radio "can do much to minimize fear by putting events into a proper perspective," and that when an incident breaks out there should be "a brief moratorium on reporting news" of it.

Beyond that, the Kerner Report took the media to task for a "failure to report adequately on race relations and the ghetto." The obvious implication in this is that the news media have the power to construct social situations for people, and that people will behave in accordance with these situations as they perceive them. This is the more important point at which eventual social violence can be controlled. To wait until destruction breaks out is to wait too long and to neglect the professional responsibility of the media.

REFERENCES

Seymour Feshbach, "Reality and Fantasy in Filmed Violence," in John P. Murray, Eli A. Rubinstein, and George A. Comstock (eds.), *Television and Social Behavior,* vol. 2., *Television and Social Learning* (Washington, D.C.: U.S. Government Printing Office, 1972).

Seymour Fesbach and Robert Singer, *Television and Aggression* (San Francisco: Jossey-Bass, 1971).

Joseph Morgenstern, "The New Violence," *Newsweek,* Feb. 14, 1972, pp. 66–69.

Report of the National Advisory Commission on Civil Disorders (New York: Bantam Books, 1968).

Aletha H. Stein and Lynette K. Friedrich (with Fred Vondracek), "Television Content and Young Children's Behavior," in J. P. Murray, E. A. Rubinstein, and G. A. Comstock (eds.), *Television and Social Behavior, Volume II, Television and Social Learning,* U.S. Government Printing Office, 1972.

SUGGESTED STUDY PROJECTS

1 Ask at least twenty-five children—ages about ten to twelve—to tell you which three television programs they watch most often with their parents, and then which three they watch with other children. Compile a list of the top ten programs in each category. Which has more violent programs, the list of shows viewed with parents, or the one for viewing with other children? What would you conclude about the role of other persons in the exposure of children to television violence?

2 Interview at least ten elementary school teachers to find out whether they give their students any instruction, formal or casual, in interpreting what they see on television. Do they deal with such topics as the reality (or lack thereof) of television dramatic presentations, or the role of violence versus other methods of resolving conflict? What kinds of instructional materials do these teachers think might help them to develop curriculum units on television that would be educationally worthwhile?

Chapter 17

Salvaging Our Environment

It seems strange in retrospect that widespread concern over the quality of the environment should have burst upon the American consciousness so abruptly in the late 1960s. The environment has always, after all, been with us. By definition, our physical environment is simply where we live. For years the goal of many Americans was to store up enough money and leisure so that they could "get away from it all" and "get back to nature." When they finally arrived there, they discovered that everyone else was there too and had made a fine mess of the place.

The historian Frederick Jackson Turner looked on the end of the frontier as the closing of an era in the American national story. The United States ceased to be a land of ever-expanding horizons by the end of the nineteenth century. But the concept of open land to be filled in, and of boundless natural resources to exploit, remained for another half-century or more. Now it is finally gone.

In its place is an uneasy awareness of the crisis proportions to which environmental depletion and pollution have grown. Huge regions suffer power failures on sultry summer days, when too many air conditioners are at work trying to create more pleasant indoor environments. Once-pristine waters have become unfit for drinking, or even swimming in. Lake Erie is near death, and at least one river flowing into it has been declared a fire hazard. The skies above "sunny" southern California are rarely visible through the smog. Snowmobiles, motorcycles, and dune buggies have transported the eternal noises of the city to what were once placid wildernesses. And things finally came full circle in the 1970s, as gasoline shortages began to curb the most obvious villain in the piece, the automobile. Bumper stickers tell us that "More is less."

But the search for scapegoats has turned up a surprising revelation. As the late Walt Kelly's comic strip character Pogo put it, "We have met the enemy and they are us." While it has been possible to identify and curb some environmentally unsound practices, often the cure has turned out to be as bad as the original problem. It is people who are using up our natural resources at a profligate pace, and it is people who are filling up the land with billions of tons of refuse. What is more disquieting, we are *all* at fault, the affluent at a far more voracious pace than the poor. Even worse, we don't seem to be able to stop, although the fuel shortages of the early 1970s at least convinced many of us to slow down.

Of all the abstract concepts that our culture has reified and treated as real and palpable, the goodness of Mother Nature is probably the most ingrained in our thinking. Prescientific physicists stated that "Nature abhors a vacuum," and nineteenth-century naturalists argued that we should not upset "the balance of Nature." (Others have asserted that it is nonetheless "human nature" to do so.) But looking at things scientifically we are hard put to identify Nature, much less to control it. Nature doesn't abhor anything; vacuums are simply a function of air pressure. Nature has no necessary balance; the central theme of natural history is constant change. And there is nothing "naturally" inherent in human beings that requires that they do foolish things to their physical surroundings.

If science finds other aspects of "Nature" hard to control, there is still a widespread faith in human ability to control humankind. One of the principal methods of self-control as people fight to save their physical environment is mass communication.

ECOLOGY AND THE STEADY STATE

Academic disciplines are filled with arcane and pedantic terms, many of them of Greek origin and quite incomprehensible to the lay person. Much of the content of introductory college survey courses consists of becoming conversant with such terms. In biology, one of the key over-arching concepts has for years been "ecology"—the study of the physical space surrounding human beings and other living things. But now ecology has gone public; it has become a shorthand reference for the totems and taboos of a new pantheism. As long as environmental resources seemed plentiful, they were taken for granted. Now that they have become scarce, they are worshiped. The environmentalist movement is no simple public fad. Some of the most distinguished scientists in the nation are enlisted in its cause. Before we turn to the role of communication in furthering that cause, it is worth our while to consider how this environmentalist ethic has come to be diffused so deeply and rapidly into the American social structure in the first place.

E-Day: A "Pseudo-event"

The historian Daniel Boorstin wrote in the early 1960s a provocative book entitled, *The Image: or What Happened to the American Dream?* In it, he introduced the concept of the "pseudo-event," which he argued had become the characteristic method of gaining access to the channels of communication in the age of the mass media. A pseudo-event is not something that really happens, but rather a contrivance to make it appear that something has happened in order to gain publicity for some business, institution, or cause. Thus, when a luxury hotel announces its twentieth birthday and throws a gala celebration in honor of the occasion, it is creating a pseudo-event that might, for no substantial reason, gain the hotel some free ink in the local newspaper or a short item on the evening television news. In the years when Hollywood dominated the film industry, movie studios hired publicity agents whose job was to create pseudo-events such as rumored romances linking two stars who just happened to be appearing together in a new picture.

Boorstin's image of a society functioning largely on pseudo-events turned out in the 1960s to be more prophetic than he could possibly have anticipated. Demonstrations against symbolic targets as well as the scheduling of observances of nonevents became the workaday tools of every cause, from the revolutionary left to the entrenched conservative "establishment." Indeed, the very term "demonstration" has come to imply an activity that is staged in order to attract public attention to some issue. This technique, along with the ubiquitous birthday observance, has been widely used on both sides of such issues as white racism, American prosecution of the Vietnamese war, and sexual inequality. The apotheosis of the "birthday" pseudo-event is the enormous expenditure of federal funds to celebrate the bicentennial of the American Revolution in 1976. The occasion is not, of course, an occasion at all, except in people's minds. It is seized on by the government as a plausible pseudo-event only because we happen to use a decimal mathematical system, so that the number 200 has a nice, round feel to it. Well-contrived pseudo-events seem to have a power to legitimize themselves no matter how outlandish they may appear to an outside observer of our national behavior. Indeed, as the sociologist Kurt Lang has pointed out, they become real events as soon as they occur—more real, in fact, than those that actually "happen" but fail to attract publicity.

Now a pseudo-event is not necessarily a bad thing, or even a silly one. There may be important and substantial ideas that cannot be brought out in any other way. News in the mass media tends to focus mostly on events and individuals. When concepts such as racism, sexism, or the abstract principles underlying the American Revolution are at stake, it is difficult to make "news" about them. This had been the core problem with environmental pollution for years. It was not easily recognizable and it was not newsworthy, so for any practical purpose it did not exist in the public mind. Then in the spring of 1970, all that was changed by a single well-planned pseudo-event. It was called, with ingenious simplicity, Earth Day, or E-Day. It is difficult to overestimate the changes it wrought in American society.

E-Day was a nationally organized and coordinated event, celebrated in different ways at university campuses such as Harvard, Texas, Pennsylvania, and Stanford, and at some 3,000 high schools and 1,000 colleges. Coming as it did in an era of sometimes violent campus anti-war demonstrations, it focused the country's attention on young people's capacity to appeal to the nation's conscience for a cause on which everyone could agree. Included in the day's activities were political leaders such as Senators Gaylord Nelson and Edmund Muskie and Mayor John Lindsay of New York, plus leading architects and environmental designers, among others. Students all over the country could be seen sporting large green "E" buttons for months afterward.

The environmental crisis had, of course, been building long before E-Day. Warnings had been sounded in best-selling books such as Rachel Carson's *Silent Spring* and Stewart Udall's *Quiet Crisis* in the decade before E-Day. But only when it "went public" could much be done about it. For some kinds of societal problems, it might be enough to have a small but devoted group of reformers hard at work on solutions. But the individual acts that add up to massive pollution do not seem like much in themselves. It probably would not matter much if one small town emptied its wastes into a large river like the Hudson; but when every town on the river takes that position, the river soon becomes hopelessly fouled. It is hard to tell an individual motorist in a city that his car is responsible for air pollution; he is likely to look about him and ask, "What about all those other cars?" And that is precisely the point that has had to be made. We have *all* had to come to look on ourselves as part of the problem.

Energy versus Environment

An even stranger twist to the story came with the energy crisis, which had also been building for some time, but struck the public consciousness with full force in the late fall of 1973. In this case the vehicle for making the point that oil, gasoline, and natural gas—and hence electricity, which is made mostly from fossil fuels—were in dangerously short supply was a speech on national television by Richard Nixon. In this case, there was no need for a pseudo-event, because citizens could already see signs of an imminent crisis—gas stations raising their prices and closing their doors, delayed fuel oil deliveries, and regional power failures.

Many immediate outcomes of the energy crisis were detrimental to the environmental cause. Such power-generating mechanisms as dams, transcontinental pipelines, and nuclear plants had been fought by environmentalists as damaging to water and wildlife. But the need for energy tended to override, in many minds, the desire for a pristine physical environment in locations remote from most population centers. A new politics came into being, pitting those who demanded new sources of energy against those holding out for preservation and restoration of the natural environment. The former took the play away from the latter, and they did it largely through the mass media—to which they had not had much access in the short years when environmentalism was riding high.

Two Voices, One Message

It is interesting to note, though, that while these two forces were clashing over major public works projects to generate power, they were recommending much the same courses of individual action to their mass media audiences.

Drive less often, more slowly, in a smaller car, the environmentalists pleaded; that will reduce air pollution. With the advent of the energy crisis, oil companies put ads on television and in magazines that said much the same thing, but for a different reason: to "help us through the energy crisis."

Keep your thermostat lower in the winter and minimize air conditioning in the summer, power companies begged; otherwise we will not be able to supply anyone with sufficient power. For some time the environmentalists had been making the same recommendations—to avoid the need for new sources of power, which would damage rivers and lakes and destroy wild areas.

Calls for reduced home use of electricity and restricted recreational use of fuels came from both sides, and they were echoed by politicians of both persuasions—those who had championed the environmental concern and those, like President Nixon, who had been considered something less than close allies by most environmentalists.

Countervailing Factors

When the contending parties on both sides of a public issue are advising people to do the same thing, it might seem that this alteration in individual behavior is practically inevitable. But it is not. For one thing, there are many industries that stand to lose a great deal if the anti-consumption recommendations are adopted permanently on a widespread scale. Tourist centers, manufacturers of large automobiles, and distributors of home appliances, to list three examples, will be hard hit if many people reduce their energy consumption significantly, whether in the interest of fuel conservation or environmental protection, or both. These and similar industries have for years maintained heavy advertising budgets to encourage people to do the very things that both the environmentalists and Big Energy are trying to discourage. It is unlikely that they will cease in this effort, although they must necessarily soft-pedal it as best they can while their erstwhile allies from the energy-producing industries are having to advertise *against* consumption of their own products.

Individual use of energy, and even depletion of the environment, is not nearly so individually determined as might seem the case on the surface. Suburbanization has separated workers' homes from their jobs by many miles and has all but killed public transportation in many urban areas. A worker cannot leave his car in the garage and take a bus to work when there is no bus; nor can he easily sell his suburban house and buy a smaller or older one that costs as much, simply because it is nearer his job. Similarly, those who work in new sealed-in buildings cannot do without their heating and cooling systems; the buildings have been designed on the presupposition that energy would continue to be available in unlimited supply.

Smaller cars will not be immediately adopted in a country whose manufacturers are reluctant to make them, which has erected tariff barriers to discourage foreign imports, and whose citizens have long been accustomed to measuring social prestige in terms of wheelbase, chrome, and horsepower. Many uses of natural resources that are not even common in many countries are required by law—to enforce a minimum standard of living—in the United States. (Flush toilets provide a homely example.) And of all the "convenience appliances" that could be turned off without a major loss in physical well-being in most homes, the television set is one of the greatest consumers of power. In a similar vein, one industry that contributes a great deal to water pollution through its heavy demand for wood pulp products is the daily newspaper.

THE ROLE OF THE MEDIA

As we have said, we do not seriously expect—or advocate—that people cease watching television and reading newspapers in order to reduce pollution. It seems a wiser course of action to take advantage of the fact that these media will continue to be attended by huge audiences; they can be used (1) to inform the public about energy-saving and pollution-abating steps individual citizens can take and (2) to provide various kinds of social support for those who alter their habitual consumption patterns accordingly.

Since this involves asking people to reorganize their lives in some ways, and to pass up a number of available conveniences, it is no easy matter. We will not attempt here to suggest which new behaviors people should adopt and which ones they should abandon. Feasible changes will vary from person to person and from place to place. Driving more slowly is a reasonable suggestion for pleasure motorists, but not for emergency ambulances. One could ask homeowners to give up their power lawnmowers and lawn fertilizers much more readily than one could make similar demands regarding farmers' tractor-drawn plows or pesticides.

The key to ensuring equity at the individual level is to enlist the support of the broad population in the general cause and then provide different audiences with specific suggestions that they *might* be able to put into effect. Everyone can recycle old newspapers, bottles, and cans, or turn out lights in empty rooms. But not everyone can ride a bicycle or bus to work or do without electrical equipment.

The concept of a "media mix" will not serve very well in this case. The audience is everyone, and all of us need to be reached through our particular media. Both kinds of content—general support for the goals of energy conservation and pollution abatement, plus specific suggestions of individual efforts that will help—need to reach each consumer. If they do not, those who give up pleasures and conveniences will be surrounded by others who fail to do so, and the total program will collapse.

The mass media have proved admirably effective at persuading individuals to do things—buy products, go places, enjoy themselves. While this has helped build a high-production, high-consumption economy, it has also created the crisis of energy and environment. So a new challenge arises. Whether the media can contribute to controlling these problems they have helped create, by encouraging people to be more selective in their patterns of consumption, is an open question.

As the media industries are presently constituted, there is good reason to doubt that they will meet this challenge. In the past, many factors, chiefly economic ones, have combined to make the media tools of pro-consumption interests. The crisis atmosphere created by environmental depletion and energy shortages has reversed this to some extent, but probably only temporarily. What seems to be needed is not so much a reversal—followed by an eventual counter-reversal into the traditional pro-consumption mode—as the achievement of a new "steady state" of more selective and judicious consumption of our national resources. The media could both engineer and reinforce this needed adjustment in American social behavior. The crises of the seventies provide the occasion for such a change, but they do not guarantee it.

There is another way in which the communication industry can help meet this challenge, and that is by providing alternative methods of bringing people together, other than physically transporting them to one place. Since transportation is a major user of consumer energy and polluter of the environment, there is likely to be a major effort to develop communication systems that will replace transportation systems in the future. We take up this possibility in Chapter 21, which deals with technological innovations in the communication industry and their impact on society.

REFERENCES

Daniel Boorstin, *The Image: or What Happened to the American Dream?* (New York: Atheneum Publishers, 1962).

Chapter 18

Mass Communication
and Sex

The story is told of a medieval monarch who had tried unsuccessfully for years to rid his empire of prostitution. Out of desperation, the emperor finally decreed that when known prostitutes died, their corpses would be carried—nude—through the streets. Prostitution soon was virtually eliminated.

In complex and more libertarian societies, control of undesirable sexual activities poses dilemmas more difficult than those faced by the desperate emperor. In America, our virtuous yet vague desire to control certain types of sexual behavior is matched by a lack of consensus on *what* to control as well and *how* to do it.

Most, if not all, societies, perceive some types of sex-related activity as detrimental to the public good. And governments have usually obliged by trying to offically control those activities. The emperor in the little anecdote above determined the sex norms for his society and marshaled his unrestricted powers to enforce compliance. But even the emperor had problems devising an effective program of control. Sex is a potent drive, and sexual activity is a vastly personal experience. So individuals with different backgrounds and personal norms quite naturally fail to agree completely on what may constitute a sex taboo.

Some American psychiatrists, psychologists, and sociologists have joined the patrons and practitioners of prostitution (the oldest profession in the world, by some accounts) in the view that it is functional for society. It provides, they argue, a sought-after service, helps curb other forms of sexual "deviance," and keeps prostitutes and vice squad detectives employed. Other influential people argue vociferously that prostitution is immoral, and they have convinced governments to make it criminal. Nor do Americans share a wide consensus about the social harmfulness of adultery, fornication, and homosexuality. Yet, most jurisdictions officially list those fairly common activities as "sex crimes."

"Controversial" seems to be an apt term to describe American attitudes toward those and similar "crimes." Research conducted for the Commission on Obscenity and Pornography indicated that Americans are divided on what types of sexual activity their governments should control. Other studies, such as the well-publicized research by A. C. Kinsey, suggest that a substantial portion of Americans do not behave as though they supported control of adultery, prostitution, and fornication. Yet a considerable segment of American society roundly condemns (at least verbally) sexual promiscuity. A minority of the Commission on Obscenity and Pornography called the research misleading and President Richard Nixon called the commission's conclusions "morally bankrupt." One thing does seem pretty clear: There is no real consensus about controlling many forms of sexual behavior.

There seems to be even less consensus on *how* to control genuinely undesirable sexual activity. Americans, for example, probably approach a consensus on the disdain for rape and on the need to control it. But what sorts of control mechanisms will our society tolerate? And which ones are likely to be effective?

Probably the most ideal control is prevention. We make rape a serious crime with heavy penalties, hoping that fear of punishment will deter the behavior. (Yet even making rape a capital offense did not seem to cause a decline in its occurrence in this country.) Societies frequently try to prevent illicit sexual behavior by controlling symbolic stimuli—including material in the mass media—which might provoke the behavior. We could, for example, prohibit discussion or depiction of rape in our newspapers, movies, and television programs. (That approach raises constitutional problems of freedom of expression. Moreover, there are serious doubts as to whether such controls would be effective preventatives.) American media could, and do, attempt to regulate their sex-oriented content. The code of Self-Regulation of the Motion Picture Association of American states, for example: "Illicit sex relationships shall not be justified. Intimate sex scenes violating common standards of decency shall not be portrayed. Restraint and care shall be exercised in presentations dealing with sex abberrations." (Such statements are, of course, vague; and the fact that compliance with self-regulation is basically voluntary makes the pronouncement little more than a platitudinous suggestion.)

Another preventative approach is to utilize (rather than control) communication to influence persons to limit their sex activities to the more commonly accepted versions. A basic thrust of "sex education" programs in schools and churches is that sex is a normal, healthy activity which can be especially rewarding when practiced conventionally. The effectiveness of such programs cannot yet be documented thoroughly, since they have only recently become widespread. Opposition to sex education programs is, of course, better established.

The major alternative to preventative controls has been coercion. Coercion inevitably takes the form of legal punishment for engaging in illicit sex-related activities. Long jail sentences force some rapists out of business, at least for a while. The electric chair was used to force some of them out of business for good. But there are at least two serious drawbacks to coercive controls: They only work after the fact, and they have not clearly been effective deterrents to future violations.

We are not trying here to plan a program for controlling rape or any other illicit sexual activity. Our point is that controls are probably most effective and least offensive when (1) there is some degree of consensus as to what, precisely, should be controlled, and (2) acceptable forms of control can be employed. Once a society establishes the need to control something, it has several options with regard to that control. These options have to be weighed against other social values (some of them in the form of constitutional guarantees). And they ought to be considered in terms of their likely effectiveness.

Controlling sexual behavior becomes a more acute problem if a society tries to control activities which many citizens do not view as particularly evil, with methods not generally conceded as appropriate. Mass communication has played a central role as both an object and a mechanism of control of sexual activity in this country.

MASS COMMUNICATION ABOUT SEX: CONTROL OF WHAT?

Most Americans would probably condemn public masturbation as an offensive activity and agree that efforts should be maintained to control such public displays. Suppose that a freewheeling newspaper published a cartoon depicting a judge masturbating behind the judicial bench. Under what, if any, conditions should a symbolic depiction of an offensive activity be restricted? Would it be sufficient to *presume* that the cartoon *might tend* to corrupt community standards of decency? Would penalties against the newspaper be justified on grounds that the cartoon seemed to glamorize masturbation? Would it make any difference if the publication were distributed primarily to adolescents? Or if the cartoon were an illustration for an article dealing with alleged judicial corruption? Or if the caption to the cartoon said: "Here come de judge!"?

American courts, which traditionally have been the arbiters of disputes over attempted regulation of sex portrayals in the media, have tried for nearly two centuries to come up with the answers to questions like that, but the status of legal doctrines governing such matters has remained fluid and doubtful.

Legal Views

The situation of the cartoon described above is not purely hypothetical. Such an illustration actually was published in 1969 by an "underground" publication in Washington, D. C.; it accompanied an article charging a judge with conflict of interest in certain trials over which he presided. A "hawker" for the publication was arrested in a Maryland suburb of the nation's capital for selling obscene material. A Maryland appeals court later overturned the vendor's conviction after finding the cartoon was not obscene and was protected by the First Amendment's guarantees of freedom of speech and press. The issues raised in that particular case *(Dillingham v State of Maryland)* illustrate some of the persisting problems of trying to control sexual behavior by regulating portrayals of sex in the media.

A key to those legal problems involves the connection between an actual offensive deed (in this case, public masturbation) and some symbolic representation of that deed (whether it be by gesture, photograph, cartoon, movie film, or words). In most legal areas involving restriction of mass communication, American courts have required that would-be suppressors demonstrate the connection to be unmistakenly present. Not so with communication dealing with sex-related material, however.

Our legal doctrines have *assumed* that certain sex-related communications (labeled by the law as "obscene") are obviously detrimental to society. Obscenity, in short, has never been protected by the First Amendment. And that, in the long run, has caused confusion about *what* can be legally suppressed. In other words, just what *is* "obscenity"?

Throughout its tangled history, obscenity has been a term without precise legal definition. Not until the 1950s did the Supreme Court attempt a comprehensive definition of that nasty unmentionable. Early American statutes described obscenity only in terms of synonyms: material which was "vile," "indecent," "lewd and lascivious," or "filthy." When courts had to interpret those statutes, they looked to the English-inspired "Hicklin rule" for guidance. The Hicklin rule said that material was "obscene" if it had a "tendency" to "deprave and corrupt those whose minds are open to such immoral influences and into whose hands a publication of this sort may fall."

Such a doctrine, of course, allowed sweeping suppression of material dealing with sex. For one thing, government only had to allege that the material "tended" to "deprave and corrupt" public morals. For another, it presumed that overall public standards of morality were no higher than those of the most susceptible, depravable member of society; if something was likely to be harmful to one reader, it should be kept away from everybody. As though the Hicklin rule were not repressive enough, American courts tacked on a "partly obscene" doctrine which allowed an entire work to be declared obscene on the basis of isolated parts. So it became possible to ban an entire book as obscene because of a single passage.

Works including Whitman's *Leaves of Grass* and Voltaire's *Candide* were banned as obscene under these doctrines. But the unholy combination of the Hicklin rule and the "partly obscene" doctrine sustained American obscenity law until the 1930s. From the mid-1930s to the mid-1950s, courts chipped away, with some notable marks, at the old doctrines. In 1933, a federal judge ruled that James Joyce's *Ulysses* was not obscene. Something is obscene, the judge said, only if it

> tends to stir the sex impulses or to lead to sexually impure and lustful thoughts. Whether a particular book would tend to excite such impulses must be the test by the court's opinion as to its effect (when judged as a whole) on a person with average sex instincts.

The 1933 definition was an improvement. It eliminated the "partly obscene" doctrine and declared that the "average" person—rather than the most susceptible—should be considered when defining obscenity. But it did retain the old notion that judges were gifted enough to determine whether material would tend to stir someone else's sexual impulses or lead to lustful thoughts.

Then, in 1957, the Supreme Court of the United States handed down a new legal definition of obscenity. In its famous *Roth v United States* decision, the Court said that portrayals of sex in mass communication could be prosecuted as obscene if "to the average person, applying contemporary community standards, the dominant theme of the material taken as a whole appeals to prurient interest."

The *Roth* definition, though widely quoted in statutes and subsequent court decisions, is not as libertarian as it looks. It retains elements of the "tendency to corrupt" theme of the Hicklin rule. And it opened up new questions that begged for clarification, such as: Who is the "average person"? What are "contemporary community standards," and how do you ascertain them? What is necessary to show "appeal to prurient interest"? American courts struggled with such questions for a decade after *Roth,* and the Supreme Court gradually added new elements to the definition. In 1962, the Court held that in order to be judged obscene, material had to be "patently offensive"—that is, it had to affront community standards of decency to such a degree that the material was offensive on its face. In that particular case *(Manual Enterprises v Day),* the Court ruled that magazines portraying nude males and aimed primarily at homosexuals were not obscene. In 1966, the Supreme Court held that to be obscene, material had to be lacking any "redeeming social value." That decision overturned attempts by at least four states to ban John Cleland's classic *Memoirs of a Woman of Pleasure* (also known as *Fanny Hill*). The Court held that the book, which candidly described Fanny's sexual escapades, had social value (and was therefore not obscene). The Library of Congress apparently saw its value too; it had previously asked permission to translate the book into Braille.

For a four-year period beginning in 1966, the Supreme Court seemed to be giving up trying to define obscenity. The Court started to look at the *behavior* of the purveyors of allegedly offensive material. In 1966, the Court upheld the conviction of Ralph Ginzburg, who published *Eros* magazine, a booklet titled *The Housewife's Handbook on Selective Promiscuity,* and other titillating publications. Ginzburg lost his appeal—not because the *content* of his publication was obscene, but because of his *conduct* in publicizing and marketing his merchandise. Ginzburg had advertised one of his publications as a manual for "the sexually elite"; he also had tried to have *Eros* mailed from two Pennsylvania towns named Intercourse and Blue Ball. Such behavior, the Court concluded, was "pandering" to the prurient interests of his potential readers. In effect, the Court told Ginzburg: Your publications themselves probably are not obscene, but if you promote them as being obscene, we'll take your word for it. Ginzburg thus became an unwitting victim of a new legal doctrine made retroactive to apply to him. Many observers have decried what they consider unfair treatment of Ralph Ginzburg.

A fundamental question raised by the Ginzburg case is whether regulation of conduct rather than of content is a more prudent approach to legal control of obscenity. The Supreme Court seemed to think it was, at least from 1967 to 1973. Perhaps the Justices had become resigned to the futility of trying to classify material as obscene or not obscene. Perhaps they could not agree on a legal definition of obscenity. Perhaps they were tired. In a 1967 decision *(Redrup v New York)*, the Court gave indications that it was plagued by all three possibilities. In that case, the Court hinted that in the future, obscenity convictions might be sustained only if the *conduct* of publishers and distributors consisted of (1) "pandering" in promotion, as in the Ralph Ginzburg case; (2) making offensive material available to juveniles in violation of a state statute; or (3) thrusting offensive material upon an individual against that person's will.

Redrup reaffirmed, at least temporarily, a movement toward controlling behavior of "smut peddlers" as opposed to smut itself. It also signaled a trend toward recognizing that standards of decency reside in *individuals* rather than in society as a whole or in the "average person." Within two years after the *Redrup* decision, the Supreme Court had overturned nearly forty obscenity convictions because lower courts had looked at content rather than conduct.

Congress, too, took up the conduct banner. A federal "anti-pandering" statute allows individual citizens to judge for themselves whether material they received through the mail offends them by being "erotically arousing or sexually provocative." Citizens can complain to the Postal Service, which will order the sender to stop sending such material to that citizen.

Another indication that the law might be backing away from defining broad standards of decency for all citizens was the 1969 Supreme Court decision *Stanley v Georgia.* The court held that individual citizens may possess and use obscene materials in the privacy of their homes. "If the First Amendment means anything," Justice Thurgood Marshall wrote for the Court, "it means that a State has no business telling a man, sitting alone in his own house, what books he may read or what films he may watch." But the beleaguered Supreme Court refused to extend Marshall's opinion to its ultimate conclusion. Logically, if a citizen has a right to possess obscene materials at home, should not distributors of such materials have a right to deliver the wares to customers who want to exercise that right? The Court in 1971 answered "no." Moreover, in 1973 a 5-to-4 majority headed by Chief Justice Warren Burger announced new legal guidelines for determining and controlling obscenity. The court (in *Miller v California*) went back to a *content* standard, ruling that materials are pornographic "which, taken as a whole, appeal to the prurient interest in sex, which portray sexual conduct in a patently offensive way, and which, taken as a whole, do not have serious literary, artistic, political or scientific value." In the same decision,

Burger threw out the *Fanny Hill* doctrine that to prove obscenity the government had to establish that the material was "utterly without redeeming social value." And in addition, Burger announced that varying local community standards could be applied to determine whether the material met the new definition of obscenity. The Court had hardly uttered its 1973 decision before local prosecutors and vice squads started scurrying to "crack down" on theaters, bookstores, and newsstands. In some localities, the crackdown even extended to purges of libraries and *Playboy* magazine. To many observers the *Miller v California* decision signaled a new era of repressive control.

This discussion of obscenity law conveys an impression of legal confusion. Actually, the intricacies of legal attempts to control media portrayals of sex are even more complicated than our simplified treatment of the topic here suggests. One clear theme should emerge, though: Over the years, even the Supreme Court has been unable to reach a long-term consensus regarding what kinds of sexual portrayals in the media ought to be regulated. As Professors Dwight Teeter and Don Pember aptly put it in an article in a law review (1971):

> Obscenity may not be a four-letter word, but such words are frequently the response of scholars attempting to uncover logic or meaning in this area of the United States law, in short, to interpreters of American jurisprudence—jurists, lawyers and laymen—obscenity is becoming a dirty word.[1]

Views of Citizens

American citizens, according to available evidence, do not agree on what obscenity laws should protect them from. If the lack of consensus among laymen is less pronounced than that among judges, it might be because citizens have not tried very hard to enunciate their confusion.

Numerous individuals and groups have emerged as self-appointed spokesmen for the "average citizen." Judges, as we mentioned above, have sometimes guarded their position as voice of the people on matters relating to sex-related presentations in the mass media. Organizations such as Citizens for Decent Literature frequently attempt to define and enforce standards for media portrayals of sex. Local, state, and national legislators elected by citizens pass obscenity statutes which supposedly reflect the sentiment of their constituents.

Trying to *accurately* assess public moods about what should be regulated does not usually yield clean-cut sentiments. Consider the following:

[1]Dwight L Teeter, Jr., and Don R. Pember, "Obscenity, 1971: The Rejuvenation of State Power and the Return to Roth," *Villanova Law Review,* December 1971, p. 211.

In a 1969 Gallup poll, 85 percent of American adults interviewed said they favored stricter laws regulating obscenity sent through the mails. In the same poll, 76 percent said they favored stricter control of newsstand sales of offensive sex-related material.

Research for the Commission on Obscenity and Pornography indicated that about 85 percent of adult American men and 70 percent of adult American women have viewed explicit sexual material in the media.

A majority of commission members felt, on the basis of research, that "a majority of the American people presently are of the view that adults should be legally able to read or see explicit sexual materials if they wish to do so."

A dissenting member of the commission claimed that Americans have "enough common sense to know that one who wallows in filth is going to get dirty. This is intuitive knowledge."

Such controversy should not be surprising. Neither should the apparently contradictory findings of public opinion polls. For not until recently have scientific efforts been made to find out whether citizens do indeed agree on what should be controlled.

Empirical research reviewed by the Commission on Obscenity and Pornography does shed some light on the apparent experiences of Americans with erotic material in the media. A majority of the commission's members interpreted the research as demonstrating that:

Exposure to erotic material does result in sexual arousal in substantial numbers of both males and females.

Most people reported no increase in the amount of intercourse or masturbation after being exposed to erotic materials.

Some persons reported that they felt more willing to discuss sexual matters with their marriage partners after they viewed erotic material.

Sex-oriented material appeared to have little effect on a person's established attitudes toward morality.

Convicted sex offenders have had less exposure to erotica as adolescents than other adults.

The commission's studies are only a tentative appraisal of how citizens evaluate and use erotic matter. But they suggest some important questions. Does American society want to control the private sexual arousals of its citizens? If some materials have no provable effect on standards of morality or on frequency of intercourse, should they be controlled at all? Are we engaged in overkill by controlling materials which might actually help prevent sex crimes?

Some citizens favor stronger controls over a wide range of sexual portrayals. Law enforcement officials typically take such a stand. The late

J. Edgar Hoover claimed that "indecent and pornographic literature is creating sex criminals faster than we can build jails to contain them." Letters to the Commission on Obscenity and Pornography from police officals throughout the country echoed a similar theme.

Many social workers, psychiatrists, and educators, on the other hand, feel that some types of erotic material actually help prevent sex crimes. Two psychologists, Drs. Eberhard and Phyllis Kronhausen, have been leading proponents of that point of view. The Kronhausens distinguished two basic types of erotica: hard-core pornography and "erotic realism." The latter form, they claim, is actually therapeutic for society, since it provides an outlet for open expression of ideas and feelings.

The Kronhausens characterize "erotic realism" as frank but realistic portrayals of sexual activity. Hard-core pornography, on the other hand, is that type of material based on pure fantasy and designed specifically for erotic stimulation. The Kronhausens say that hard-core pornography has three identifiable features: a constant succession of erotic scenes; a buildup of erotic excitement in the course of the text; emphasis on the physical sex responses of the participants, and the portrayal of extreme sexual activities (such as incest and flagellation) as attractive. Such material presumably could be a legitimate target for some kind of governmental control; no claim is made that it has therapeutic value.[2]

Conflict of Views

There are, then, deep and genuine differences of opinion in American society about what kinds of erotic material, if any, ought to be controlled. Our laws reflect the view that material which incites lustful thoughts or sexual arousal, or which is distributed in a pandering or intruding fashion, needs to be regulated. Some citizens would control even more types of erotica. Others would control only the sale of "hard-core" pornography to juveniles. There may be general consensus that *harmful* materials need to be controlled, but much disagreement on what "harmful" means. One result is that the various control mechanisms that our society has devised often seem to work against each other. That problem is discussed in the following section.

MASS COMMUNICATION TO CONTROL S– –

American society traditionally has employed control mechanisms to both prevent and punish undesirable sexual activity. Mass communication has become involved in both types of control because society has presumed a

---

[2]Eberhard Kronhausen and Phyllis Kronhausen, *Pornography and the Law*. Ballantine Books. New York, 1964.

connection between portrayals of sex in the media and the sexual behavior of media audiences. The law, the media themselves, and citizen groups have been used as control agents in this country.

Legal Controls

Legal sanctions against erotic material in the media involve elements of prevention and punishment. The sanctions commonly take the form of criminal statutes which allow prosecution for portraying obscene material. (Forty-eight states have such statutes; the federal government has five.) The rationale of obscenity statutes is that keeping salacious material out of circulation will help prevent moral turpitude. Violating the statutes can result in punishments that include fines and prison terms.

The notion that symbolic portrayals of sex constitute potent forces which may cause people to engage in undesirable sexual activities has been disputed by empirical studies, by the professional judgment of many psychologists and psychiatrists, and by a majority of the Commission on Obscenity and Pornography. The latter group, as a result, recommended that all existing federal, state, and local statutes prohibiting distribution of erotic materials to consenting adults should be repealed. Instead, they suggested new statutes to regulate distribution of "explicit sexual material" to juveniles and to prohibit public displays of offensive sexual materials. That recommendation was rejected by then-President Nixon.

Denmark repealed its obscenity laws in 1967 after a government commission concluded that there was no scientific evidence that pornography resulted in the commission of sex crimes by normal people. Since then, sales of obscene material have actually dropped in Denmark.

Self-Control by the Media

The mass media, of course, are subject to legal sanctions if they violate obscenity laws. But many media have imposed upon themselves stricter regulations about sexual portrayals than the law would require. A medium often sees itself as a standard-bearer for American decency and a mirror of what it views as proper conduct.

The media have therefore become agents of social control in matters concerning sexual conduct. They, in effect, attempt to define and maintain sex norms. Norm-setting activity by the media takes various themes. Some media "codes" for proper treatment of sexual topics seem to reflect past rather than contemporary sex norms. Most general-audience magazines and newspapers still refuse to spell out words they consider offensive. Germaine Greer was fined $40 in a New Zealand court in 1972 for uttering bad language in public. American news media reported the incident, but most managed to get around quoting the nasty word which brought the fine.

United Press International said she had muttered "a euphemism for sexual intercourse." Other media found other ways to avoid using the word. A few were bold enough to use "f---." And, of course, "expletive deleted" became a stock phrase in the 1974 "White House transcripts," as well as in the news reports of their contents.

The "codes of ethics" of several mass communication organizations prescribe certain standards for treating sex-related material. The Television Code of the National Association of Broadcasters states that "profanity, obscenity, smut, and vulgarity" are forbidden on television programs. The Code of Self-Regulation of the Motion Picture Association of America warns against "obscene speech, gestures, or movements." Both codes, along with the Radio Code of the NAB, state that their members should "honor the sanctity of marriage and the home" in their productions.

Sometimes media self-regulation results from fear of possible new legal controls. That was the case with the movie industry in 1969 when it introduced its "G," "PG," "R," and "X" rating system. The ratings, it was argued, would keep juveniles away from sexually explicit movies and therefore would curb legal attempts to censor or ban films. The rating system has been controversial from its inception. Some critics say it promotes pornography by allowing X-rated movies. Others say it stifles free expression because many theaters refuse to show X-rated films and many newspapers refuse to accept advertisements for them.

Self-regulation by the media may be preferable to government control, from the standpoint of the First Amendment. But both involve censorship, a negative form of control.

Communication as a Positive Control

In recommending repeal of existing obscenity statutes, the Commission on Obscenity and Pornography stated its belief that

> much of the "problem" regarding materials which depict explicit sexual activity stems from the inability or reluctance of people in our society to be open and direct in dealing with sexual matters.

The Commission seemed to be supporting the viewpoint of the Kronhausens and others (discussed earlier in this chapter) that more frank and unrestricted communication about sex might actually help control sex crimes. But prospects look dim for repealing obscenity statutes in the near future, although forms of "positive controls" through increased communication are still possible; some already exist. The commission suggested three possible "positive controls":

A massive sex education effort for both young people and adults. The programs presumably could utilize several existing social institutions, including the mass media. The aims would be to develop healthy attitudes toward sex; to get people to accept sex as natural and normal; and to acquaint people with the differing attitudes in this country toward sex and sex behavior.

Increased open discussion about control of obscenity, based on factual information about its effects. The commission stated that research on the uses and effects of erotic materials contradicted many widely held assumptions. It also suggested more research in that area.

Widespread participation by citizens in organizations devoted to discussing and debating sex behavior and sex portrayals. "People tend to assume," the commission noted, "that most people's opinions are similar to their own." Citizen groups composed of a wide spectrum of persons could thus promote accurate knowledge about a community's attitudes toward sex.

In addition, the mass media might exert a positive control by treating sex more naturally and frankly. The movie industry and publications such as *Playboy* have helped divert discussion of sex from clandestine media to more public forums. Reluctance by other media to use certain words or portray certain scenes under any circumstances probably bolsters the notion that sex is unnatural and illegitimate.

SEX, COMMUNICATION, AND FREEDOM

The "positive controls" suggested above will not eliminate sex crimes. The negative controls imbedded in our legal system certainly have not. The key to complete prevention might well lie in an ingenious scheme like the one devised by the anti-prostitution emperor.

American attempts to control illicit sex behaviors by restricting communication often clash with constitutional guarantees of freedom of expression. America seems quite uncertain about its attitude toward behavior and media portrayals of sexual themes. We need to ponder whether our present legal controls are counterproductive. We need to consider whether a system of positive controls might also be counterproductive.

Most of all, perhaps, American society needs to consider whether our present system of negative controls offends our standards of f-----m.

REFERENCES

Books and Articles

The Report of the Commission on Obscenity and Pornography (New York: Bantam Books, 1970).
William Rivers and Wilbur Schramm, *Responsibility in Mass Communications* (New York: Harper & Row, 1969).

Harold L. Nelson and Dwight L. Teeter, Jr., *Law of Mass Communications* (Mineola, N. Y.: Foundation Press, 1974).

Dwight L. Teeter, Jr. , and Don R. Pember, "Obscenity, 1971: The Rejuvenation of State Power and the Return to *Roth*," *Villanova Law Review,* December 1971, pp. 211–245.

Eberhard and Phyllis Kronhausen, *Pornography and the Law* (New York: Ballantine Books, 1964).

Suzanne Yeager, *G-PG-R-X: Forced Self Regulation:* (Columbia, Mo.: Freedom of Information Center, 1971).

John McCormick and Mairi MacInnes (eds.), *Versions of Censorship* (New York: Doubleday, 1962).

Court Decisions

Dillingham v State of Maryland, 267 A.2d 777 (1970).

United States v One Book Called "Ulysses," 5 F.Supp. 182 (1933).

Roth v United States, 354 U. S. 476 (1957).

Manual Enterprises v Day, 370 U. S. 378 (1962).

A Book Named "John Cleland's Memoirs of a Woman of Pleasure" v Attorney General of the Commonwealth of Massachusetts, 383 U. S. 413 (1966).

Ginzburg v United States, 383 U. S. 463 (1966).

Miller v California, 93 S. Ct. 2607 (1973).

Redrup v New York, 388 U. S. 767 (1967).

Stanley v Georgia, 394 U. S. 557 (1969).

SUGGESTED STUDY PROJECTS

1 Interview at least twenty students, asking them this question: "What is obscenity?" Do the responses tend to support the conclusion made in this chapter regarding lack of agreement on what the term means? How do the responses break down in terms of defining "obscenity" as *conduct* rather than media *content*?

2 Investigate the current state of the law regarding obscenity in your state, county, or city. What definitions of "obscenity" are found in your statutes or ordinances? Have there been recent convictions under these laws? On what grounds did the court convict or acquit the defendant?

Chapter 19

Mass Communication
and Radicalism

All organisms, from the simple amoeba to the complexity we call a pluralistic society, develop mechanisms for survival. The desire to keep stable in the face of serious threats is probably the most intense and powerful drive operating throughout a society. In one sense, governments exist to protect societies from dangers (both internal and external) which could bring about societal collapse if left unchecked.

Ideas and movements considered dangerous to existing political and economic institutions are often labeled "radical" by conventional usage. The radical advocates a profound, fundamental change in the way things are done. And resistance to drastic social alterations—particularly to sudden ones—is inevitable in any society.

The historian Charles Merriam, writing in 1931, observed that

> every modern state develops a far-reaching program designed to maintain the morale of its constituent members where their activities will fit in with and perform the functional activities necessary for group survival.[1]

[1]Charles E. Merriam, *The Making of Citizens,* University of Chicago Press, Chicago, Ill., 1931, p. 13.

Such programs vary from nation to nation; often they also vary within a nation over time. In most technologically developed societies, mass communication provides a natural control tool since it can reach a good share of the citizenry. The ways that mass communication becomes involved in controlling radicalism are likely to vary according to place and circumstance.

Radicalism is a particularly evasive victim for social control schemes. One reason is its macroscopic nature. An innovative idea is not usually considered radical (and thus potentially threatening) unless it seems likely to disrupt a value held dear to the whole society. Closing off a street in a residential suburb for a "block party," or even to protest heavy traffic, might bring amusement, toleration, or even cooperation from authorities. But if protestors block major traffic arteries in the nation's capital during rush hour, it is viewed as radical disruption because it strikes at the heart of a government's desire to function normally.

Moreover, radicalism takes the form of a movement built on ideology. How does a society check a group of dedicated persons? And can it control the spread of the idea which unifies them? Controlling radicalism is difficult for another reason: control mechanisms have to be developed which are productive, yet tolerable to society. Experience has shown (in this country in 1776 and in many other countries) that over-repressive controls breed even more discontent and can result in total revolution. History should also have taught us that ideas cannot be killed off through coercion.

Communication helps keep a society on an even keel by managing social tension. This task can be approached by strategies to counteract possible seeds of discontent. It can be done by confronting the words and actions considered part of the discontent itself. Or it can include elements of both approaches.

Few societies ever reach consensus on political and economic values. Human beings, left to their own talents, naturally seem to disagree about things. Social consensus, therefore, is usually an unnatural phenomenon resulting from a compulsory program such as cradle-to-grave indoctrination. Yet some societies consider absence of consensus a serious threat, and so they attempt to eradicate expression which symptomizes disagreement over goals and values. Under such a system, words which propose radical actions are a main target of the control program. The aim is to create an illusion of consensus and thereby reduce tension.

Even pluralistic societies strive for some degree of consensus on political and economic issues, knowing it can never be completely attained. A pluralistic society needs some means of cementing its diverse parts together so that it will not come apart with every small stress. What we usually call democratic societies have decentralized programs, with a host of institutions and agencies, both public and private, trying to prevent and punish threats to the political and economic order. The agencies may each employ different strategies, and sometimes they may even disagree on goals. Decentralization may make effective control more difficult, but it probably makes freedom more real.

Pluralistic, decentralized societies usually exert less coercive control over radicalism than centralized, homogeneous ones. As Professor John D. Stevens of the University of Michigan explains: "If there is not much centralized power, a society must try to avoid issues which will wreck its fragile coalition. In such a situation, a society has to endure some diversity of opinion."[2] Yet no modern society deliberately allows its control programs to become dispersed and unmanageable to the point of ineffectiveness. Controls become most overt, most noticeable, most coordinated when threats to society appear to be most grave. Consequently, control over radical expression and action is usually tightest during "rough times"—as we will illustrate later in this chapter.

The ways a society uses communication to manage tension can be a good gauge of the character of the society and of the time. A free society may have to *try* to avoid tension by tolerating dissent, as Professor Stevens suggests. But complete avoidance is never likely to occur. So in times of stress, dissident expression is frequently viewed as a poison rather than a safety valve, and suppression is more likely to be considered an appropriate antidote.

MASS COMMUNICATION AS A CONTROL

Societies rely on mass communication to deal with radicalism and the tensions it may cause. Three communication strategies are common, and pluralistic societies such as America develop programs which combine all three. First, mass media can be used to *integrate* citizens' political values. Second, mass media are used to help citizens *evaluate* their values and those of other citizens. Finally, the media are tools for those who wish to *advocate* values.

Integration—"The Melting Pot"

If asked to describe the "ideal democracy," most Americans could probably rattle off a list of conditions which are supposed to represent the "American way of life." The list would no doubt include citizen sovereignty through voting, a governmental structure which provides for majority rule but protects minority rights, and an economic system independent of total government control. The abstract democratic ideals of most Americans have been

---

[2]John D. Stevens, "Freedom of Expression: New Dimensions," in Ronald T. Farrar and John D. Stevens (eds.), *Mass Media and the National Experience*, Harper and Row, New York, 1971.

fairly well integrated; there is considerable consensus about what our country is supposed to stand for. Such agreement on abstract goals does not happen by accident or coincidence. It is largely a product of a deliberate program of civic training whose ultimate goal is to inspire allegiance toward the political system and to discourage radical dissent.

As a communication strategy, integration stresses formality and symbolism. Several American institutions in various ways use communication to help promote conformity and consensus on political values. In the schools, advocates of the "integrative-consensual" model of formal education championed by John Dewey and his followers seek to perpetuate the notion of America as a pot in which differing values can be melted down into a harmonious blend. Conventional information about American traditions and government institutions is utilized to dampen subcultural loyalties and radical ideas. The mass media provide supplemental material for that kind of civic training. Besides textbooks, the news and entertainment content in the media often emphasize the desirability of harmony and allegiance to our political and economic institutions. Traditional Fourth of July parades and patriotic speeches are scarcely underplayed in the media. Nor would a television network think of interrupting the national anthem which inevitably precedes athletic events.

Some families also use integrative communication strategies in bringing up children; the parents try to teach their children to avoid controversy by limiting dissent in the home and by restricting children's access to those mass media which might provoke alternative ideas. Other institutions such as churches, employers, and voluntary organizations use communication to inculcate loyalty.

Integration, then, tries to promote agreement among citizens on certain basic political values. Integrative communication channels are usually formal and structured—the schoolroom civics lesson, the Sunday sermon, the pledge of allegiance. Its content makes liberal use of patriotic symbols. Information is controlled because integrators think too much information will create doubt.

Evaluation—"Work within the System"

If America's tension-management programs were strictly integrative, we would be hard pressed to claim freedom. Consensus on ideals may well be useful, but widespread agreement on how to carry out those goals is antithetical to a society which values citizen input and freedom of expression. Many educators, politicians, and other "control agents" argue that radicalism can best be managed by an informed, enlightened citizenry. If citizens have accurate knowledge about the political system, including its weaknesses, they can use constitutional channels to correct shortcomings. That, in the long run, is considered the best safeguard against a drastic radical upheaval. The overall goal is to increase the political efficacy of the citizenry—to make a society of intelligent, questioning citizens who can guide society toward its goals.

Evaluative communication strategy is largely unstructured and informal. Some would even call it "permissive." Many educators prefer to discuss concepts (rather than transmit "hard facts") and encourage students to analyze and compare alternatives. Likewise, some parents encourage children to seek out alternative viewpoints on a wide range of matters; often these parents allow children to participate in family decision making as a means of learning to evaluate conflicting ideas.

The mass media provide a plethora of contrasting viewpoints on a multitude of subjects, including the status of our political system. The news media, through interpretative reporting, prod citizens into evaluating complex controversies. Mass communication therefore is a mighty tool for citizens and groups who see evaluation as the best means for America to deal with social tension, for the media allow citizens to compare society's ideals with its actual performance.

While integration seeks to achieve consensus, evaluation seeks to achieve *accuracy* and *understanding* in society. It tries to give each citizen a correct and complete picture of society's goals and a report of society's performance in meeting those goals. It also tries to get citizens to acquire skills in comparing (i.e., understanding) different viewpoints about goals and performance. An important tenet of evaluative communication strategy is that information, in the long run, will reduce (rather than create) doubt about the worth of our political and economic institutions. Evaluation embodies the classic philosophy of a "free marketplace of ideas" expounded by John Stuart Mill in his nineteenth-century treatise *On Liberty*. That idea has provided the framework for much of our theory concerning freedom of expression, from court interpretations of the First Amendment to newspaper slogans like "Let the people have the truth and freedom to discuss it and all will go well."

Advocacy

If there is to be a free marketplace of ideas, that is, if citizens are to have access to all possible opinions about the viability of their government and its policies, persons of all persuasions, from the most conventional to the most radical, need to have the means to communicate their views. One sign that a society is mature and self-confident about its survival is that it permits such advocacy. Of the three types of tension management, advocacy is the most risky for society, especially for a pluralistic one which has no wide consensus on political values. But many societies, including ours, take the risk to some extent. Supreme Court Justices Louis Brandeis and Oliver Wendell Holmes, writing in a 1927 court opinion *(Whitney v California)*, explained why we should take it:

> Those who won our independence believed that the final end of the state was to make men free to develop their faculties. . . .They believed that . . . the greatest menace to freedom is an inert people. They recognized the human risks to which all human institutions are subject. But they knew that order cannot be secured merely through fear of punishment for its infraction . . . that the path of safety lies in the opportunity to discuss freely supposed grievances and proposed remedies. . . .

Advocacy can be a good control strategy. It may be safer to let political radicals advocate their causes through mass communication than to force them into clandestine tactics. Yet America has not granted total license in this area. No society ever has. In this country a system of controls ranging from formal legal sanctions to harassment helps keep the voices of radicalism from talking too loud or advocating things considered too dangerous for "democratic" ears.

Radical advocates have been among the country's most prolific users and developers of mass communication vehicles. Nearly every radical movement worth its salt has to produce materials for the media. Leaflets, underground newspapers, and underground films are common staples of the radicals' media "menu." Journalists have been known to scoff at what they consider the amateurish and uncouth quality of some radical attempts at mass communicating. Legal authorities, on the other hand, have often taken a more serious and stern stance. Judging from the legal actions taken against some types of radical advocacy, American officials have felt threatened by the so-called amateurs.

Much constitutional law has been molded through American society's efforts to restrain radical expression. Some of the greatest victories for an expanding freedom of speech and press have come from unsuccessful attempts to punish promoters of radical causes.

GOVERNMENT CONTROL OF RADICAL EXPRESSION

America's establishment media should be grateful to radical communicators for at least one fact: "rabble-rousing agitators" have been at the forefront of many important victories for freedom of the press. Often the confrontations took place during periods of great national tension, when most conventional media considered it their patriotic duty to support consensus and oppose radical advocacy.

For those who would suppress radical expression, a panoply of legal tools have been available throughout our history. Though scarred and blunted by court opinions over the years, some of the tools still remain. We examine these tools next.

Sedition

Sedition is really a catch-all term encompassing a number of related crimes. Generally speaking, it is the offense of endangering the safety of the state through verbal or other expression. Historically, sedition has worn several hats in America.

The oldest and most pernicious was the common-law crime of seditious libel. Simply stated, it forbade criticizing the government or its officials. The idea of seditious libel was transplanted to the American colonies from England, where it had sprouted from the notion of the absolute right of the monarchy; criticism of the monarch was akin to blasphemy under old English law. In colonial America, that doctrine remained in force through the Revolutionary War and was employed to stifle expressions of disenchantment.

Under seditious libel, malcontents who made factual charges against colonial rulers were subject to greater penalties than those who uttered false charges. The rationale was that criticisms based on facts were especially likely to stir up feelings of scorn against the government. The famous but somewhat overrated trial of printer John Peter Zenger in 1735 is illustrative. Zenger printed (but did not author) a verbal attack on a New York colonial governor and was prosecuted for seditious libel. By most odds he should have been convicted. Instead, he was acquitted by a "lawless" jury which, among other things, refused to consider truthful attacks on government as more harmful than false ones. Zenger's trial did not change the law of seditious libel, but it underscored a lack of consensus among colonial Americans about the efficacy of that legal doctrine.

Decades later, with the success of the American Revolution and the subsequent adoption of the Constitution and Bill of Rights, new questions about the legitimacy of seditious libel were raised. Should common-law sedition persist in America after independence? Through the closing years of the eighteenth century, state courts and legislatures continued to use the doctrine to punish their critics. In 1816, the Supreme Court held that the federal government could not prosecute common-law crimes, including seditious libel. That still left the door open for common-law prosecutions by the states, and both state and federal prosecutions continued under a new form of sedition law, the sedition statute.

One of the most infamous chapters in the history of American restraints on free expression was the two-year experience with the Alien and Sedition Acts. A Federalist Congress passed the statute in 1798 to punish criticism of Federalist president John Adams and his administration. Fourteen Republican writers were indicted, prosecuted, and convicted under the act for publishing uncomplimentary comments about the President and his entourage. The statute expired in early 1801 and was not reinstated by the Jeffersonians, who had captured control of the government in the election of 1800.

Hostile public reaction to the Alien and Sedition Acts helped bring about the demise of common-law seditious libel in the states. A telling blow was cast in 1804 when the state of New York prosecuted a Federalist editor named Harry Croswell. A dedicated agitator, Croswell made his *Wasp* deliberately vicious; respectable Federalists even disapproved of his tactics. Croswell was brought to trial for printing an article charging that Thomas Jefferson had paid a journalist to smear the integrity of George Washington. He was convicted of seditious libel, despite brilliant libertarian rhetoric by his defense lawyer Alexander Hamilton. Believing that the charges which Croswell had printed against Jefferson were true, Hamilton argued that factual reports, no matter how scandalous, should be protected. Although the court disagreed and Croswell lost his case, Hamilton's arguments were soon picked up by state legislatures; state after state passed statutes making truth a defense against libel. And statutes began replacing common law as the tool for controlling sedition at the state level.

Once American legislatures stated enacting sedition statutes, it was hard to stop them. Subsequent statutes, as well as prosecutions under them, coincided with periods of national tension. During the 1830s and 1840s, there was a flurry of attempts in Southern legislatures to outlaw abolitionist expression. In the first twenty years of the twentieth century, advocates of socialism, anarchism, and syndicalism became targets of new state sedition statutes. World War I saw enactment of more sedition laws, most notably the federal Espionage Act of 1917. Almost 2,000 prosecutions under that act—and the banning of about one hundred newspapers from the mails—attested to the political paranoia of the period.

Then the Supreme Court, under the guidance of Justice Oliver Wendell Holmes, began to protect radical expression. In 1919 Holmes coined the phrase "clear and present danger" as a test of which radical expressions could be successfully prosecuted. The case *(Schenk v United States)* involved a leftist pamphlet which advocated draft resistance. The Supreme Court upheld Schenk's conviction. But Holmes saw a need to deviate from the old "bad tendency" rule which allowed convictions for radical expression on a mere assumption that they might injure society. He wrote:

> We admit that in many places and in ordinary times the defendants in saying all that was said in the circular would have been within their constitutional

rights. *But the character of every act depends upon the circumstances in which it was done. . . .*The question in every case is *whether the words are used in such circumstances and are of such a nature as to create a clear and present danger that they will bring about the substantive evil. . . .* (Emphasis added.)

Holmes had set the stage for a dramatic shift in legal control of radical advocacy. It took two decades before Supreme Court majorities started using his "clear and present danger" formula to overturn convictions; but when they eventually did, the result was more constitutional protection for the mere advocacy of radical action. Expression, in other words, became protected unless it produced a threat that was real (not assumed) and imminent (not remote). The development of the "clear and present danger" requirement, coupled with a 1925 Supreme Court decision *(Gitlow v New York)* which for the first time held that the states cannot infringe upon First Amendment rights, signaled a twenty-year period of relaxation. Sedition prosecutions nearly became extinct between the late 1920s and the late 1940s. Congress did pass a new sedition statute in 1940. It was called the Smith Act, and it became the first federal peacetime sedition law since the Alien and Sedition Acts of 1798. Prosecutions under the Smith Act's sedition provisions didn't occur until the pressures of the Cold War and Mc-Carthyism gripped the country in the early 1950s. The Supreme Court, by deviating from the "clear and present danger" test, did uphold one sedition conviction against Communists *(Dennis v United States)* in 1951, but later it returned to the Holmesian formula to overturn convictions of others.

Since the late 1950s, sedition gradually faded from our legal vocabulary. But sedition-like prosecutions, brought under statutes prohibiting "syndicalism," "conspiracy," and other abstractions, remained in use as a potential control over radical advocacy. In 1969, the Supreme Court considered the case of Clarence Brandenburg, who had been convicted under Ohio's syndicalism statute. Brandenburg, a Ku Klux Klan leader, had urged persons attending a rally to "bury the niggers" and "send the Jews back to Israel." Ohio's syndicalism statute prohibits advocacy of crime, sabotage, violence, or unlawful methods of terrorism as a means of accomplishing industrial or political reform. The Supreme Court overturned Brandenburg's conviction because there was no proof that his remarks provoked a "clear and present danger" to public order.

Another form of sedition deserves brief mention: criminal libel. Originally a common-law offshoot of seditious libel, it allows the government to prosecute someone for making a false, damaging statement about the government or its officials. Prosecutions for criminal libel peaked between 1890 and 1900 and nearly vanished after the end of World War I. So-called group libel, a special form of criminal libel, allows states to prosecute persons who defame ethnic or religious groups. Such statutes have been held constitutional, but for one reason or another legislatures have repealed them from the lawbooks; currently, no state has such a statute.

Desecration laws, which in many ways resemble criminal libel laws, prohibit the casting of contempt or ridicule upon the symbols of government, such as flags and monuments. While criminal libel and group libel have pretty much been laid to rest in America, a noticeable upswing in the number of prosecutions for desecration in the late 1960s, some of them successful, suggests that some restriction remains alive, if not well.

Contempt

Courts, legislatures, and some administrative agencies possess powers to punish actions or expressions which pose a "clear and present danger" to their functioning. Contempt can be a potent control, since the contemptor is not arrested and usually not given a jury trial. He often is merely "cited" for contempt, and his punishment is announced; contempt citations, however, can be appealed to higher courts. Most contempt of court citations are of the variety known as "direct contempt"—disruptive behavior in the presence of a judge. (The contempt citations issued against reporters who refuse to reveal news sources, are examples of "direct contempt.") Another form known as "constructive contempt" is of some concern to us in this chapter. It allows punishment for words and activities which take place outside the courtroom. Until 1941, state judges were able to use "constructive contempt" liberally as a means of punishing their detractors. Words, whether spoken or published, that cast doubt upon the integrity of a judge or the judicial system could be considered a threat to the proper and orderly administration of justice. During the turbulent years preceding and encompassing World War I, citations for "constructive contempt" were particularly numerous. The Supreme Court put the brakes on this in 1941 when it ruled (in *Bridges v California*) that "constructive" contempt cannot hold up unless a "clear and present danger of" interference with court business can be demonstrated.

A disturbing trend toward using "direct contempt" to control radicalism appeared on the horizon in the early 1970s. Federal and state governments intensified their investigations of "politically radical" groups such as the Black Panthers and of the so-called drug culture. As part of their investigations, the government subpoenaed journalists who had established contacts with such groups and demanded that they testify before grand juries. Refusal to testify would usually be cause for a "direct contempt" citation; agreeing to testify, on the other hand, would likely blunt the reporter's contacts with those groups and consequently would threaten the reporting of their activities. A 1972 Supreme Court decision *(Branzburg v Hayes)* dealt with three reporters who had declined to testify before grand juries. One of them, a reporter for *The New York Times,* had gained the confidence of a Black Panther group in California. Another, a reporter for the Louisville *Courier-Journal,* had gained access to organizers of illegal marijuana activities in Kentucky. The third, a newsman for a television station in New Bedford, Massachusetts, had been given permission to stay inside Black Panther headquarters during civil disorders in 1970. The three reporters, supported by an impressive list of Who's Who in American Journalism, asked the Supreme Court to hold that the First Amendment forbids contempt citations against journalists in such circumstances. The Court refused to do so.

Other Legal Restrictions

In their drive to stamp out radical expression, overzealous American governments sometimes resort to a wide assortment of legal miscellanea when the conventional laws don't seem to apply. Supreme Court decisions resulting from some of those attempts have become landmarks for freedom of the press. Minnesota, for example, had a statute declaring publication of "malicious, scandalous, and defamatory" materials to be a "public nuisance." Although "public nuisance" statutes are fairly acceptable methods of controlling illegal dumping of garbage, officials used the Minnesota law to get an injunction against a Minneapolis weekly, the *Saturday Press,* which had been smearing public officials during the late 1920s. The state put the newspaper out of business, but the Supreme Court (in *Near v Minnesota*) held that the statute constituted unlawful prior restraint and therefore violated freedom of the press. Another incident arose in 1936 when Louisiana political boss Huey Long became displeased with what the state's large newspapers were saying about him. He had his legislature pass a special tax on newspapers which circulated 20,000 or more copies. (There were thirteen such papers in the state, and twelve of them opposed Long's policies.) The Supreme Court (in *Grosjean v American Press Co.*) held that Long's attempts to silence his critics by placing a "tax on knowledge" violated the newspapers' First Amendment rights. Two years later, the city of Griffin, Georgia, tried to use a peddler's ordinance to stop Jehovah's Witnesses from distributing pamphlets. The ordinance required that distributors of literature get written permission from the city manager. The Supreme Court (in *Lovell v City of Griffin*) ruled that the First Amendment protects the right to distribute as well as the right to publish and that freedom of the press applies to pamphlets and leaflets as well as to conventional mass media.

In 1971 the federal government used the federal Espionage Act to attempt to stop newspapers from publishing the "Pentagon papers," a mammoth government-sponsored study of United States involvement in

Vietnam. The media initially obtained the study (which was officially classified as secret) from anti-war citizens who removed them from government files without authorization. The Court held (in *New York Times v United States; United States v Washington Post Co.*) that the media could not be prevented from publishing the materials; some justices, however, hinted that they would go along with an espionage prosecution against the newspapers for publishing secret documents.

HARASSMENT AS A CONTROL

Particularly during tense times, extralegal intimidation can be used as an effective, though repugnant, way to shut up radical advocators. During the years just before the Civil War, more than one abolitionist editor lost his possessions to pro-slavery mobs. One of them, Elijah Lovejoy, lost his life to Illinois vigilantes. During the Civil War, "copperhead editors"—those in Northern states who opposed the policies of the Union in general and Abraham Lincoln in particular—became targets for mob violence.

Intimidating unpopular advocates by anonymous threat and very identifiable violence spans the history of this country. As a widespread form of control, public harassment probably was greatest during the Civil War years and the "Communist scare" years of the 1940s and 1950s. In the latter period, the House Un-American Activities Committee and the late Senator Joseph McCarthy were able to discourage leftist expression by publicly casting shadows of doubt upon the "loyalty" of its advocates.

Continuing stress brought on by the war in Vietnam was accompanied by charges that police used harassment tactics frequently and brazenly against anti-war advocates. Offices of "underground newspapers" were raided, but police usually claimed they were searching for illegal drugs or pornography. Staff members of radical publications almost unanimously consider themselves victims of harassment. In a 1972 study by the Twentieth Century Fund, the journalist Fred Graham suggested a reason for the situation:

> Obviously, the doubts and suspicions that the public feels about militant left radicals and the so-called "counter-culture" . . . are reflected in its attitude toward the organs of these elements in society and their personnel. And although the same public is apparently willing to tolerate established left- or right-wing publications—e.g. *The* (Communist) *Worker*—it is not so willing to accept the legitimacy of the un-established, or underground press.[3]

[3] *Press Freedoms under Pressure: Report of the Twentieth Century Fund Task Force on Government and the Press.* Background paper by Fred P. Graham. Copyright 1972 by The Twentieth Century Fund, New New York, p. 107.

Then Graham speculated on implications of unfettered intimidation of underground papers:

> By permitting public officials to use their authority successfully against publications that incurred their displeasure, the established press has allowed legal precedents to be set that may someday haunt the entire journalistic profession.[4]

That statement also would have been appropriate for 1800, 1860, or 1920. And it will probably be an accurate assessment of efforts to stifle whatever vehicles of radical expression may exist in 1984.

REFERENCES

Books and Articles

Charles E. Merriam, *The Making of Citizens* (Chicago: Univ. of Chicago Press, 1931).

Edgar Litt, "Education and Political Enlightenment in America," *The Annals*, September 1965, pp. 32–39.

John D. Stevens, "Freedom of Expression: New Dimensions," chap. 2 in Ronald T. Farrar and John D. Stevens, *Mass Media and the National Experience* (New York: Harper & Row, 1971).

Harold L. Nelson (Ed.), *Freedom of the Press from Hamilton to the Warren Court* (New York: Bobbs-Merrill, 1967).

Press Freedoms Under Pressure: Report of The Twentieth Century Fund Task Force on Government and the Press. Background paper by Fred P. Graham (New York: The Twentieth Century Fund, 1972).

Supreme Court Decisions

Brandenburg v Ohio, 395 U. S. 444 (1969).

Branzburg v Hayes, 408 U. S. 665 (1972).

Bridges v California, 314 U. S. 252 (1941).

Dennis v United States, 341 U. S. 494 (1951).

Gitlow v New York, 268 U. S. 652 (1925).

Grosjean v American Press Co., 297 U. S. 233 (1936).

Lovell v City of Griffin, 303 U. S. 444 (1928).

Near v Minnesota, 283 U. S. 697 (1931).

New York Times Co. v United States; United States v Washington Post Co., 403 U. S. 713 (1971).

Schenk v United States, 249 U. S. 47 (1919).

Whitney v California, 274 U. S. 357 (1927).

---

[4]Ibid.

Part Five

Social Change

Chapter 20

Looking at Social Change

In France, where one revolution has followed another since 1789, political critics have often wryly observed, *"Plus ça change, plus c'est la même chose"*: roughly "The more things change, the more they stay the same." One could easily say the same about the great problems of American society. The kinds of issues we have raised in this book seem urgent to us today—but they have also seemed so to generations past, and no doubt they will in the future.

We would not want to leave our readers with the impression that the complex of media institutions, individual and group needs for information, and societal problems that we have been analyzing here are somehow frozen into immutable forms as we have described them. Rather, we would like to end on a note of change—in the media and in society.

This final section of the book will necessarily be briefer than those that have preceded it. We have no crystal ball, and there has been no research on the future. We can, however, examine patterns of change that have occurred in the past and anticipate some innovations that have been widely predicted; this will at least address the question of change. While we would not pretend to have answers to such a question, our hope is to encourage our readers to look for answers themselves.

To this end, we offer two chapters. Chapter 21 deals with innovations that are at least technically foreseeable within the communication field. In this case, the question becomes: What changes in society might we anticipate if various new communication technologies are adopted on a widespread scale? Chapter 22, the final chapter, looks at a few selected trends that may be leading toward changed relationships among different segments of society. Here our question will be: What new demands on our communication system might result from these projected patterns of social change?

As a broad guide to the reader's own thinking on these topics, we offer one unresolved issue in the field of communication and social system analysis. Many writers have taken the position that the communication system within a society is a mechanism or force that creates change—in the goals, processes, and tensions through which the society operates. An alternative viewpoint is that societies change for historical reasons that are well beyond the scope of communication to influence; the role of a communication system is simply to hold the larger social system together, keeping it functioning smoothly while it changes. Finally, there is the somewhat intermediate position that communication does not directly create change, but that the structure and efficiency of the communication system determines how rapidly change in the society will occur.

There is no certain method for choosing among propositions of this level of abstraction. By this point, the reader should be sufficiently familiar with the communication structures of American society that he or she will be able to arrive at an independent judgment as we examine some possible points of change in our national life.

SUGGESTED STUDY PROJECTS

1 Select a major innovation in the history of American media, such as the introduction of a new medium or a new method of gathering or processing news. What technical and economic changes helped lead to this innovation? What changes in individual lives and social interaction did it bring about?

2 Suppose an Organization for the Preservation of the Status Quo existed, with the aim of maintaining social and economic relationships in the United States as they are today. What advice would you give members of such an organization regarding a "communication program" to help them achieve this goal? What use should they make of mass media? What do they need to know about individuals' reactions to information? What about interpersonal communication processes?

Chapter 21

Innovations in Communication

Let us summarize the communication system of the United States at this point in history. In terms of the media that are in use, what they transmit, the scope of regions they cover, the audiences that use them, and their capacities for speed and storage, the following list covers ten of the principal components of our system:

1 Television Transmits entertainment (mostly light) nationally, and advertisements and capsule news locally and nationally. Used extensively by almost everyone, more so by the poor, the young, and the old. Broadcasts major news and sports in real time; stores other materials for broadcast according to a fixed schedule. Programs cannot be stored by audience.

2 Newspapers Transmit local and national news and mostly local advertising on a scheduled daily basis, and micro-local news or advertising weekly or semiweekly. Used primarily by adults and the more educated, plus those closely tied to the local community. Time delays of eight hours or more in reporting; storage of information by audience possible but limited by bulk and by impermanence of newsprint.

3 Radio Transmits music, advertising, and news capsules locally, repetitively, and continuously. Used occasionally by most people, and regularly by a few in association with other activities. Time and storage capacities similar to television.

4 Magazines Transmit national news and advertisements weekly, and information on major specialized topics at least monthly. Newsmagazines used mostly by the well-educated and semi-elite; specialized magazines geared to their respective audiences. Mostly limited to occasional summary or feature articles. Have good storage capability and compensate for lack of speedy reporting with depth coverage of special topics.

5 Films Transmit light and serious entertainment. Used by young adults mostly, with occasional selective use by other groups depending on cost and interest. Excellent storage, although somewhat expensive since user lacks storage control.

6 Books Transmit fiction and both general and specialized information of all types. Used by the well-educated and specialized audiences. Time lag of at least one year, with a few exceptions. Excellent storage and low cost permit user control of exposure.

7 Telephone Transmits discussions between two (or more) persons. Used extensively by almost everyone. Limited to real time transmission (i.e. as it happens) without storage, except when taped.

8 Formal organizations Transmit information one-way or interactively between persons physically present at meetings. Used by members on scheduled occasions. Ordinarily limited to real time without storage, except for minutes of meetings or taped recordings.

9 Conversations Transmit thoughts and feelings between persons physically juxtaposed. Used by everyone frequently. Almost always limited to real time without storage.

10 Thought Intrapersonal processing and organization of information, ideas, feelings, and intuitions. Used by everyone continuously. Real time only, with fallible storage (memory) that involves some loss over time and some error in recall.

If the foregoing list covers less than the total range of human communication (it does) and is mildly facetious (it is), nevertheless it demonstrates the range of psychological and sociological phenomena we are concerned with here. It extends from the major mass media, which differ in terms of content, speed of transmission, storage capabilities, and access for audiences, to universal forms of communication which have characterized the human race for hundreds of thousands of years and provide the real stuff from which the media should distill and preserve the best for society.

Technological innovations in communication have been introduced at an accelerating rate, and there is no reason to believe that this will not continue. The sociologist Melvin DeFleur has shown that each new mass medium has "diffused" into society at a faster rate than did those that preceded it. It took the daily newspaper about a century to reach its peak level of use, whereas radio was widely adopted within fifteen to twenty years after its invention. Television saturated the nation in less than ten years from the time it was made commercially feasible.

It is easy enough to see in our own lives some differences in social organization that are caused by new media. Films encouraged people to leave their houses for entertainment; radio encouraged them to stay home. Then came television, which modeled its programing after radio but also made films available at home. Combining major features of the two older media, television largely replaced them as a "functional equivalent"—that is, it performed functions for the person that were equivalent to many of those performed by radio and film. The older media survived mainly by shifting emphasis onto those functions they serve that television does not. For instance, films are aimed at people (mostly young and unmarried) who want to get out of the house; and radio has converted its evening programing from story-line drama and comedy to music and casual talk shows, which make a better background for other activities (house chores, studying, parties, driving) than television does—since television demands visual attention and constant following of a plot.

But the more significant impact of new media technologies comes not from simply providing a functional equivalent to existing media, but from serving new functions that lead to changes in social organization. To anticipate these, it is necessary to analyze media in terms of such basic parameters as storage capacity, access, speed of transmission, amount of information that can be stored or transmitted, and distortion of information. We have referred to a few of these things in our capsulized rundown of our present communication system to show how much they vary from one medium to the next. New technologies will be most socially significant to the degree that they extend our communicatory capacities in these ways.

Since basic interpersonal communication is primarily conducted through just two channels, sight and sound, it does not seem that technological media innovations that would bring in other senses—such as "smellovision" or "feelies"—would have much social impact. In the early 1950s, for instance, Hollywood produced several three-dimensional movies, but this innovation was abandoned almost immediately; it was technologically quite feasible, but it did not add sufficient communicatory value beyond that of the two-dimensional film to be worth the cost and bother. A variant of the technique survives in a few round-screen theaters that provide tourist attractions in urban areas. But no significant film has ever been made with the 3-D effect.

INTERACTIVE MEDIA

Two-way interactive communication, on the other hand, seems to be one of the greatest needs of the mass media. We are near to having the hardware—coaxial cables, computers, satellites, and fairly cheap sender-receiver sets—for two-way (and even multi-way to some extent) telecasting technology for the general public. Social scientists have scarcely begun, though, to experiment with the human "software" that will be necessary before, say, a board of directors could hold its annual "meeting" by means of interactive television, rather than by all the members traveling to a single point in space.

On the face of it, a widely available interactive television system through which all sorts of groups could meet and discuss without coming together physically sounds economically unfeasible. But cost has not been an insuperable barrier to the adoption of any new media technology for which social conditions were otherwise appropriate. Broadcast television, after all, requires a much greater immediate investment by users (a few hundred dollars for a color receiver) than any other medium, yet it has been adopted faster than any other mass medium into American homes. Cable television subscriptions are easy to sell in remote areas, but few cable systems have done well in channel-rich (and entertainment-rich) metropolitan centers; the price is the same in each place, but the social context is different.

Eventually, multi-way (or *n*-way) interactive television could provide a functional equivalent not just for another form of communication, but *for transportation* as well. Transportation is by far the most expensive activity Americans engage in. Many families spend more on their cars than on their homes. Suburbanites spend as much as one-half of their leisure time in daily transit, and central cities devote a similar amount of their precious ground space to the automobile and to transportation systems. Most experts see transportation as the key variable in both the environmental and the energy crises. Not all of this is going to be solved by communication media alone, quite obviously. But a good share of the moving about that people do today is essentially for the purpose of communicating with other people at the place where they are going. This should at least provide powerful motivation for efforts to develop multi-personal audio-video hookups that might serve as functional substitutes for face-to-face discussion and formal meetings. As transportation becomes less feasible economically, due to food shortages and environmental pollution, communication alternatives to transportation become relatively more feasible—even without major breakthroughs in communication technology.

Television has already demonstrated that it can reduce transportation, although it has not been interpreted in those terms. Every Saturday in the fall, for instance, football games are held at colleges and universities across the country. Many of them draw crowds of 25,000 to 100,000, which means that they put on the road twice that day enough cars to equal the evening rush hour of a large city. Very few of these games are televised, but when one is, the crowd may well drop off 15 to 50 percent (depending on weather). This is looked on as a calamity by athletic directors, anxious for the spectator dollar. But it might not be an outrageous idea, from the viewpoint of environmental and energy conservation, to *require* television broadcasting of all spectator events that are likely to draw, say, 10,000 or more persons to see them.

Interactive media could further extend the capability of communication to render travel unnecessary. This is not idle musing about the twenty-fifth century. A number of interactive systems, many of them including video display, are already in use. A few examples will suggest some of the changes in social organization that we might expect as this technology diffuses. The telephone, especially with its highly improved long-distance service, has made the physical separation of family members much easier to bear; this has encouraged people to accept jobs away from the place they consider home. Interactive computer-user systems permit a scientist to sit at his office (or home) desk and carry on a kind of conversation with data that are stored on a tape miles away. Doctors hundreds of miles from the nearest hospital can feed in a description of a patient's mysterious collection of symptoms to a central data terminal and almost immediately receive back a probable diagnosis based on thousands of like cases. Banks use interactive systems for rapid credit checks, stockbrokers use them to keep up with the current state of the Wall Street market, and airlines use them to route passengers quickly.

Professor E. B. Parker of Stanford University sees the issue of widespread public access to these new technologies as critical to the future of American society. So far, as he points out, use of interactive telecommunication systems (beyond the level of the telephone itself) has been restricted to certain elites, in the worlds of science and finance, for instance. This gives them a technological advantage that can enhance their power within society by making others more dependent on their skills. On the other hand, mass use would democratize the communication system, so to speak, thus helping to liberate the broad general public from manipulation or exploitation by controlling elites.

One can foresee some important changes in formal organizations if *n*-way interactive video systems were widely available. We should not assume that meetings held by means of such a hookup would be exactly the same as meetings for which all members assemble in one place. There would be some confusion at times about who had the floor, and some loss of conviviality, or even of a sense of "belonging" to the organization. Sub-conversations, for either personal or business purposes, would probably have to be made separately, by telephone perhaps.

But there would be some gains, too. Total time devoted to business, as a proportion of all time expended for the meeting (including travel, seating, etc.), would be quite high. Members who wanted only to casually observe, rather than to participate, would be free to "listen in" while doing other things at the same time—much as they would during any other television show. Those interested in only part of the meeting would not have to sit through the whole thing.

More importantly, since this form of televised meeting would not be particularly tied to transportation or even spatial constraints, it could encourage more frequent meetings and could make viable organizations that cover wide geographical areas. It could also permit some decentralization of the population, which is mostly crowded around a few metropolitan centers today. Artists and writers have always enjoyed the luxury—afforded by the special properties of their media technologies—of living and working "away from it all" in pleasant remote settings like the shore, woods, or mountains. New communication technologies could extend this possibility to other kinds of workers, by freeing them from the need to be physically adjacent to the other people with whom they interact in their daily business.

This is not blue-sky prophecy, but rather a recognition of a pattern of social change that has already begun. A person can sit at his home telephone and, via a simple keyboard, ask questions interactively of a file of data in Ann Arbor, Michigan, or play chess with a computer program in Cambridge, Massachusetts. What is important is not that we *can* do these things, which few of us are much interested in doing, but that we can do them *just about anywhere.* As more forms of activity are brought into this kind of format, more kinds of workers will be freed from the spatial constraints that exercise such control over our lives today.

Building a mass system of this type would, of course, require enormous amounts of risk capital and almost certainly several kinds of governmental aid—subsidies, tax breaks, technical assistance, etc.; there is ample precedent for these kinds of public support in the development of such industries as railroads in the nineteenth century and air transportation in the twentieth.

The First Amendment's guarantee of free speech and a free press puts some limits on the kinds of governmental intervention that are permissible within the communication industry—and, particularly, it limits the contents of communication. But there has already been a great deal of governmental input when it comes to the development of new communication hardware. There undoubtedly are ways in which the development of social organizations for wide public utilization of new media technology can be fostered by government without infringing on our essential freedoms.

STORAGE AND RETRIEVAL SYSTEMS

As we have already mentioned in several connections, the ability to store information within a system and then retrieve it when it is needed is an important parameter of communication technologies. Publications provide our dominant mode of storage today, and librarians are experimenting with computer-controlled systems to improve indexing and access to them. Information can also be stored on tape or other computer-readable media; this generally saves space but makes access and usage quite a bit more difficult for those who lack appropriate training—which includes most of us.

Lack of storage and retrieval capacity has been one of the most glaring deficiencies of the broadcast media. A program that comes on television at 7:30 P.M. is simply not available to a person who happens to be away from a receiver set at that time. There is, then, an understandably high interest in the development of cassette systems that would allow a person to record a program at one time and watch it later. The necessary technology for this is available, but it has not yet been developed to the point where it can be commercially marketed on a mass basis. It requires a fairly expensive television receiver and some recording tapes, plus a few operating skills. Cassette television will probably diffuse fairly slowly into society, since those who would be most able to adopt it (high-income, well-educated people) are the ones who rely least on television as part of their daily lives. But once it has diffused to a sizable number of homes, we can expect some changes in the television industry to adjust to this different type of customer. Cassette recordings of "adult" films that would not be shown on broadcast television, for instance, would very likely be made available for purchase or rental. This would be so near to a functional equivalent of in-theater film that the theater industry might vanish entirely, leaving young couples out on dates to search for other forms of entertainment.

Storage permits access on an occasional rather than a scheduled basis. There are some obvious advantages to this for the individual, but there are also some losses for the society when everyone is on his own schedule.

It may not be terribly consequential that when someone asks, "What did you think of that Dick Cavett Special last night?" the response might be, "Oh, I'm not going to watch that until this afternoon." Still, the coordination of American social life is partly predicated on the assumption that many of us will be laughing at the same joke, or learning the same bit of bad news, at the same time.

Somewhat less obviously, the print media also are schedule-bound. We receive a newspaper in the morning and/or one in the evening, daily and/or on Sunday—no more, no less. Other periodicals—the word "periodical" is instructive—arrive on a set schedule, weekly or monthly or quarterly. This pace is geared to the publishing industry's needs and to postal regulations, not to the stream of events in the outside world that the media bring to us. We adjust our lives and coordinate them with others' lives accordingly. Even books, the medium most amenable to occasional access, are scheduled to an extent; it is not unusual for two office-mates to discuss the latest Book-of-the-Month Club selection that they have both just read. If they read it at widely different points in time, or if they did not read the same book, something would be lost, namely, the discussion (which could well be an important element of the book's impact on society in the longer run).

When "everyone is talking about" a book (film, television program, or news item), society is at work on the thing, defining its broader meaning. This may be a subtle social outcome of scheduled media access, but we suspect that it is a more important one to society than appears to be the case on the surface. We should be wary of losing it. Since a great deal of current technological effort is going into the development of storage and retrieval capabilities for all media, society watchers might well keep their eyes out for this kind of social loss. It may turn out to be the case that people will coordinate their schedules for using media even when this is not forced on them by the media system; if so, they could continue to interact about media content.

SPEED, REAL TIME, AND SIMPLICITY

The need for speed in information transmission has dominated the news industry historically. It was perhaps never so well demonstrated as in the Battle of New Orleans in the War of 1812—which was won by Andrew Jackson several weeks after the peace treaty with the British had already been signed, but before the news of the treaty had reached New Orleans. Pheidippides died (so Herodotus tells us) after running the twenty-six-or-so miles to Athens with the news of the great victory against the Persians on the plain of Marathon. In their haste to get "scoops" on one another, the United Press erroneously reported the end of World War I before there was an armistice, and the Associated Press did somewhat the same thing in World War II. The *Chicago Tribune* made headlines in all the newspapers it had "scooped" with its own headline "Dewey Defeats Truman" the morning after the presidential election of 1948. (Truman won.)

Haste may not make waste in news communication, but it certainly increases the likelihood of error. It also creates an emphasis on simple interpretations of events and on superficial reporting. Thus news reports tend to tell who won and what the score was, rather than why. This may seem trivial when sports fans complain about it. It certainly is not trivial when the news is about a war, and the information channels are dominated by "official body count" statistics, as was the case with the Vietnam war in the late 1960s. A reporter who does a lengthy analysis of the shifts in morale, strategic position, or logistics that the day's (or week's, or year's) fighting has brought is unlikely to have the article published by many newspapers. The daily news media want material (to fit their schedules) that arrives punctually (they often will publish the first article they receive on a topic) and lends itself to a clear headline (hence simplicity). The media are too inclined to report superficialities (for example, "Jones scores two touchdowns," or "President carries Los Angeles County") rather than to explain some of the underlying processes that account for the surface outcomes (for example, the Tigers forced State out of its zone defense, or only 60 percent of the Chicano vote turned out). The premium on speed exacerbates this problem, and many technological innovations in the media are adopted mainly because they save time—the telegraph and telephone, faster printing presses, streamlined production techniques, and so forth.

The ultimate in speed, of course, is transmission of an event in real time—that is, as it happens. This had been the special province of the broadcast media, as was first demonstrated to the nation in 1912 when a young wireless operator named David Sarnoff began sending out news of the sinking of the great ship *Titanic* even before the ship went down. Sarnoff went on to found and dominate the National Broadcasting Corporation, and radio went on to bring people football games, FDR's fireside chats, and spot news, all in real time.

Radio's practice of featuring "live" events enabled a skillful Mercury Theater group headed by Orson Welles to present a dramatization in 1938 of H. G. Wells's *War of the Worlds* that many listeners mistook for a news report. The dramatization was so vivid that many people in New Jersey left their homes seeking shelter or escape from the invading Martians who were supposedly wreaking havoc across the river in New York City.

Television has in its time treated its viewers such "live" events as Gen. Douglas Mac Arthur's parade through Chicago after being fired by President Harry Truman; the four debates of 1960 between Richard Nixon and John Kennedy; and the on-camera murder of Kennedy's assassin, Lee Harvey Oswald, by Jack Ruby. A good firsthand picture of the United States government in action was afforded by telecasts of the Ervin Senate Select Committee hearings in the summer of 1973, the House Judiciary Committee's hearings on impeachment a year later, and the consequent resignation speech of Richard Nixon and swearing-in of Gerald Ford as his successor.

Real-time transmission is often cited by admirers of television as a major reason why they find it a more "credible" medium than the press. The thought is that there is less chance of being misled about an event if one is allowed to witness it directly than if it is described by someone else. This is true enough for athletic contests, but not so true for events in which the significant action is not amenable to photography or sound recording.

The emphasis on real-time observation leads television to portray those elements of events that *are* televisable. A candidate may be giving the same bland speech in city after city. There's not much news there. He may also be losing or winning, say, the Irish vote in Boston because of something in that speech. Now that's important, and a good reporter would find out about it. But it is hard to photograph support from Irish voters. So the speech (or more often a couple of sentences from it) gets taped and broadcast that night (so that it seems like real time to the viewers), and the reporter may mention in passing that the Boston Irish have been reacting to the campaign in an odd way. The availability of a real transmission of a trivial event (the tape of the speech) is seen by viewers as "straight" information, but they may look askance at the seemingly unsubstantiated comment on the Irish vote as the product of a biased reporter.

The reporter has his biases, of course, but most of them are aimed at getting a favorable response from his audience (and hence advancement in his reporting career). So he starts looking around for something photogenic by which he can document the Boston Irish bit. Sure enough, there is a public opinion poll that shows this trend, and he gets someone to make him a bar graph that he can put on the screen for tonight's show. These figures are, of course, dated and subject to both random error and sampling biases; and at best they show what has happened in Boston, but not why. But they are certainly better than nothing when competing with on-scene and "live" coverage, which is so well suited for television.

There are a number of technological innovations being developed that will expand the real-time, as-it-happens capabilities of the broadcast media. These will tend to enhance the social role of those media and hence to enhance the kinds of information they transmit. In turn, such innovations will diminish the role of the kinds of information that are not well suited for broadcast transmission—including sophisticated analysis of complicated human events.

As a simple example, weather satellites beam constant information back to earth in real time. This can be simultaneously transformed to a television-screen display that shows the range of cloud cover over any section of the country, large or small. Weather satellites cannot, on the other hand, read surface barometric pressures, which have much more to do with local weather conditions than cloud cover. It would be somewhat foolish,

If we define "old" as being beyond the working years, people are getting to be old at a younger age than they used to, because of early-retirement plans. Housing developments for "senior citizens" are removing many old people from the family home and locating them in homogeneous age groupings. The general economic prosperity of the past twenty-five years has left many of them comfortably fixed. And medical advances are keeping them alive longer.

For all these reasons, the old are going to constitute an increasingly large proportion of the media market. So far there has been little adjustment by the media to this trend, but the potential is there. We should expect to see the gradual introduction of television programs featuring older characters, of more specialized magazines for the old, of cable channels devoted to cultural content favored by older people, and even perhaps the development of new communication arrangements designed to service senior citizen villages or retirement homes.

BLACK, BROWN, RED, YELLOW, AND WHITE

The concept of race has been discredited for serious scientific purposes. That is, the genetic differences between various racial strains in America— or anywhere else in the world—are marginal, trivial, and presumably vanishing ever so gradually. But the social fact that there is widespread *belief* in race is too massive to be avoided. One approach to changing this has been to try to abandon race as a focal concept and instead to discuss the larger notion of "ethnic groups" and "minorities" (even those that constitute numerical majorities) in the population. From the perspective of communication practices, this is all to the good. But it should not be taken as evidence that race itself has ceased to be the most critical and volatile social division in American society—and hence the most overwhelming challenge to our communication system. The problem of racism can neither be defined away nor communicated away.

Race serves two general functions for us. The more obvious function is that it is used by one person as an indicator of what to expect from another person. When a white meets a black, he has some stereotyped set of beliefs about what the black is likely to do; when he meets someone of Oriental extraction, a different stereotype is called to mind, and he reacts differently. These stereotypes can be terribly inaccurate, and unfair to the other person, of course; so they constitute a major social problem. But stereotypes are not going to vanish, nor are observable physical differences between races. So we should expect racial stereotyping to be with us into the foreseeable future, and we should consider what we might do to allay it rather than hope to eradicate it.

The second function of race is to help us define ourselves. Because of historical, physical, and social separation, the different races of America have maintained different cultures and different role definitions, such as differing ideas of the part a father should play in raising his children. Until very recently it was widely believed that these "ethnic" differences, which exist within races as well, would gradually vanish in the "melting pot" of a single homogenized American culture. It was further assumed that the characteristics of the unified culture would be pretty much those of the dominant white race of European origin. The media set the standardized tone: ethnic accents and appearance were limited by radio, film, and television to comic or character roles. Nonwhites scarcely existed at all, in either entertainment media or news columns before the 1960s, save for the faithful ethnic sidekicks of such white superheroes as the Lone Ranger, the Green Hornet, and Mandrake the Magician. Still, white performers portraying nonwhite races (Al Jolson, Amos and Andy, Charlie Chan, and almost all the Indians in the cowboy movies) outnumbered members of those races in the entertainment world.

White racism, as the Kerner Report of 1968 put it, was and is the controlling fact of American interracial life, and nowhere has it been so manifest as in the mass media. The American racial revolution of the 1960s got several important messages across to the media from black, red, brown, and yellow Americans:

1   They wish to maintain their ethnic cultures and identities and to be permitted to take pride in their differences from white America. (Black is beautiful, it was pointed out.)

2   They wish to be portrayed by the media in the full range of variation of human behavior, not as racial stereotypes. (There should be good Indians and bad Indians in westerns, not just wild Indians and dead Indians.)

3   They wish to have access to all jobs in the media equal to those of whites. (Chicano reporters should be assigned to all kinds of news beats, not just the barrio.)

4   They wish to have their cultural heritages, along with the problems and achievements of their communities and peoples, explored and explained and preserved by the media in the same ways that white America is treated. (A lot of Chinese helped build the West, but the children of their descendants today have no way of knowing that.)

5   They wish to have their own media channels, operated for (and preferably by) their subcommunities. (When the President addresses the nation on an important matter, there should be simultaneous translation into Spanish for the hundreds of thousands who do not understand English well enough to follow him.)

These are not outrageous demands, since all that is being asked is parity with whites. But they are radical demands, in that they get very near the root of the problem. There has been some progress on all five points, but mainly it has been limited to the first three. That is, the media have begun to acknowledge that we have a multiracial society and that different ethnic cultures are of equal validity; nonwhites are being cast in nonstereo-typed roles; and many more nonwhites are being employed by the media and assigned to a wider range of duties than was the case ten years ago.

Developing full-blown treatment of these ethnic cultures in the media is more difficult, because it is a process that takes many years to build. It requires training and sensitivities that simply have not been available within the mass communication industry in the past. It also requires a market that would make this kind of effort economically feasible. Since nonwhites generally have far less money (total and per capita) than whites, media content that will attract white faces to consumer ads is likely to continue to thrive at the expense of material for nonwhites.

Channels for nonwhite communities are also in short supply. The ethnic newspaper, once common in our cities, has practically vanished; less than half a dozen dailies are printed today for the nation's nonwhite minorities. A few large cities have "soul music" radio or FM stations and Spanish-language UHF television stations (but unfortunately only a small percentage of Spanish-speaking homes receive UHF). But generally nonwhite Americans are agglomerated in huge ghetto districts of our cities; mass media, on the other hand, are organized and distributed at the broader level of the total urban community. So there has been little headway, despite some considerable effort, in the establishment of media channels for communication within racial subcommunities.

The demands, however, are clear, and the cause is an imperative one. It appears that the media have given up waiting for a racism-free millennium to arrive in America and are moving (with some prodding) toward accommodating our multiracial society. At the risk of sounding apocalyptic, we would hope to see substantial changes in the organization and content of the media regarding the racial divisions of American society before it is too late.

CITY, SUBURB, AND COUNTRYSIDE

There have been three broad phases in American history. The first was the filling in of the land with people, farms, and towns. This was accomplished in the early nineteenth century in the East and later in various parts of the West. The second was the era of urbanization, as people left the country for jobs and other attractions of the city. This trend characterized the period up through the 1920s. Since World War II we have shifted to a remarkable pattern of suburbanization, with central cities barely holding population about level, while new towns sprout up all around them. This has been rough on the newspaper, which developed and thrived in the era of urbanization. It was organized to emanate from the center of a city, bringing the activities of City Hall and ads for downtown stores to the homes of the citizenry. With suburbanization, however, that doesn't work so well. It takes a long time to get the paper out to the suburbs, and then it is being delivered in a locale that contains citizens of another town entirely—one that in many ways is likely to be at odds with the central city and that has a very different ethnic and social constitution, plus its own local newspaper.

Los Angeles is the country's most suburbanized (and de-urbanized) region. The *Los Angeles Times* has emerged as one of the nation's greatest newspapers by adjusting its operation to take advantage of suburbanization. For instance, there is a second *Times* printing plant in suburban Orange County, and each suburban zone around the city gets a different daily "zone section" covering local news. Such coverage is not on a par with that of established local dailies; but most suburban papers are faced with mini-versions of the problems suburbanization poses for the metropolitan papers. For instance, before suburbanization there were four cities in Orange County large enough to sustain local dailies; all four papers survive, but only two of them have been able to penetrate seriously into the county's many new cities that have sprung up where only villages and orange groves existed a few years ago.

Suburbanization is not an inevitable trend. Other changes in society may well slow it, or even reverse it. But while it exists, we can expect the media to adjust their operations in accord with suburbanization's demands. One that has been particularly remarked on by many observers of the suburban scene is the loss of a sense of *community*.

The newspaper, and to a lesser extent the broadcasting station, has long been a source of community identity. A recent survey in Wisconsin showed that farmers who live outside municipalities tend to think of themselves as members of the communities whose newspapers they read, even when other communities are nearer for such activities as shopping and schools. Within large cities, neighborhood semi-weekly "throwaway" shopping ad newspapers perform a similar function, giving residents a sense of belonging to Oak Park or Westchester, rather than just to the huge and remote metropolis.

Two characteristics of suburbanized America that operate to destroy a sense of community are mobility (suburbanites frequently move to other suburbs) and a pervasive sameness—chain stores, tract names like Prestige Gardens and Sunshine Heights, architecture that seems all to be cut from a single mold, and all the other trappings that make the outskirts of Chicago look so much like the outskirts of Washington, D. C., or St. Louis or Dallas or Minneapolis.

This is television country, by and large. The national culture provided by network television is built around the commonality of life that exists between Shaker Heights, Scarsdale, and Van Nuys. Television has not done much to foster a local sense of community, partly because its audience has not provided much of a market for it and partly because it is not very well suited, as a medium, to that task.

But as people get used to their suburbs, and have spent sizable portions of their lives in them, manifestations of community identity should grow. Local government, which tends to be impotent in new suburbs, will gather power and will require communication channels. There are few local merchants in suburbia, and those in the cities are gradually getting squeezed out by corporate chains, just as independent farmers are being replaced by corporate farming. These trends do not augur well for the sense of community in city, suburb, or countryside. And yet we suspect that any medium that can offer community through communication will tend to thrive in the coming years, particularly if suburbanization begins to wind down.

The concept of community is an old one in Western society, but it takes on new meanings in different historical periods. In the eras of filling in the countryside and of building our cities, there were close relationships between the organization of media and the development of communities of various sorts. Suburbanization seems to have come upon us too fast and to have burgeoned at such a pace that the media have not yet adjusted to the new needs for community identification and functioning that this phenomenon has created. The success of the *Los Angeles Times* in comparison with many collapsing metropolitan dailies is almost certain to encourage both mimicry and further innovation.

DOLLARS

Finally, we should consider that most classic problem of human organization, the distribution of wealth. Not only do the rich have more money than we do and the poor less, but both groups seem very conscious of that fact. (Or is it only us? Most likely it is everyone.) Redistribution of wealth may sound vaguely subversive to some, but it is a constant and very American activity. Money is flowing daily from hand to hand in exchange for goods and services, and at the end of each day a few hands hold most of it and many hands are virtually empty.

This economic fact is at the heart of the politics of all modern nations. Most of them have taken much more serious steps to force a more equitable distribution of wealth than the United States has. This country's approach has been more in the direction of enlarging the total wealth and trying to ensure that all citizens get a least minimal amounts to live on, while some few are able to accumulate far more than they can possibly put to good use.

The mass media are not geared to either the poor or the overly wealthy of American society, but rather to the massive middle class—certainly the most affluent group of workers in history. The content of the media, as we have repeatedly stressed throughout this book, is designed to appeal to this vast sea of consumers and thus deliver them to advertisements for products they might otherwise not buy. This is the "mass" to which the mass media address themselves. It is not an underprivileged proletarian mass of the Great Unwashed, but an overprivileged bourgeois mass that in fact spends more money on cleansing agents (for body, mouth, teeth, clothing) than perhaps all previous civilizations combined.

Mass media are obviously closely intertwined with the transfer of money from one hand to another in our society. So let us consider some possible patterns of change in the distribution of wealth in the United States and the effect these might have on the organization and operation of the media.

If the very wealthy grow even richer, it will probably not mean much to the media. There might be expanded markets for luxury media; but in a nation where more than half the homes already have color television sets or stereo hi-fi systems, or both, the luxury market seems to be fairly well saturated already. A contraction of affluence among the wealthy might be more consequential, in that it would make less risk capital available to underwrite mass media. This could be particularly serious for newspapers, many of which are not profitable businesses but are run out of family fortunes that make up the difference through less glamorous enterprises.

The American mass media have always been run by well-to-do people, and in many cases they have been profitable, helping the rich get that much richer. They have been used by their owners to further the interests of the wealthy, most obviously in the case of newspapers that endorse pro-business candidates and policies. Television is a bit different, partly because it is corporately owned (rather than family-owned, as many newspapers are) and partly because its fortunes are so closely tied to the interests of its middle-class audience. Changes in the estate of the very rich would probably not alter television's operation in major or obvious ways. The wealthy are largely able to insulate themselves from news coverage and are not a very popular topic for entertainment media these days. In the 1930s, though, movies and novels seized on the theme of the rich man who lost everything in "the crash" as a basic story plot. (Presumably this was some comfort to the poor man, who, though he too had lost everything, had of course lost so much less.) There is also a minor market for the saga of the wealthy man who is unfairly deprived of his goods due to a socialistic forced redistribution of wealth, as in the book and film *Doctor Zhivago*. But generally the ups and downs of the wealthy do not interest Americans in the 1970s as much as the details of the personal lives of the very few who are so conspicuously rich as to be major public curiosities—Howard Hughes, J. Paul Getty, and Aristotle Onassis being three examples.

The poor are out of fashion too. They do not appear on television, although they spend a great deal of time watching it. Any improvement in their lot is bound to be given great attention by the media. There is little indication in the media that it is even conceivable that the relative status of the poor will remain static, much less get worse. If it does improve, the poor will simply join the middle class, becoming part of the viable media audience. In fact, the poor are already in it, of course, to the extent that they buy at least the necessary products that are advertised, such as soaps and dentifrices. Since the poor are disproportionately represented by nonwhite ethnic minorities, those who become more affluent will be more tempting advertising targets, and consequently there will be more media content suitable to them.

But it is the shifts in the fortunes of the middle-income consumer that will affect the media the most. Sponsor-supported media, that is, television, radio, and most periodicals, assume that a large amount of discretionary income exists within the audience and that it can be controlled via advertising. Media supported by users, such as films and books, require that there be sufficient discretionary income to pay their full fees. When that pool of middle-income money expands relative to inflation, the media thrive. When it contracts, those media that are most dispensable are most likely to suffer, while those that are considered daily necessities probably will not. A general recession that temporarily set back the middle class economically would probably hurt user-supported media most, since the consumer's investment in sponsor-supported media is not so obvious or direct. On the other hand, an economic squeeze on corporations and the wealthier people who head them would hit hardest at sponsor-supported media, since advertising would be an expense that a firm would likely reduce in times of belt tightening. We saw some hints of these effects in the economic "stag-flation" of 1974.

Growth and diffusion of the mass media have proceeded at a fairly steady rate throughout this century, in good times and in bad. It is much more likely to be altered by an event such as a war—which diverts production capacity to other industries—than by a general economic recession or by major shifts in the distribution of wealth in our society.

AND SO . . .

We've been asking, "In what ways will our mass media system have to adapt, in order to service our changing society?" We couldn't give any definitive or comprehensive answer to such a question, of course. But it was worthwhile to ask it anyway and to play with a few ideas along that line. That way, we will not be taken totally unawares when societal changes do indeed impel reorganization of the media—even though the changes that occur might not be the ones we considered here.

SUGGESTED STUDY PROBLEMS

1   Keep track of all the advertisements on a television channel from 6 to 7 P.M., and then again from 10 to 11 P.M. Make notes on the products advertised and the kinds of appeals that are used. From the differences between the two time periods, what guesses can you make about the different audiences that are being addressed in terms of such factors as age and wealth?

2   Identify two different ethnic subcommunities within one city, one white and the other nonwhite. Keep track of a week or more of coverage in the city's newspaper of people and events in these two subcommunities. Do your findings bear out the charge that the media are guilty of white racism?

Index

Index